Houston's skyline changes every
year as the city continues to
grow and develop. This 1982
view of the downtown area was
taken by Story J. Sloane III.

HOUSTON

A Chronicle of the Supercity on Buffalo Bayou by Stanley E. Siegel

Picture Research by Patrick H. Butler III
"Partners in Progress" by Gerald Egger

Produced in cooperation with the

Harris County Historical Society

Windsor Publications, Inc.
Woodland Hills, California

Windsor Publications
History Books Division
Publisher: John M. Phillips
Editorial Director: Lissa Sanders
Production Supervisor: Katherine Cooper
Senior Picture Editor: Teri Davis Greenberg
Senior Corporate History Editor: Karen Story
Corporate History Editor: Phyllis Gray
Marketing Director: Ellen Kettenbeil
Production Manager: James Burke
Design Director: Alexander D'Anca
Typesetting Manager: E. Beryl Myers
Proofreading Manager: Doris R. Malkin

Staff for *Houston: A Chronicle of the Supercity on Buffalo Bayou*
Editor: Annette Igra
Picture Editor: Teri Davis Greenberg
Editorial Assistants: Susan Block, Patricia Buzard, Evelyn Harkless, Judith Hunter, Patricia Morris, Pat Pittman
Sales Managers: Marcus Black, Ernie Fredette
Sales Representative: Walter Black
Layout Artist: Don Gould
Production Artists: Ellen Hazeltine, Shannon Strull
Proofreaders: Henriette Folmer Henderson, Leslie King, Kaylene Ohman, Phyllis Rifkin
Typographers: Barbara Neiman, Cynthia B. Pinter

Library of Congress Cataloging in Publication Data

Siegel, Stanley.
Houston, a chronicle of the supercity on Buffalo Bayou.

"Produced in cooperation with the Harris County Historical Society."
Bibliography: p.
Includes index.
1. Houston (Tex.)—History. 2. Houston (Tex.)—Description. 3. Houston (Tex.)—Industries. I. Butler, Patrick H. II. Egger, Gerald. III. Harris County Historical Society. IV. Title.
F394.H857S53 1983 976.4'235 83-17067
ISBN 0-89781-072-4

Published 1983
Printed in the United States of America
First Edition

TO THE HISTORIANS OF HOUSTON
WITH GRATITUDE FOR
THEIR SCHOLARSHIP AND INSIGHT

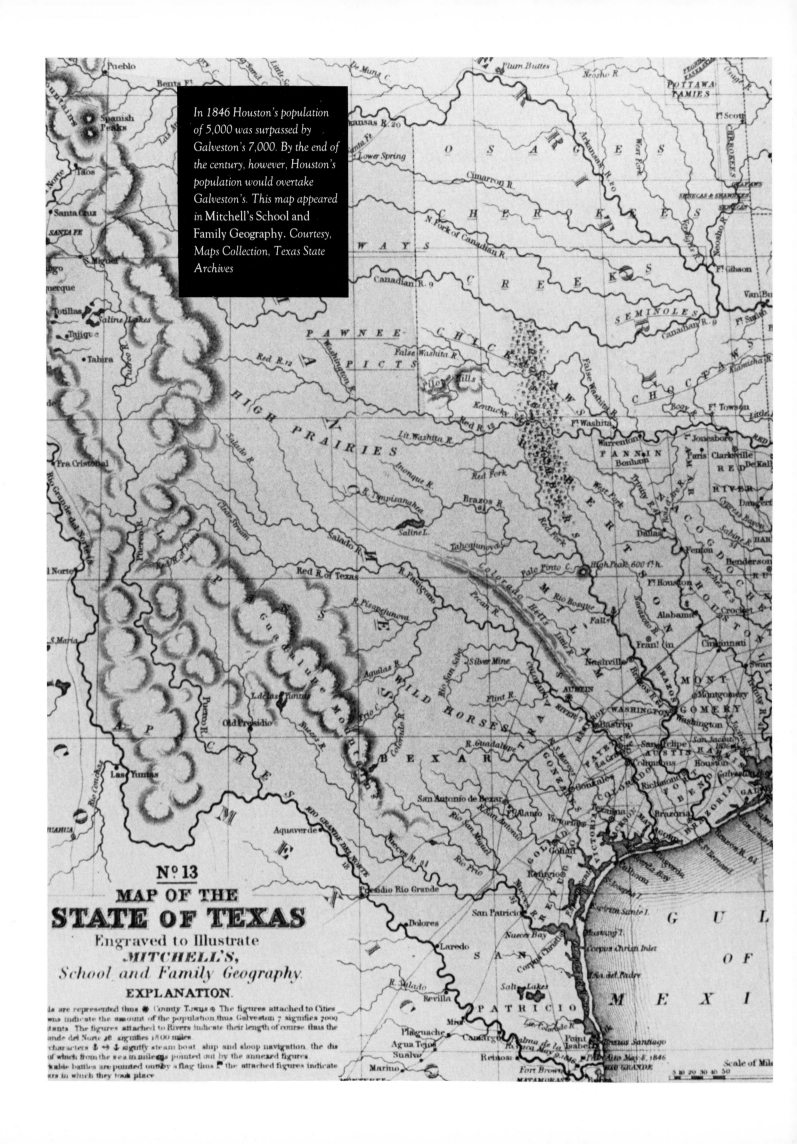

In 1846 Houston's population of 5,000 was surpassed by Galveston's 7,000. By the end of the century, however, Houston's population would overtake Galveston's. This map appeared in *Mitchell's School and Family Geography. Courtesy, Maps Collection, Texas State Archives*

N⁰ 13

MAP OF THE
STATE OF TEXAS
Engraved to Illustrate
MITCHELL'S,
School and Family Geography.
EXPLANATION.

...als are represented thus ✱ County Towns ⊕ The figures attached to Cities
...wns indicate the amount of the population thus Galveston 7 signifies 7000
...tants. The figures attached to Rivers indicate their length of course thus the
...ande del Norte 18 signifies 1800 miles.
...characters ⟱ → ⟱ signify steam boat ship and sloop navigation the dis
...of which from the sea in miles is pointed out by the annexed figures
...kable battles are pointed out by a flag thus ⚐ the attached figures indicate
...rs in which they took place

CONTENTS

PREFACE

This work seeks to acquaint the general reader with the history of a unique city, Houston, Texas. Founded in the immediate aftermath of the Texas War for Independence and named for the conquering hero of that struggle, the city prospered as the first capital of the Republic of Texas. Annexation culminated in statehood and, facilitated by railroad construction, the city emerged as a leading trade and market center. Spared Union invasion during the Civil War, Houston adapted to Yankee occupation during the postwar Reconstruction era. Symbolically, the final quarter of the century culminated with the fabulous Spindletop oil discovery, which cast the future of Houston in the present century.

The completion of the Houston Ship Channel in 1914 marked the fulfillment of a dream that had commenced virtually with the founding of the community. Direct access to the Gulf of Mexico and the attainment of "deep water" in time placed the Bayou City among the five leading ports in the nation. Two World Wars fueled even greater economic advancement, and by 1950 Houston had become the major petrochemical center in the country. Perhaps it was only inevitable, given its past record of growth and development, that the Houston-Harris County area would be chosen as the space exploration capital of the United States.

While the above constitutes an enviable urban record of accomplishment, there have been problems along the way. Only relatively recently has adequate attention been devoted to the artistic and cultural side of city life. Also, standards of public education languished somewhat, and the city was guilty of evasive and delaying tactics on the issue of integrating the public schools. The text of this work describes the earlier second-class status of blacks and Hispanics in Houston, and later the hard won gains in civil rights and political expression that have been realized. New minorities are present today and appear to be more easily welcomed into the mainstream of community life.

Finally, some attempt has been made to forecast Houston's role in the future. Certainly if the next 150 years are anything like the previous period, the results will be noteworthy, even by Texas standards.

Stanley E. Siegel

The Houston Fair and Exposition of 1921 was intended to demonstrate Houston's modernity to the world. The symbol of the fair, Miss Houston, was dressed in the latest costume, inviting the country to see all that her city had to offer. Courtesy, Special Collections; Houston Public Library

The territory that would encompass Houston and Harris County was a part of the grant made to Stephen F. Austin by the Mexican government. Austin worked to maintain his colony, although his travels left the development of the colony in the hands of his secretary, Samuel May Williams. Austin attempted to solve the problems that grew up between Mexico and Texas, but eventually decided to support those who favored the break. Courtesy, San Jacinto Museum of History

CHAPTER I

ON BUFFALO BAYOU: THE TURBULENT ERA

In 1519 the Spanish governor of Jamaica commissioned a navigator to explore the west coast of Florida and map a possible route westward. In pursuit of this commission, Alonzo Álvarez de Piñeda mapped the Texas coastline for the first time.

After sailing up the west coast of Florida, Piñeda proceeded to map the northern Gulf Coast. He discovered the mouth of the Mississippi River and also sketched the coastline, bays, and rivers of the Gulf of Mexico all the way south to Tampico. Returning from Tampico, he landed at the mouth of a river that he named "Rio de las Palmas," generally believed to be the Rio Grande.

The first recorded impression of the Houston vicinity and its inhabitants was left by explorer Alvar Núñez Cabeza de Vaca. Left shipwrecked on the Texas coast in November 1528, he was captured by Indians on Galveston Island. Cabeza de Vaca managed to escape and travel to the mainland, where he became a trader among friendly Indians in the future Harris County vicinity. These Indians have been identified as Karankawas, a ritually cannibalistic tribe that inhabited the marshes and inlets of the Gulf of Mexico for thousands of years prior to the coming of the Americans. Other Indian tribes that roamed the area of the future city of Houston included the Bidais and the Orcoquisacs, a tribe of hunters and primitive farmers who spent the winter in small villages along Spring Creek in what is now northern Harris County.

Settlers from the United States began to migrate to Texas in substantial numbers following the Panic of 1819 in the United States. A few were already there, having crossed over illegally from the "neutral ground" between Spanish Texas and American Louisiana, their presence winked at by Spanish authorities in San Antonio and Nacogdoches. However, the economic dislocation occasioned by the depressed financial conditions in the United States prompted the heavy migration of the early 1820s. State and federal statutes sanctioned imprisonment for indebtedness, so for those in debt a new start in Mexican Texas was particularly attractive. "G.T.T." scribbled

on a farmhouse door informed the local sheriff that he had missed out on a foreclosure and that the former occupant had "Gone To Texas." Also, as a result of the nation's first major depression, the United States Congress decreed that land could no longer be purchased on time, but only for cash. While the American price of $1.25 an acre was not excessive, it was beyond the reach of most who dreamed of getting on their feet again on new land, and free land was available for them in Texas.

Fortunately, the intensive desire of Americans to move to Texas coincided with Mexico's willingness to receive them as colonists. Attaining its independence from Spain in 1821 after 10 years of bitter civil war, Mexico felt that the time was now propitious for the settlement of its outlying provinces. Where Texas was concerned, Mexican leaders felt particularly secure since in 1821 Spain had ratified the Adams-Onís Treaty with the United States. Negotiated by Secretary of State John Quincy Adams and Spanish ambassador to the United States Louis de Onís, the agreement defined the Sabine River as the northeastern boundary between Spain and the United States, indicating to Mexico that it had nothing to fear from American frontiersmen.

Mexico also sought to attract European immigrants. French, German, and British colonization schemes were proposed, but with few concrete results. Then the Imperial Colonization Law of 1823 was passed. Foreigners were invited to settle in Texas if they would become Mexican citizens, accept the Roman Catholic faith, and agree to defend Mexico against all enemies, internal and external. Grants of land could be secured by applying to the local *ayuntamiento* (town council) or by employing the services of an empresario licensed by the Mexican government. The maximum grant of land was the traditional Spanish "league and a labor." In stark contrast to the United States policy at the time, the land was free, subject only to nominal empresario fees.

The correspondence of Stephen F. Austin, the leading empresario in colonial Texas, reveals the concerns of the early

DOMINGUEZ' GRANT.

 N°   **4428** $\frac{120\ \text{English}}{1000\ \text{acres.}}$

I, JOHN DOMINGUEZ, OF THE CITY OF MEXICO,

Do hereby certify, That under and by virtue of a certain Grant of Land in TEXAS, made to me by the GOVERNMENT OF THE STATE OF COAHUILA AND TEXAS, with the approbation of the SUPREME GOVERNMENT OF THE UNITED STATES OF MEXICO, on the 6th day of February, A. D. 1829, for the purpose of colonization as an Empresario, I do hereby authorize and empower   of   to locate for his own use and benefit, and to receive a title therefor, and to hold the same to himself, his heirs, executors, administrators and assigns, in accordance with and subject to the terms of the said Grant, so made to me as aforesaid, and to the laws of the United States of Mexico and of the state of Coahuila and Texas, one SITIO of land, within the limits of the said Grant, which are as follows, viz. :

Commencing on the RIVER ARKANSAW, at that part which is crossed by the twenty-third degree of longitude west from the CITY OF WASHINGTON, which is in fact the boundary line between the MEXICAN REPUBLIC and the UNITED STATES OF NORTH AMERICA; thence the line runs to the south, along the said twenty-third degree of longitude or boundary line, a distance of FORTY LEAGUES ; thence the line strikes TWENTY LEAGUES to the west, which is the limit of the reserve referred to in the Colonization Law of the 18th of August, A. D. 1824. From the point at which the said last mentioned twenty leagues terminate, a line is to be drawn to the north parallel with the said twenty-third degree of west longitude from WASHINGTON, till it reaches the said RIVER ARKANSAW, which forms the boundary line between the MEXICAN REPUBLIC and the UNITED STATES OF NORTH AMERICA. Thence the said grant runs along the western bank of the ARKANSAW for TWENTY LEAGUES, till it comes to that part at which it is crossed by the before mentioned twenty-third degree of longitude west from the CITY OF WASHINGTON, which is the place of beginning.

The rights and privileges hereby conveyed, may be assigned and transferred by delivery of this CERTIFICATE, after its indorsement by the original holder. Dated November 11th, 1831.

John Dominguez

By his Attorneys:

A. D. Days

C. V. S. Kane

The lands to be located by the Agent of the Empresario, who will reside upon the premises.

Texas pioneers. Succeeding to the grant originally held by his father, Moses Austin, Stephen went to Mexico City in 1823 to receive reassurance that Mexican officials were serious in their intention to settle Texas. Once back north of the Rio Grande, he informed all those who wrote to him that the colonization laws did not prohibit slavery. Also, while admitting that conversion to Roman Catholicism was a formal requirement, he doubted that adherence to that religion would be vigorously enforced. Their fears eased, Austin brought the "Old Three Hundred"—the 297 original colonial families—to Texas, and located them on choice lands between the Brazos and Colorado rivers.

Between 1823 and 1835, on the eve of the Texas War for Independence, some 25,000 Americans settled in Texas. Most settled between the Sabine and Colorado rivers. Confined to what would today be the eastern and Gulf Coast sections of the state, they endured Comanche raids from the west and the depredations of Karankawa Indians along the coast. In time, Austin was forced to recruit a militia company of colonists to fight off the Indians, and many Texas historians believe that this mounted corps constituted the beginnings of the famed Texas Rangers.

One disappointment encountered by migrants to Texas was the absence of broad and deep rivers for transportation. Texas rivers tended to drift leisurely to the Gulf Coast where they dropped their silt deposits, creating dams across their mouths and sandbars that effectively blocked passage. The Brazos River, for example, which seemed to be the natural waterway to Austin's colony, was rendered virtually useless by a sandbar at its mouth.

By contrast, the harbor leeward of Galveston Island was the best in Texas. Austin had an official survey made of the island and harbor, and Mexico designated Galveston as an official port of entry. Buffalo Bayou ran deep and wide from Brays Bayou to its confluence with the San Jacinto, which then emptied into Galveston Bay. In 1828 J.C. Clopper, an early pioneer,

recorded his impressions of the waterway:

. . . this is the most remarkable stream I have ever seen—at its junction with the San Jacinto is about 150 yds. in breadth having about three fathoms water with little variation in depth as high up as Harrisburg —20 miles—the ebbing and flowing of the tide is observable about 12 miles higher the water being of navigable depth close up to each bank giving to this most enchanting little stream the appearance of an artificial canal in the design and course of which Nature has lent her masterly hand.

Unlike most Texas waterways, Buffalo Bayou ran east-west. What was thought to be the head of navigation on the bayou was only some 20 miles from the center of the fertile Brazos agricultural region and less than 40 miles from the capital of Austin's settlement at San Felipe.

The area's commercial and trade possibilities excited the imagination and initiative of John Richardson Harris, who had first moved from New York to Missouri and then settled in Texas in 1824 as a member of Austin's original colony. From the Mexican government Harris received a league and a labor of land at the juncture of Buffalo and Brays bayous in the vicinity of modern-day Houston. At that site, in 1826, he plotted a small town called, not surprisingly, Harrisburg. Harris then erected a steam-powered sawmill, and Harrisburg became known in colonial Texas as a "timber town."

With the help of his brother David, who followed him to Texas, John Harris then established a trading post at Bell's Landing on the Brazos River. Their sloops and schooners plied between Texas and New Orleans; one, the *Rights of Man,* carried 84 bales of cotton to New Orleans in 1828. However, the principal business of Harrisburg was as a supply depot for the colonial settlers in the Galveston Bay area and at San Felipe. Trade with Austin's colony was further facilitated when in 1830 Mexican officials permitted the laying out of a primitive overland road from Harrisburg to San Felipe. Finally, on

December 30, 1835, the revolutionary Provisional Government designated the town as the "place for transacting the judicial and municipal business . . . and for the deposit of the Archives of the Municipality of Harrisburg." Unfortunately, John Harris did not live to see the little prominence his town achieved. While on a trip to New Orleans to purchase equipment for his sawmill, he contracted yellow fever in that swampy city, leading to his death on August 21, 1829.

The fortunes of Harrisburg, like those of all the burgeoning communities in colonial Texas, were tied to the winds of political change. Repeated and persistent attempts on the part of the United States to relocate the Texas boundary further to the south fed a growing apprehension in Mexico that an American invasion was imminent. To combat this possibility, Mexico instituted the Law of April 6, 1830, which barred further immigration from the United States, increased the complement of Mexican soldiery throughout Texas, and located customs garrisons at points along the Gulf Coast to ensure the collection of taxes.

One such garrison at Anahuac was commanded by John Davis Bradburn, a Kentuckian serving in the Mexican military who was despised by the local settlers for his oppressive measures. When he arbitrarily arrested attorneys William Barrett Travis and Patrick C. Jack in mid-1832, the thoroughly alarmed American community reacted in two ways. At Brazoria a peaceful demonstration took place and a call for a protest convention was issued; at Velasco bloodshed resulted when American colonists seeking to sail back up along the Gulf Coast to Anahuac clashed with Mexican troops blocking their way.

Fifty-eight delegates representing all of the American colonists in Texas convened at San Felipe in October 1832 to discuss a response to the Mexican measures. Meeting in the capital of Austin's colony, it was fitting that the delegates chose Austin as their presiding officer. A cautious revolutionary at best, he counseled moderation and respectful protest. The delegates passed resolutions urging repeal of the ban against immigration,

a reduction in taxes, and use of the English language in judicial and commercial transactions in Texas by wide margins. Then, in defiance of Austin's moderate course, the "radicals" led by William Wharton and William Barrett Travis demanded separate statehood for Texas. This measure carried, but had no practical effect, since it was studiously ignored by Mexico.

The period from October 1832 to April 1833 was one of tranquility, the altercations at Anahuac and Velasco seemingly forgotten. However, in January 1833 another convention was called to meet on the first of April at San Felipe. Those who wished to move more rapidly in the direction of independence or at least separate statehood pushed for this assemblage, and the election of radical William Wharton as presiding officer reflected their strength. One of them, recently arrived in Texas and elected from the Nacogdoches district, was Sam Houston.

In a real sense the history of Texas from the Independence period through the Civil War is the history of Sam Houston. Perhaps only the growth and future prospects of his namesake city can rival the story of his colorful life. Born in Virginia in 1793, Houston moved to Maryville, Tennessee, in 1807. Young Sam's formal schooling was brief; he preferred to live among the Indians and as the adopted son of a Cherokee chieftain took the name the "Raven." A lifelong friendship with Andrew Jackson developed when, in 1813, he enlisted in the United States Army under Jackson's command. He subsequently practiced law and then ventured into the hurly-burly of Tennessee politics, winning the gubernatorial race in 1827.

After a brief and unsuccessful marriage in 1829 to 16-year-old Eliza Allen, Houston resigned as governor of Tennessee and left by steamer for Little Rock, Arkansas. Traveling by land and water, Houston reached a trading post at the falls of the Arkansas, where he took up Indian life again with some of his former Cherokee friends. Drinking certainly more than he should have, Houston set up as an Indian trader and took an Indian wife, Tiana Rogers; later humorist

Will Rogers would be proud to claim descent from her.

Over the span of the next four years, 1829-1833, Houston was frequently in Washington, often the guest of his friend, President Jackson. Ostensibly "Ambassador from the Cherokee Nation to the United States," historians believe that he and Jackson discussed the ripening political controversy in Texas. In 1832, at the request of President Jackson, Houston crossed the Red River at Jonesborough and made his way to San Antonio. His commission was to report on Indian affairs in Texas and to urge the Comanches to cease their raids on American soil across the Sabine River. Some believe that he was in Texas to test the political waters and gauge the climate for revolution. He returned to Texas the next year to stay, and went on to represent Nacogdoches in the 1833 convention.

As chairman of a committee empowered to draft a state constitution, Houston made his presence felt almost immediately. The document provided for slavery and on paper established a government much like that of most Southern states. Resolutions similar to those passed the previous year were endorsed, and Stephen F. Austin was designated to present them at Mexico City. From there, Austin wrote home advising that steps be taken to form a separate state within the Mexican Republic. The letter was intercepted, and he was imprisoned without formal charge until mid-1835.

As Austin languished in prison, a political change was effected in Mexico that had a direct bearing upon Texas. In April 1834 dictator Antonio López de Santa Anna seized power, abolishing the republican principles of the government by declaring the Constitution of 1824 invalid, and demanding oaths of allegiance from the governors of the 19 states of Mexico. When Governor Francisco García of Zacatecas, a northern mining state, refused to swear fealty to Santa Anna, the tyrant himself led an army to coerce the disaffected state.

In the state of Texas-Coahuila, Governor Augustine Viesca announced his support for the old constitutional ideals of the Mexican

Facing page:
Houston's founders named their town after Sam Houston (1793-1863), the hero of the battle of San Jacinto. Houston served as president of the Republic of Texas from 1836-1838 and from 1841-1844. From Thrall, Texas *1879*

Left:
Antonio López de Santa Anna assumed dictatorial power in Mexico during April of 1834. After seeing his forces defeated by Texans in 1835, he began a campaign that would end at San Jacinto with his defeat and capture by Sam Houston. Courtesy, San Jacinto Museum of History, San Jacinto Monument

rebellion against Spain and rejected Santa Anna's grab for power. General Martin Perfecto de Cós, brother-in-law to Santa Anna, repaired to the state capital at Saltillo to crush the last pocket of opposition. Colonel Domingo de Ugartechea, Cós' deputy, was sent to San Antonio where he called for the arrest of William Travis and Lorenzo de Zavala, a Mexican opponent of Santa Anna who had taken refuge in Texas. This precipitated yet another protest convention, scheduled to meet in November 1835 at San Felipe. At just this juncture Austin returned to his colony, following his release from prison, and sanctioned the convention.

Before the elected delegates could convene, war broke out in earnest. The settlers at Gonzales had a cannon that had been given to them earlier as protection against Comanche raids. Ugartechea sent an underling to Gonzales to confiscate it. The colonists, aided by volunteers from neighboring settlements, were determined to resist. After

On March 16, 1836, David G. Burnet (1788-1870) was elected president of the ad interim government of the Republic of Texas. The night of the day he was inaugurated, he received the news of the fall of the Alamo. From Cirker, Dictionary of American Portraits, Dover, *1967*

a second demand by Mexican officials, the inevitable armed clash took place on October 2, 1835.

Two weeks later, on October 16, 1835, delegates to the third convention, known as the "Consultation," gathered at San Felipe. The delegates were still chary of complete independence and opted instead for separate statehood within the Mexican nation. Henry Smith was named governor and James Robinson, lieutenant governor, while Sam Houston was appointed commander-in-chief and ordered to raise and recruit a regular army. Pointedly, Houston was given no authority over the volunteer army that had formed after the clash at Gonzales and was at that moment marching against San Antonio. Finally, the land offices were closed in order to prevent speculation during the fighting, and Austin, William Wharton, and Branch T. Archer were ordered to the United States to speak for Texas while raising men and money.

The "Army of the People," as the volunteer force was appropriately called, then lay siege to Bexar. In the resultant battle General Cós was compelled to surrender and was required to retreat beyond the Rio Grande, a point of demarcation that future Texas governments would claim as their southwestern boundary. Texas was cleared of Mexican troops and on February 1, 1836, elections were held throughout colonial Texas to select delegates to one last convention.

Feelings ran high for a declaration of independence and the creation of an independent nation. While the delegates assembled at Washington-on-the-Brazos, the Alamo garrison was under siege by Santa Anna, and other Mexican forces were moving in to Attack. Also, the Texas commissioners, Austin, Archer, and Wharton, were writing from the United States that volunteering would cease and financial assistance would dry up unless Texas legitimatized its cause.

On March 2, 1836, independence was declared and the Republic of Texas was born on Sam Houston's birthday. The declaration of Texas independence, based on

Jefferson's more famous statement, was written by George Childress, a friend of Andrew Jackson from Tennessee. Patterned after the United States Constitution, a state constitution was written, to become operative after ratification by the people of Texas. Houston was again commander of the military forces, this time both volunteer and regular army. Land was offered to those who would fight for Texas, while transactions in land were suspended until the war's end. David G. Burnet was named president of the ad interim government and Lorenzo de Zavala, one of three Mexican signers of the independence declaration, was chosen as vice-president. The task of this body was to prosecute the war; it would relinquish office and popular elections would be held when Mexican troops had been driven beyond the Rio Grande.

When the Army of the People captured San Antonio in December 1835, Texas was the only state in Mexico not yet under Santa Anna's heel. Santa Anna had to crush the rebellion in Texas in order to secure his political base in Mexico City. Accordingly, preparations were made to cross the Rio Grande with an army of 6,000 men. The campaign began on a high note when General José Urrea surrounded and then destroyed a Texas force commanded by Francis W. Johnson at San Patricio. The main body of the Mexican army, led by Santa Anna, marched from Laredo to Bexar, arriving at the Mission of San Antonio de Valero on February 23, 1836.

The mission (named for the "alamo" cotton flower that grew nearby) housed a garrison of 152 men, but should not have been used as a fortress. General Houston had, in fact, directed Travis and Bowie to evacuate the troops; neither would carry out the order. When James Walker Fannin refused to march his troops from Goliad to relieve the garrison, the men inside were doomed. Teenage volunteers from Gonzales swelled their number to 183 before the final Mexican attack. When the carnage was complete, not a defender was alive and some 500 attackers also perished.

On March 11, 1836, Fannin, still at Goliad, was ordered to abandon his position and retreat to the northeast. Here he would join forces with an army General Houston was assembling to make a final stand in the area of the Sabine boundary line. Fannin delayed following Houston's instructions in order to assist civilians fleeing before the Mexican army. He finally began his retreat on the morning of March 19, 1836, by crossing the San Antonio River and moving east toward Victoria

When he stopped to graze his oxen, he was surrounded and attacked by the cavalry of General José Urrea. A fierce battle continued until late afternoon and Fannin was severely wounded. He and his men spent a miserable night on the open prairie without water.

Urrea renewed his attack on the morning of March 20. When the Mexicans moved cannon into the battle and began bombardment of the Texans' exposed position, Fannin was forced to surrender.

Following his triumph at the Alamo, Santa Anna divided his forces. Some units began the march back to the Rio Grande,

the campaign seemingly won, while the remainder, under the dictator's command, started in pursuit of General Houston. Santa Anna reached San Felipe on April 7, but finding the Brazos impassable at that point, he headed downstream seeking a more favorable crossing. Mexican intelligence then reported that the personnel of the ad interim government had taken refuge at Harrisburg, which was serving as a temporary capital. For Santa Anna, the opportunity was irresistible; the campaign could be won at one swoop with the arrest of the civil leaders, who would be compelled to negotiate. The only Texas force of any consequence was beyond the Brazos and seemed to be retreating toward the United States.

In March of 1836 matters became desperate for the Texas cause. In an effort to rally the people to the defense of Texas, Sam Houston published his Army Orders, which were issued from Washington-on-the-Brazos on March 2, four days before the fall of the Alamo. Courtesy, Special Collections; Houston Public Library

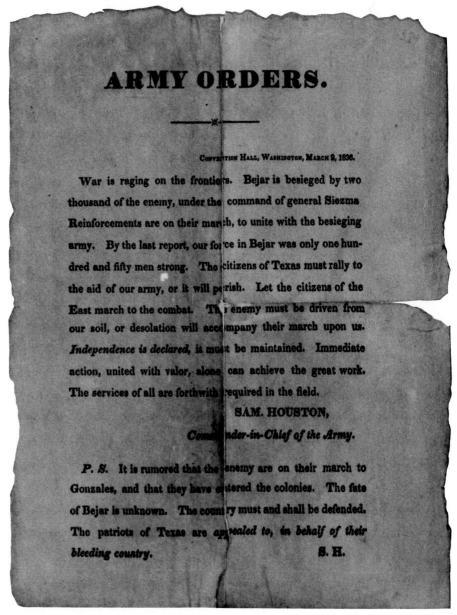

ARMY ORDERS.

CONVENTION HALL, WASHINGTON, MARCH 2, 1836.

War is raging on the frontiers. Bejar is besieged by two thousand of the enemy, under the command of general Siezma Reinforcements are on their march, to unite with the besieging army. By the last report, our force in Bejar was only one hundred and fifty men strong. The citizens of Texas must rally to the aid of our army, or it will perish. Let the citizens of the East march to the combat. The enemy must be driven from our soil, or desolation will accompany their march upon us. *Independence is declared, it must be maintained.* Immediate action, united with valor, alone can achieve the great work. The services of all are forthwith required in the field.

SAM. HOUSTON,

Commander-in-Chief of the Army.

P. S. It is rumored that the enemy are on their march to Gonzales, and that they have entered the colonies. The fate of Bejar is unknown. The country must and shall be defended. The patriots of Texas are appealed to, in behalf of their bleeding country. S. H.

Relaying word to his other units to link up with him, Santa Anna and about 750 men streaked toward Harrisburg.

They arrived too late. The government and some refugees had fled a few hours earlier on board the steamer *Cayuga,* seeking the safety of Galveston Island. He did encounter three printers who had fled San Felipe with the press of the first newspaper in Texas, the *Telegraph and Texas Register.* Disgusted, the Mexican commander ordered the printing press thrown into the bayou and the town of Harrisburg burned to the ground, amidst much looting and general destruction by Mexican soldiers. Thus ended the history of the pioneer community founded by John Harris; the city of Houston would rise upon its ashes.

General Houston learned of the disaster at Goliad on March 25. Fannin's defeat permitted General Urrea to join forces with General Ramirez y Sesma, who was advancing toward the Colorado River, and Houston sought to avoid a pitched battle with the combined Mexican forces. Retreating along the Brazos, Houston expected to fight a single decisive battle and thus waited for the most opportune time to attack. His motives were suspect and accusations of cowardice were hurled against him. His men, learning that Santa Anna had reached Harrisburg, demanded that Houston march to meet the enemy. The retreat was halted and on April 18, not far from the site of the present Houston Ship Channel, the "Raven" ordered his men to make camp.

When Santa Anna discovered the approach of the Texas force, he directed his army upstream. Houston broke camp, led his troops a few miles down Buffalo Bayou, crossed to its south side, and encamped in a wooded area near the juncture of Buffalo Bayou and the San Jacinto River. At four o'clock in the afternoon, on a bright, sunny

For 13 days a force of 187 Texans commanded by Colonel William Barret Travis defended the Alamo against General Santa Anna and approximately 5,000 men. When reinforcements for the Texans failed to arrive, the Mexicans stormed the Alamo, killing all of the troops within. From Thrall, Texas 1879

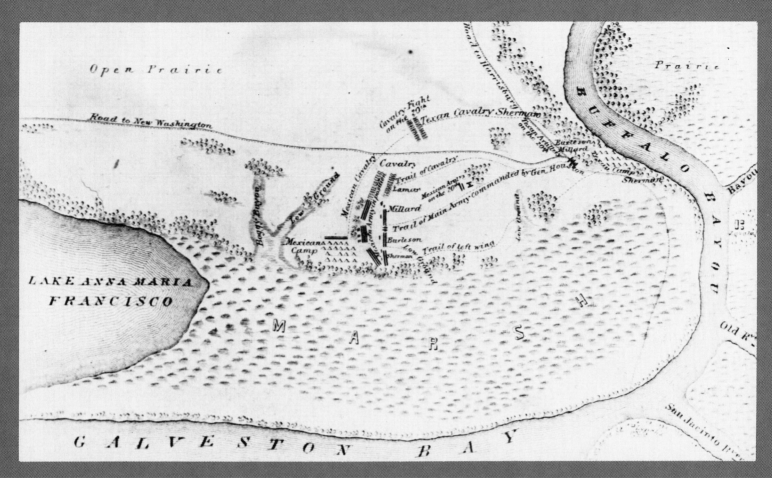

At four o'clock on the afternoon
of April 19, 1836, Houston
ordered his army forward.
Catching the Mexican forces
unaware, the Texas army
smashed straight into the
Mexican lines and ended the
dreams of a Texas empire for
Santa Anna within 20 minutes.
Courtesy, Harris County
Heritage Society

Augustus Chapman Allen (pictured here) and his brother, John Kirby Allen, saw new opportunities for wealth in Stephen F. Austin's colony. After spending four years searching for the right moment and playing a role in bringing independence to the Texans, the Allens founded Houston. Augustus Allen survived his brother, but in the 1840s problems stemming from the difficulty of settling his brother's estate and his growing differences with his wife forced him to leave Houston. He later served as a U.S. diplomat and in 1864 he died in Washington. Courtesy, Harris County Heritage Society

Charlotte Allen, the wife of A.C. Allen, remained a dominant force in Houston for many years in the mid-19th century. Though separated from her husband, she administered most of the Allen holdings until her death in 1895. Courtesy, Harris County Heritage Society

day, the command to attack was given. Enjoined to "Remember the Alamo," the Texans won the battle of San Jacinto in less than 20 minutes. The Mexican losses were some 600 dead and almost 750 captured. Among them was Santa Anna, the "Napoleon of the West," who fled the field of battle disguised as a common infantryman. In gratitude for his life, which Houston spared, Santa Anna signed the Treaty of Velasco and recognized the independence of Texas.

The Texans came through the battle with only six dead and a handful wounded. Among the latter was General Houston, who had been shot in the ankle. Houston, now the "Hero of San Jacinto," left for New Orleans on the advice of his doctors to seek medical treatment. On July 23, 1836, ad interim President Burnet issued a proclamation stating that elections would be held the first Monday in September for president, vice-president, and members of the Texas congress. The 1836 constitution drafted at the Independence Convention would be ratified and a straw ballot taken on the desirability of annexation. After a spirited campaign, Houston was elected president of Texas by a wide margin over candidates Henry Smith and Stephen F. Austin, and Mirabeau B. Lamar was designated vice-president, defeating Alexander Horton. The

constitution was overwhelmingly ratified and by the same margin the citizens of the Republic stated their preference for union with the United States. At West Columbia, another temporary capital site, Houston took the inaugural oath and pledged to seek annexation while at the same time maintaining the borders of Texas against any possible future threat from Mexico.

With independence from Mexico a reality and the Republic of Texas established, John Harris' widow anticipated that Harrisburg would be quickly rebuilt. It might have been, had not two enterprising pioneers from New York founded another town on Buffalo Bayou. Augustus Chapman Allen and his younger brother, John Kirby Allen, came to Texas from upstate New York in 1832. Reared by their parents to value real estate, the brothers became involved in land speculation in Texas. They settled in San Augustine and moved to Nacogdoches in 1833. Although neither brother served in the army during the 1835-1836 campaign, they did, at their own expense, outfit a ship that carried volunteers from the United States to Texas. Immediately after the San Jacinto campaign, they sought to buy land at Galveston and build a port city, but conceded failure when title difficulties could not be resolved.

Because the Galveston location did not work out, the Allen brothers determined to look further upstream. The former site of Harrisburg, at what was then considered to be the head of navigation on Buffalo Bayou, was their next choice. There land and water routes converged, but that location was also tied up in litigation due to the claims of John Harris' widow and others to his estate. Speed was of the essence to the Allens, who feared that the Brazos River could be made navigable before the Buffalo Bayou route to the interior.

After further searching, a tract of land at the juncture of Buffalo and White Oak bayous was selected. Buffalo Bayou was still deep above Harrisburg, and extensive sounding revealed that White Oak rather than Brays Bayou marked the head of navigation. John Austin (no relation to Moses or Stephen F.) had acquired title to the land in question in 1824, and his heirs were willing to sell. Here there were no thorny title questions; the cost was $5,000 for the southern half of two leagues along the southwest bank of the Buffalo. To demonstrate their honesty and sincerity, the Allen brothers paid $1,000 down, with the balance due in 18 months. The purchasers confidently expected that the sale of town lots would defray the remaining debt.

Other speculators were also at work founding would-be towns along the banks of Buffalo Bayou and Galveston Bay, spurring the Allen brothers to work ever faster. Title was conveyed early in August 1836, and by the end of that month an official survey had been prepared by a firm of New Orleans engineers and town lots were offered for sale. Wisely, the promoters named their future city "Houston" in honor of the victor at San Jacinto. That Sam Houston might well be elected first president of the Republic of Texas also figured in their planning. On August 30, 1836, they began advertising the sale of town property in the Columbia *Telegraph and Texas Register*. Their vision for Houston was not modest:

The town of Houston is located at a point on the river which must ever command the

trade of the largest and richest portion of Texas, and when rich lands of this country shall be settled, a trade will flow to it, making it, beyond all doubt, the great interior commercial emporium of Texas.

There is no place in Texas more healthy, having an abundance of excellent spring water and enjoying the sea breeze in all of its freshness. Nature seems to have designated this place for the future seat of government. It is handsomely and beautifully elevated, salubrious and well-watered and is now in the very center of population and will be so for a long time to come.

The Allens soon had an opportunity to fulfill their dream when the congress of the Republic decided the location of a permanent seat of government. Nacogdoches, San Jacinto, Matagorda, Fort Bend, Washington, and Columbia were all considered, but a consensus could not be reached. Then John K. Allen, an elected member of the house, presented the case for Houston. After four ballots Houston was finally chosen by a slender majority as the seat of government until the conclusion of the 1840 legislative session, conditional upon the promise of the Allen brothers to erect a $10,000 capitol at their own expense.

At the time Houston was founded, the Allen brothers commissioned Gail Borden to produce a map of the new city. Reproduced on the 1869 Wood map, the original map shows a city of 62 blocks hugging Buffalo Bayou with space reserved for a courthouse, the congress of the Republic, churches, and schools. Within 10 years, the city had outgrown the original site. Courtesy, Texas Room; Houston Public Library

The Allens now stepped up their advertising campaign, referring to the "City of Houston" and "The Present Seat of the Government of the Republic of Texas." Space was taken in leading Southern newspapers, and newcomers began to arrive in January 1837. Francis R. Lubbock, a future governor of the state, came to Texas intending to remain only until he could locate a brother who had volunteered in the Revolution. He visited Houston and later recorded in his memoirs:

My stay in Texas was short, but I had found my country. The strong, massive character of the people and apparent grandness of the country impressed me greatly. So thoroughly was I persuaded of the bright prospect ahead for those who would settle promptly, that I at once made up my mind that if my young wife would give up New Orleans and follow me, Texas would be our home.

The Allen brothers had boasted that their city was situated at the head of navigation on Buffalo Bayou. Challenged to prove their assertion by critics who insisted that the fledgling community was in fact 15 miles above the head, the promoters felt compelled to prove their claim. They chartered the steamboat *Laura* with Captain Thomas W. Grayson aboard to sail from Columbia to Houston and convinced a group of leading citizens to make the trip. The *Laura* was then the smallest steamer operating in Texas, indicating that the Allens themselves had some reservations. Although the distance to Harrisburg was traversed with ease, it took three days to get from that site to Houston; logs, moss, and other snags made progress difficult and painfully slow. While early historians of Houston disagree as to the exact day of arrival, the most likely date was January 22, 1837. The first sailing vessel to reach Houston, the *Rolla*, arrived on April 21, 1837, just in time for many of its passengers to attend the first San Jacinto anniversary ball. It encountered the same navigational hazards from Harrisburg to Houston as had the *Laura*. The channel above Harrisburg was narrow and obstructed; widening and improving Buffalo

Bayou was essential to the future prospects of Houston.

Despite these inconveniences, the city continued to grow. Perhaps with pardonable pride, Francis Moore, Jr., the new editor of the *Telegraph and Texas Register*, now published at Houston, noted that the city had become the "focus of immigration from all directions" and the "center of most of the spirit and enterprise of Texas." Within a few months of its inception, the city had more than 500 inhabitants. An anonymous visitor recorded his impressions in the following way:

Houses could not be built near as fast as required, so that quite a large number of linen tents were pitched in every direction over the prairie, which gave the city the appearance of a Methodist camp ground. Some of these tents, such as were used for groceries, were calculated to surprise one from their great size. A number of them measured more than a hundred feet each in circumference, with conical tops, thirty or forty feet in height, supported by means of poles in the center.

For the early period of Houston's history, trade rather than manufacturing was the most significant commercial activity. However, some Houstonians were involved in manufacturing; in 1841 the *Telegraph and Texas Register* pointed with pride to two new sawmills and W.K. Kellum & Company's brick foundry on the outskirts of the city. The next year the newspaper commented on the opening of a brass foundry and J. Wilson's Company's fabricating shop, which made stills, bells, stirrups, and spurs. During the era of the Republic, prior to statehood, a saddlery, lard-oil factory, corn mill, and pottery mill also opened for business.

Houston merchants exchanged goods such as furniture, clothing, farm tools, books, medical supplies, and groceries, for the produce of the countryside, principally cotton, lumber, livestock, and hides. Some merchants maintained permanent places of business and cultivated a regular clientele, but auction sales were common as well. Such firms as Hedenberg and Vedder and Davison and De Cordova sold real estate, dry goods, slaves, and other "commodities" at auction. The trading and auction season lasted approximately from September until April. Country produce came into Houston by wagon and later by railroad. Purchased by local merchants, the goods were then shipped down Buffalo Bayou to Galveston for transfer to oceangoing ships. Then, to complete the business cycle, Houston businessmen frequently journeyed to Mobile, New Orleans, and New York to purchase

Houston's first mayor, James S. Holman, was an agent for the Houston Town Company and was involved in banking and business activities. After serving as mayor, he remained politically active but continued to develop his business career. Like many of Houston's mayors, he had strong ties to, and was part of, the business establishment. Courtesy, Texas Room; Houston Public Library

The government of Texas soon developed a series of engraved notes, which were issued from Houston. Designed with the image of a classical goddess and an Indian shooting buffalo, these five dollar notes were typical of the currency issued to foil counterfeiters. In all, $650,629 in notes ranging from one dollar to $50 were issued. Courtesy, San Jacinto Museum of History

new merchandise and arrange for shipment to Houston.

Amidst all this business activity, cotton remained the principal item of trade. Trains of oxen carried cotton from plantations along the Brazos and Colorado rivers to stores at the foot of Main Street, there to reload goods bound for the interior. Shipped down Buffalo Bayou to Galveston and then out to Northern ports, cotton provided an economic link between the Republic of Texas and the United States. The Allen brothers had dreamed of making their city one of the great cotton markets of the world and, indeed, its beginnings were auspicious.

In addition to envisioning Houston as a leading port, the Allen brothers also forecast the development of the city as a railroad center. The August 30, 1836, edition of the *Telegraph and Texas Register* predicted the following:

As the country shall improve railroads will become in use and will be extended from this point [Houston] to the Brazos and up the same also to the headwaters of the San Jacinto embracing that rich country and in a few years the whole trade of the upper Brazos will make its way into Galveston through the channel.

The Texas Railroad, Navigation, and Banking Company was the first railroad company chartered not only in Texas, but west of the Mississippi as well. It contemplated the construction of a railroad linking the Sabine River and the Rio Grande with Houston as the midway terminus. But opposition to the company arose almost immediately because of the company's banking privileges. With this political controversy, and with the shortage of capital caused by the economic Panic of 1837, the company never completed a mile of track. In May 1838 the Republic congress awarded a charter to the Brazos and Galveston Railroad Company, which sought to link Galveston with the trade of the interior. The promoters hoped to reach the settlements along the Brazos and Colorado rivers by following Buffalo Bayou to Harrisburg

and then overland to the Brazos region. This enterprise also failed, and nothing was accomplished on land or water, but it did alert some of the leading citizens of Houston to the dangers posed by Galveston's railroad ambitions. Then in January 1839 a charter of incorporation for the Houston and Brazos Railroad Company was granted. Augustus C. Allen was the principal organizer and stockholder of this projected road, which was to run from Houston to points along the Brazos River. Advertisements for laborers appeared and the spot where the road was to begin was marked by a slab with an appropriate inscription. However, a threatened Mexican invasion forced the project to be abandoned and no trace can be found of any actual grading.

Andrew Briscoe, a signer of the Texas Declaration of Independence and the first chief justice of Harris County, strongly believed in railroads, and with financial backing from investors in Harrisburg and Galveston, he received a charter for the Harrisburg Railroad and Trading Company in 1841. Designed to revive Harrisburg as a rival of Houston, a prospect that pleased his Galveston backers, Briscoe's charter designated the Brazos River as the western terminus of his projected road. However, he had no intention of stopping there. The doughty Briscoe actually planned a transcontinental railroad and employed an engineer to survey a route to the Pacific Coast. Two miles of roadbed were completed before the Harrisburg project collapsed, though 40 years later the Southern Pacific would follow its contemplated route to California.

In addition to rail connections, dirt roads and Buffalo Bayou linked Houston with the interior of the Republic. In truth, many of the roads leading to Houston were nothing but dirt pathways following an uncertain route; often a compass had to be employed to pick up the trail once again. The roads were dusty in the summer and became quagmires after a slight rain. During the period of the Republic one traveler, Samuel A. Roberts, recalled, "they were then impassable, not even Jack-assable." The Brazos prairie west of Houston was particularly

CONSULATE OF THE REPUBLIC

OF TEXAS.

I WILLIAM BRYAN, Consul for the Republic of Texas, for the port of New Orleans, State of Louisiana, and United States of America, do hereby certify that the annexed order or Draft drawn by Barnard M. Johnson on Messrs J.H. Phillips &c in favor of Thos. Jenkins for one thousand dollars, dated Saint Augustine May 5. 1840, was presented this day to several persons by the Name of Phillips, and other Merchants of this City, and also a reference made to the Mercantile directory, and no Knowledge could be obtained of the existence now, or anytime heretofore of any such firm or House as J.H. Phillips &c in the City of New Orleans

Given under my hand and seal of office, at the City of New Orleans, this Twentieth day of September eighteen hundred and ~~thirty~~ forty and the Independence of Texas the Fifth

Wm Bryan
by Edward Hall
Consular Agent

hazardous and prone to flooding in rainy weather, and the roads from Houston to the north were almost as bad. The lack of adequate roads most likely hampered immigration to Texas.

While horses and mules were used, ox teams hauled most of the goods coming into the city. Less expensive than draft horses, oxen could subside on prairie grass and could cover from 10 to 15 miles daily when the roads were not flooded. Upon reaching Houston the wagoners would deposit their goods and rendezvous at a wagon camp on the outskirts of the city to prepare for the return trip. Houston had two wagon camps, one of them on Main Street, where it is said that revelry and whiskey flowed late into the night. Although most of the teamsters were white, occassionally a Brazos cotton planter would send his wagon to Houston driven by a black slave. Because freighting was basically the work of planters and wagoners, attempts were also made to establish regular passenger service in and out of the city. The Texas Stage Line and the Houston-Austin line offered service to Richmond, Austin, and San Antonio. The prospective traveler was charged $15 and promised that he would reach Austin in three days; the pledge was rarely honored.

Buffalo Bayou would remain Houston's link to the outside world until the rail connections of the post-Civil War era. Writing in May 1837, Francis W. Moore, Jr., complained, "the principal objection to this place is the difficulty of access by water; the bayou above Harrisburg being so narrow, so serpentine and blocked up with snags and overhanging trees that immense improvements will be required to render the navigation convenient for large steamboats." Accordingly, in 1839, the Buffalo Bayou Company was organized by John D. Andrews, one of Stephen F. Austin's "Old Three Hundred" settlers, to dredge and clear the water route. Five miles of channel were cleared above Harrisburg, though snags and obstructions continued to be a persistent problem. Early in 1840 two ships, the *Emblem* and the *Brighton*, sank and partially blocked the channel. The *Brighton* was salvaged and renamed the *Sam Houston*, but

Established in 1825 on the banks of Buffalo Bayou, Harrisburg was a major competitor of Houston for trade in the late 1830s and 1840s. The city, incorporated under a trust to the Harrisburg Town Company in 1839, attempted to fund its development as a transportation center serving the Brazos. Although the first railhead in Texas, the city lost out to Houston after the Civil War. In 1926 it was annexed by Houston. Courtesy, Special Collections; Houston Public Library

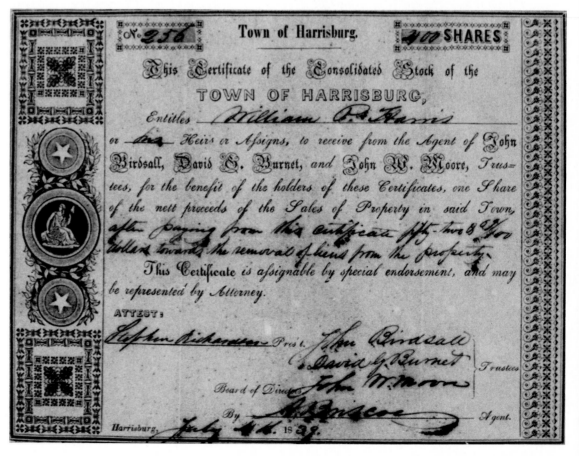

even with its new name it sank again shortly thereafter.

The accomplishment of a deep-water channel able to accommodate oceangoing ships was still in the future, but a positive step was taken in 1840 when the Republic congress authorized the city to build and maintain wharves. In 1841 the Houston City Council created the Port of Houston, which consisted of all wharves and landing facilities along Buffalo and White Oak bayous. The city then proceeded to tax merchants using the channel to raise funds for bayou maintenance; free wharf space was also permitted to certain businessmen in return for their efforts to keep Buffalo Bayou navigable. Primitive roads, railroad projects, and works to widen and clear the water path to the Gulf of Mexico were all attempts on the part of Houston's leaders to solve their city's transportation difficulties.

Locating the seat of government at Houston had been greatly responsible for the city's initial surge. A number of small towns had been chartered by ambitious promoters along Buffalo Bayou and Galveston Bay, but Houston prospered while they failed. Colonel James Morgan, a Galveston booster with shipping interests in that city, sarcastically observed in a letter to a friend:

The new town of Houston cuts a considerable swell in the paper. I wish its projectors and proprietors success with all my heart . . . As for New Washington and Lynchburg, Scottsburg and all the other burgs, not forgetting Powhatan, all must go down now. Houstonburg must go ahead in the *newspaper at least.*

However, complaints about the Republic's capital were voiced almost from the start. Many legislators insisted that the Allen brothers had not provided the facilities they had promised. Irritation with the humid, muggy weather that often afflicted the Bayou City was widespread, and its location so close to the Gulf made the incidence of yellow fever a frightening specter. In exasperation a congressman wrote to his wife that, "Houston was the most miserable place

in the world," while a young attorney, John Hunter Herndon, castigated the city as, "the greatest sink of dissipation and vice that modern times have known." Yet this must not have been the prevailing sentiment, for Houston continued to grow and prosper.

The issue of the location of the permanent seat of government was ultimately decided by the 1838 presidential election campaign. Candidate Mirabeau B. Lamar favored moving the capital and campaigned on that issue. On December 1, 1838, President Lamar delivered his inaugural address at the capitol, the site of present-day Houston's Rice Hotel. He made no mention of his intention to work for removal, but the matter was never in doubt. Lamar's supporters quickly passed an act through the Republic legislature stipulating that the new capital would be called "Austin" and that it would be situated at "some point between the rivers Trinity and Colorado, and above the old San Antonio road." The legislative requirements effectively secured the bypassing of Houston and meant that the new capital would be located in Central or West Texas. Since Sam Houston's political base was essentially in the east and along the Gulf Coast, Lamar intended to cultivate the frontier.

After an intensive search, commissioners appointed by congress recommended the embryo village of Waterloo, a settlement on the east bank of the Colorado. Understandably, boosters of the city of Houston were displeased. One who had been a Lamar partisan during the campaign was the editor of the Houston *Telegraph and Texas Register,* Francis W. Moore, Jr. While noting that "the climate was remarkably healthy" in Austin, Moore also observed that it was "almost entirely uninhabited, and what is worse probably, more exposed than any other point on the frontier to the depredations of hostile Indians." Yet these sentiments were mild compared to the bitter comments of the editor of the Houston *Morning Star:*

The idea of *permanently* locating the seat of Government by commissioners appointed by Congress, seems to be entirely absurd—the only satisfactory way is to leave it exclusively to the people. That there must be a called session of Congress at this place in the fall seems inevitable—for the law at present in force designating the time for the removal of the different departments to the new Capital, cannot by any possibility be obeyed.

The establishment of the permanent seat of government remained a political issue throughout the Republic period. In 1842, during his second term in office, President Houston convened congress into extraordinary session at the capitol in his namesake city. The announced purpose was to prepare for renewed war with Mexico, but many believe that "Old Sam" hoped to force the capital question once again. If so, he suffered one of his rare political setbacks when the solons met at Washington-on-the-Brazos for the next session.

The city of Houston had been compensated somewhat when it was designated as the county seat of Harris County in 1837. President Houston had named Andrew Briscoe, prominent in the Texas Revolution, as chief justice of the county. Perhaps fittingly, shortly thereafter Briscoe announced his impending marriage to Mary Jane Harris, daughter of John Richardson Harris, the founder of Harrisburg.

Among the matters falling under county jurisdiction was education. The 1836 Texas constitution guaranteed freedom of education and stressed its importance to a cultivated society, and congress passed the Education Bill of 1839, which granted to each county the proceeds from the sale of three leagues of land (13,284 acres) for the creation and upkeep of public schools. The institutions would be administered by county school boards, which were empowered to establish courses of study and set qualifications for teachers.

However, land was so abundant in Texas that it had little value for sale, and most counties did not even bother to survey the land available to them for sale. Therefore, the only schools that existed in Houston during the Republic were private. The best of these was the Houston City School, whose course of study included all disciplines taught in excellent academies. Tuition was three dollars per month, but children who could not pay the stipend were admitted free. Other smaller private schools that functioned on a somewhat regular basis in the city were the Classical School, Houston Academy, and the Houston Female Seminary. Private tutoring in the home, particularly in scientific subjects, was also not uncommon. Public education on the primary and secondary levels was still a goal for the future.

In addition to freedom of education, the Republic constitution also guaranteed freedom of religion and, in fact, prohibited clergymen from holding public office. In its infancy, Houston was home to many and diverse religious groups. The Reverend Littleton Fowler acted as chaplain of the senate in 1837-1838 and founded the first Methodist church in 1844. It eventually became Shearn Methodist Episcopal Church, South, named in honor of merchant and prominent member Charles Shearn. In 1838 the Reverend William Y. Allen started a Presbyterian congregation and also organized a Sunday School and Bible Society. The membership of the latter group included many who held political office in the city, county, and Republic governments. In the late 1830s Z.N. Morrell, an eloquent itinerant Baptist preacher, led celebrants in regular meetings while extolling the virtues of temperance. The Baptists finally built a church in Houston in 1847 on the corner of Travis Street and Texas Avenue. The Roman Catholics received the ministry of two missionary priests, Father John Timon and then Father J.M. Odin, who came to Houston from the Lazarus House in St. Louis. The first Jewish congregation was Beth Israel, founded on December 28, 1859. The cornerstone of Beth Israel synagogue was laid in June 1870 with the interdenominational cooperation that characterized Houston's early religious history. In a long procession to the new building, many religious denominations and civic groups were represented. A bless-

ing was recited by Henry S. Jacobs, chief rabbi of the New Orleans Port synagogue, and the Freemasons were in charge of the ceremonies

In lieu of regular church services and established congregations, clergymen preached to anyone who would listen in revival-style services. The privations of life in early Texas made many eager for the consolation of religion, but the excesses practiced by some ministers irritated others. With obvious distaste, Ashbel Smith, a sophisticated physician and later the Republic's ambassador to England and France, recorded these impressions in 1838 of a revival service conducted in Houston:

Methodists of this town Houston are in a state of horrible—of frightful excitement—which has lasted already eight or ten days and attracts crowds of spectators. No pen or tongue could give you an adequate description of those riotous scenes—a person must see & hear in order to be convinced of their mad extravagancies & I fancy most will distrust the evidence of their senses. They call it a revival.

Preachers railed against the evil of drink, with some effect. The Sons of Temperance, the first Houston temperance society on record, was organized on February 20, 1839, with the Reverend William Y. Allen and Sam Houston among its leading members. Speeches were delivered by many prominent citizens and even President Houston, no stranger to alcoholic excess, made an impassioned plea for temperance. Nevertheless, drunkenness was a prevalent vice in the

early days of the city.

In 1837 the Republic congress passed a law suppressing various kinds of gambling, such as roulette and rouge et noir, but in Houston this seems to have been honored only in the breach. In this connection, Gustav Dresel, a German businessman whose journals reveal much about Houston's early history, noted, "games of hazard were forbidden, but nevertheless the green tables were occupied by the gamblers for the whole night. What is more, these blacklegs even formed a regular guild, against which any opposition was a risky matter." Since thoroughbred racing was also popular in the city, this, too, increased the incidence of gambling.

Early Houston was no stranger to frontier rowdiness or violence. Francis W. Moore, Jr., editor and sometime mayor of Houston, mounted a spirited crusade against one form of violence—dueling. Legal in most Southern states at the time, it is not difficult to see why the practice took root in Houston. Moore was particularly incensed at the murder of Henry Laurens, a young man of good family, back in the States by gambler Chauncey Goodrich. The duel was provoked when Goodrich falsely accused Laurens of stealing. Contested with rifles at 20 paces, Laurens died two days later from wounds sustained in the encounter. Goodrich's death not long afterwards in San Antonio under violent circumstances enabled Moore to moralize once again concerning the high rate of bloodshed and violence in Texas. Thanks in great part to the efforts of the crusading editor, in 1840 both the city and the Republic passed anti-dueling statutes, which operated against the seconds as well as the participants in an "affair of honor."

As befitted a frontier community, the meting out of justice in Houston was swift and uncompromising. Trials were conducted in an informal manner with little attention paid to formal rules of evidence and legal procedure. William A. Bollaert, an English barrister who later practiced law in Galveston, has left this description of a trial held in Houston in 1842:

Organizing a church in 1839, the Episcopalians were one of the earliest religious groups to establish a congregation in Houston. The members waited five years to begin work on the first Christ Church at Texas and Fannin in 1845. The Gothic structure was replaced in 1893 by the present cathedral. Courtesy, Harris County Heritage Society; Litterst-Dixon Collection

There was a very gentlemanly man as Judge Morriss. The District Attorney as prosecution for the Republic was opposed by half dozen lawyers—ready of speech and loads of references—from Magna Charter upwards—the Court was over a crockery store used on Sunday for a Methodist Chapel—the Judge was chewing his quid—thrown back in his chair—his legs thrown up on his desk—the District Attorney was chewing and smoking . . . I saw the weed in the mouth of some of the lookers on—order was kept in the Court—but ever and anon there was a squirt of Tobacco juice on the floor.

If trials were sometimes conducted in a casual manner, sentencing was harsh and precise. In addition to fines and jail time, the city criminal code condoned whipping and death by hanging. Theft was routinely punishable by 100 lashes applied to the bare back of the offender, though juries could assess a greater number of lashes. Branding on the palm of the hand was at one time a recognized punishment, but the practice was later outlawed. Hanging was the sentence reserved for convicted murderers and rapists, with the execution carried out in public. The practice was defended as being salutary for the citizenry, but the large crowds indicate that there was a circus atmosphere attached to it. In 1838, amid a

Mirabeau Buonaparte Lamar (1798-1859), who had commanded the Texas cavalry at San Jacinto and had served both as vice-president and president of Texas, also served as president of the Philosophical Society of Texas. From Thrall, Texas 1879

boisterous crowd, lawyer John Hunter Herndon viewed the hanging of convicted murderers David Jones and John C. Quick. Herndon recorded these impressions in his diary:

A delightful day, worthy of other deeds— 140 men order'd out to guard the Criminals to the gallows—a concourse of from 2000 to 3000 persons on the ground and among the whole not a single sympathetic tear was dropped—Quick addressed the crowd in a stern composed & hardened manner entirely unmoved up to the swinging off the cart—Jones seemed frightened altho as hardened in crime as Quick—they swing off at 2 o'clock P.M. and were cut down in 35 minutes not having made the slightest struggle.

Not all attractions that drew crowds of Houstonians were violent. Theatrical productions, both serious and comic works, generally drew overflowing and appreciative audiences. Minstrel shows, acts featuring trained animals, and practitioners of the "science of phrenology" were also warmly received. Of a more serious nature was the formation of the Philosophical Society of Texas, chartered in 1837. Mirabeau B. Lamar served as president and Ashbel Smith as vice-president. Meeting in Houston, the first paper that the members applauded arose out of Smith's experiences as a physician in treating yellow fever cases. Admitting that Houston's climate was a factor in the dread disease, Smith stressed cooperation and the exchange of information between the Bayou City, New Orleans, and Mobile in combating the common foe.

From its faint beginnings immediately following the attainment of independence, Houston had become the principal urban center of the Texas Republic. While its citizens were chiefly concerned with the economic growth of their city, they had not neglected social and cultural attainments as well. Greater challenges lay ahead as Texans debated whether or not they wished to enter the Union as a state or pursue their independent status.

Agustín de Iturbide, the first emperor of Mexico, renegotiated the colonization laws that had been originally agreed upon by the Austins and the former Spanish government. Iturbide's legislation would serve as the basis for much of the colonization law, but he remained on the throne only a few months and was overthrown in 1824. The Republic of Mexico was established at the time of his fall. Courtesy, San Jacinto Museum of History, San Jacinto Monument

Lorenzo de Zavala was one of the important Mexican leaders of the Texas revolution. A Federalist, he had been forced to flee Mexico in 1830 and then again in 1833. Although Santa Anna's minister to France, he resigned his office and moved to Texas in 1834. His home, across Buffalo Bayou, served as a hospital for the wounded of San Jacinto. He served as vice-president of Texas from March 17, 1836, until October 17, 1836. Shortly after his resignation, he died, having played an important role in bringing his liberal ideals to Texas. Courtesy, San Jacinto Museum of History

This beaded cigar case was brought by Stephen F. Austin to Texas upon his release from a Mexican prison in 1835. Austin had been imprisoned by the government of Mexico for suspicion of inciting insurrection when he traveled to Mexico at the behest of the Convention of 1833 to protest the Law of April 6, 1830. Courtesy, San Jacinto Museum of History, San Jacinto Monument

Built in 1830 for trade on the upper Missouri River, the steamer Yellowstone was purchased in 1835 for use in Texas waters by the Texas bankers McKinney and Williams. During her trip to Texas, she carried 47 Mobile Grays who volunteered for the Texas army. On March 31, the retreating Texas army crossed the Brazos aboard her. Thirty-nine days later she would carry members of the Texas government and their prisoner, Santa Anna, to Velasco. After the war she carried cargo and passengers up and down Buffalo Bayou between Houston and Galveston. Courtesy, San Jacinto Museum of History, San Jacinto Monument

Right:
Commander of the left wing of the Texas army at San Jacinto, Sidney Sherman would play an important role in the development of Texas in the 1840s and 1850s. A leader in the community of Harrisburg and the representative for Harris County in the Seventh Congress of the Republic, Sherman also believed in the need for rail development in the region. In 1850 he became a leading promoter of the Buffalo Bayou, Brazos and Colorado Railway. Sherman later served as commandant of Confederate forces on Galveston Island until ill health forced his retirement. Courtesy, San Jacinto Museum of History, San Jacinto Monument

Far right:
Having come to Texas in 1821 and settled in San Antonio in 1822, Erastus "Deaf" Smith had been a neutral at the beginning of the Texas revolution, but was kept out of San Antonio by Mexican soldiers and then decided to join the forces of the revolution. At San Jacinto Smith was the leader of the scouts and destroyed Vince's bridge before participating in the battle. He later commanded a company of rangers. Courtesy, San Jacinto Museum of History

Left:
The wife of the man credited with the cry "Remember the Alamo," Catherine Cox Sherman, lived a life typical of an entrepreneur's wife on the Texas frontier. Her husband brought her to Texas from Ohio, finding a home in a one-room cabin near San Jacinto. Sidney Sherman later served in the Congress of the Republic, and after annexation tried many different enterprises, none of which quite worked. His wife supported him in all things, moving from San Jacinto to Harrisburg and finally to Galveston, where she died in 1865. Courtesy, San Jacinto Museum of History

Carried by the Texas forces at San Jacinto, this flag was brought to Texas by a company from Newport, Kentucky. Made of white silk with an embroidered figure of Liberty, the flag served a nation that did not yet have its Lone Star flag. Courtesy, San Jacinto Museum of History

In less than 20 minutes, the forces of Sam Houston destroyed the detachment of the Mexican army under Santa Anna. The painter Henry McCardle interviewed veterans of the battle in the 1870s so he could paint this detailed work, which is on permanent display in the Texas State Capitol. McCardle depicts the moment at which the Texans broke through the Mexican line. Courtesy, Texas Department of Highways

On May 8, 1846, U.S. forces
under the command of Zachary
Taylor met members of the
Mexican army under Mariano
Arista at Palo Alto, 12 miles
from Brownsville. The victory of
the U.S. forces was the first in
the two-year Mexican War that
confirmed the annexation of
Texas by the U.S. The war was
celebrated in a series of Texian
Campaign plates produced in
England. Photo by Story J.
Sloane III, Harris County
Heritage Society

CHAPTER II

STATEHOOD, GROWTH, AND CRISIS

Shortly after Texas achieved independence from Mexico, the issue of annexation to the United States came to the fore. Voters in the Republic's first presidential election cast a straw ballot for or against union with the United States, and a great majority of the electorate preferred annexation. In his 1836 inaugural address, President Houston promised that the issue would have first priority.

In fact, overtures to the United States had already been made by the ad interim administration of David G. Burnet. In response to a Texas request, Henry Morfit, a clerk in the State Department, visited the Republic in the late summer of 1836. Upon his return to Washington, he advised President Jackson against immediate recognition of Texas in light of the threat of Mexican invasion in response to annexation. This was sage counsel in a Presidential election year, as Northern opposition to the annexation of Texas had begun to manifest itself on anti-slavery grounds. Once Democrat Martin Van Buren was safely elected, Jackson announced the appointment of Alcee La Branche as charge d'affaires from the United States to the Republic of Texas. It was the last official act of his administration and Jackson celebrated it by sharing a glass of wine with William Wharton, appointed by President Houston to represent Texas at Washington. Throughout the period of independence, the American government maintained its diplomatic headquarters at Galveston, resisting all suggestions from leading Houston merchants that it move to that city.

In contrast to his predecessor Sam Houston, President Mirabeau B. Lamar opposed annexation, but following Sam Houston's reelection in 1841, the annexation issue became viable once again. On April 4, 1841, John Tyler succeeded William Henry Harrison as President, and shortly thereafter Abel Upshur, an ardent expansionist, became Secretary of State. As a Southerner, Upshur favored annexation, and he was also suspicious of British interests in the area. President Houston responded to the more congenial atmosphere in Washington by dispatching Isaac Van Zandt and James Pinckney Henderson as envoys to Washington, empowered to conclude annexation talks. On April 12, 1844, a treaty was signed by the Texas representatives and John C. Calhoun, who succeeded Upshur. However, all was held in abeyance as the summer approached and with it the party conventions to nominate candidates for the 1844 U.S. Presidential campaign.

Both the Whig and Democratic parties held their conventions in Baltimore. The Whigs named Henry Clay as their standard-bearer, and James K. Polk captured the Democratic nomination. Clay indicated that he favored the annexation of Texas but not at the cost of war with Mexico; Polk, catching the nation's mood of expansion, pledged to acquire Texas and Oregon. Anti-slavery feeling in the North helped spawn a third party. James G. Birney, the Liberty Party's nominee, vehemently opposed the admission of the slave state of Texas as fatal to sectional harmony. Texas and expansion were the issues that would determine the election.

In June 1844 the treaty for the annexation of Texas reached the Senate floor for a decisive vote. The Texas pact was overwhelmingly defeated—the first time a major treaty was rejected in United States history. Rather than attaining the constitutionally required two-thirds approval in the Senate, the treaty was rejected by almost precisely that count. Five months later, in November, Polk won a narrow victory at the polls and thus the electorate popularly endorsed the admission of Texas into the Union. However, the Congressional elections had resulted in only a slight change in the makeup of the Senate and thus the treaty's rejection could be anticipated upon a second vote.

At this juncture the Texan envoy, James Pinckney Henderson, suggested the "joint resolution" approach, requiring only a simple majority in the House and Senate, rather than a two-thirds vote of approval in the Senate. With the assistance of Senators Thomas Hart Benton and Robert Walker, a bill was quickly drafted. By its terms the State of Texas was guaranteed a republican

The Democratic Presidential
and Vice-Presidential
candidates in the 1844
campaign, James K. Polk and
George M. Dallas, favored the
annexation of Texas to the
United States. Annexation was
the major issue of the campaign.
From the Collections of the
Dallas Historical Society

form of government and was permitted to retain title to its public lands. Slavery would continue as a legal institution and the state reserved the right to divide itself up into as many as five states, with slavery outlawed in any state north of the 36.30 line. After intensive debate and by a close margin in each chamber, the bill for the annexation of Texas carried.

Houstonians overwhelmingly supported union with the United States. The city's leading newspaper, the *Telegraph and Texas Register,* portrayed this sentiment in the following editorial comment:

The news of the passage of the annexation resolutions was hailed with a burst of enthusiasm by our citizens that has never been exceeded. The news of the victorious battle of San Jacinto scarcely excited such general and enthusiastic rejoicing. The sound of the drum and other musical instruments, the roar of the cannon, the loud shouts of the multitude resounding long after midnight, indicated the ardent longing of our citizens to return . . . under the glorious eagle of the American union.

The annexation legislation required that the people of the Texas Republic accept the proposal by January 1846, and that a state constitution acceptable to the federal Con-

gress be written by that time. After 10 years of struggle and privation the citizens of the Republic were willing enough to accept the benefits of American citizenship, but suddenly there was an alternative. Seeking to avoid war between the United States and Mexico over annexation and fearing that such a conflict would result in a decisive American triumph and additional territorial gains, Britain and France urged Mexico to recognize the independence of Texas. At virtually the same time that Andrew Jackson Donelson arrived to convey the American proposal of annexation to Texas, Charles Elliot returned from Mexico bearing an offer of independence from that nation. Under pressure from both camps, President Anson Jones agreed to submit the two plans to the vote of a specially elected convention. On July 4, 1845, at Austin, the delegates expressed their preference for union with the United States with only one dissenting vote. In Houston the decision met with celebrations in which the Stars and Stripes were raised and resolutions of approval were adopted. In rapid sequence a state constitution was written and ratified by the people, and Texas was admitted as the 28th state in the Union on December 29, 1845.

The annexation of Texas by the U.S. was viewed by Mexico as the taking of Mexican soil, which, the Mexican government had warned earlier, would lead to war. The moment annexation was finalized, diplomatic relations with the U.S. were broken off. While annexation was the principal cause of the Mexican War, it was not the only one. Northern maritime interests avidly sought to acquire California and its choice Pacific Coast ports at San Francisco and San Diego, and all efforts to purchase California had failed. After an unsuccessful attempt to present a plan for the American purchase of land north of the Nueces River, including California, President Polk insisted that he had made every reasonable sacrifice in the cause of peace and ordered American troops to take up a position along the Rio Grande. A patrol unit of American soldiers commanded by General Zachary Taylor was engaged by Mexican troops along the border on April 24, 1846. In a statement that later became famous, President Polk demanded war to avenge, "American blood shed upon American soil," and on May 11, 1846, Congress rallied to the support of the Chief Executive and declared a state of war to be in existence between the United States and Mexico.

Between 125 and 150 Houstonians volunteered for military action in the war with Mexico, and wartime activities brought increased traffic through the Port of Houston. Tons of arms, cotton, and foodstuffs passed through the port, boosting the city's growth. After almost two years of fighting, Mexico finally yielded its claims to Texas and many other future American states in the treaty of Guadalupe Hidalgo, signed on February 2, 1848.

As Houston developed economically with the coming of annexation, the Mexican War, and statehood, the old Houston-Galveston rivalry flared up. At the time of Houston's origin, there was no town on Galveston Island. Although in the planning stage earlier than Houston, a major storm in 1837 delayed the founding of the city until the next year. Despite the boasts of the Allen brothers, few oceangoing vessels could make their way up Buffalo Bayou to Houston; therefore most ships of that size landed their cargoes at Galveston. However, Houston's designation as the first capital of the Republic was an honor not shared by Galveston. As Professor Marilyn Sibley points out in her book, *The Port of Houston*, the rivalry between the two young cities at

This 1859 drawing depicts a cargo of cotton being loaded at Main Street.

this point in their mutual history was a friendly one. Many Houstonians maintained business operations in both cities and many tended to view Galveston as principally a depot for goods ultimately destined for consumption in Houston.

At the inception of statehood, however, Galveston's population was almost twice that of Houston. The Bayou City's growth, which had been very rapid from the time of its founding, had begun to slow somewhat. The federal census of 1850 placed the city's population at 2,397, an increase of less than 400 over the count taken by the Republic 10 years earlier. Still, in 1850, Houston was the state's third-largest city, ranking behind Galveston and San Antonio. While somewhat disappointing to local boosters, the above tally did not take into account a floating population, temporarily resident in the city and dedicated to trade. In the latter category, the cotton trade appeared to be particularly booming. According to figures compiled in 1842 by the *Telegraph and Texas Register,* 4,260 bales of cotton were carted to the city from plantations along the Brazos and shipped out from Houston. By 1854 that figure had reached 11,359 bales, proving conclusively that Houston had established itself as a trading center where land and water routes converged.

The city took steps to improve its port facilities, and with the encouragement of the municipal council, wharves were built on the banks of Buffalo Bayou within the city limits. An ordinance was passed on June 10, 1841, creating the Port of Houston and placing all wharves and landings within the political jurisdiction of the city. Also, it was stipulated that the waterfront area between Main and Fannin streets would be held in reserve for large ships to dock while smaller craft would be given other locations. Then, in compliance with the ordinance, Charles T. Gerlach, a local merchant, was named to be wharfmaster. Encouragement was also given to efforts to clear the channel above Harrisburg and to prevent pollution along the route from Harrisburg to Houston.

In 1849, as the scramble to California to find gold reached its intensity, the city lay

astride one of the most frequently traveled routes to the Pacific Coast. No less an authority than General Stephen Kearney, the Mexican War conqueror of Santa Fe, recommended the Houston to El Paso to San Diego route as the quickest and most practical way to the fabled gold fields. Writing in a St. Louis newspaper, Kearney insisted that an emigrant might make the trek from Houston to San Diego for not more than $20. A few Houstonians headed for California in search of gold, but prudent proprietors of general stores and businessmen like Thomas W. House and William Marsh Rice remained behind and enjoyed temporary prosperity from the sale of foodstuffs, rifles, powder, and kits of carpenter tools purchased by the "'49ers."

As the decade of the 1850s approached, Houston was but 14 years old. At this point in its history the city faced a major, perhaps inevitable, challenge from Galveston. Leading capitalists there sought to secure the trade of the interior of Texas, principally cotton from the Brazos and Trinity river bottoms. If those rivers were made navigable, given the lack of adequate roads from the interior to Houston, the Bayou City could be effectively bypassed as a trading depot. With this aim in mind, the Galveston and Brazos Navigation Company was chartered on February 8, 1850, to build a canal connecting the Brazos River with Galveston Bay. The canal was built, but the expenses of constant dredging exceeded the profits earned. This challenge was beaten back, but the rivalry between Houston and

As a part of their successful effort to make Houston the capital of the new Republic, the Allen brothers built a peach-colored, two-story structure to house the legislature, as well as other smaller government offices. Although not complete when the government arrived, the new structure served to house a small art gallery as well as the offices of government. After the government moved to Austin, the building reverted to the Allens and they used it as a hotel. Courtesy, Harris County Heritage Society

Facing page:
The development of regular steamship service between Galveston and Houston was a major feature in Houston's growth before the Civil War. Regular runs by steamers tied the city to the world in terms of both passengers and freight. This advertisement, produced by the Houston Telegraph Company, suggests that the newspaper was the center for advertising of all types during this era. Courtesy, Special Collections; Houston Public Library

its neighboring cities then shifted to railroad construction.

Like Andrew Briscoe before him, San Jacinto veteran Sidney Sherman, a prominent citizen of Harrisburg, hoped to lure trade to Harrisburg rather than Houston through the construction of a railroad. He became the leading promoter for the Buffalo Bayou, Brazos and Colorado Railway Company, which was incorporated in 1850 with financial backing obtained in Boston. The road had been built to Richmond on the eastern bank of the Brazos by 1856, when construction was halted for lack of funds. Sherman and his partners were unable to command sufficient state assistance, and the outbreak of the Civil War doomed completion of Sherman's project. Nevertheless, he had finished some 80 miles of track from Harrisburg to the Colorado River, and the Buffalo Bayou, Brazos and Colorado could claim one other distinction; in 1853 one of its locomotives, the *General Sherman*, became the first to grace the Texas countryside.

Houston benefited from railroad construction when the Houston & Texas Central, chartered originally by the state legislature in 1848 as the Galveston & Red River, obtained a new charter in 1852 and

was granted permission to locate its terminus in the Bayou City. Houston businessman Paul Bremond was named president of the railroad in 1854. He was unsuccessful in securing Northern capital to finance the project, but state loans enabled the road to continue. By 1860 it had reached Millican in Brazos County, about 80 miles northwest of Houston. Interestingly enough, Washington-on-the-Brazos, jealous of its river traffic, refused to award the Houston & Texas Central right-of-way through the town.

In the decade before secession, two other projects were begun with Houston connections. On February 7, 1853, the Galveston, Houston, and Henderson Railroad Company was chartered with the endorsement of Houston and Galveston capitalists. Both cities gave their approval and financial groups in each city agreed to subscribe for $300,000 of the stock. Construction began just opposite Galveston on the mainland at Virginia Point and had reached the outskirts of Houston by 1859. At that point work ceased because of the outbreak of a yellow fever epidemic, but the road became the first in Texas to touch the seacoast. Triweekly train service was begun between Houston and Virginia Point. Passengers and freight were then transferred between

Conceived of by Sidney Sherman, the Buffalo Bayou, Brazos and Colorado Railway Company was the first Texas railroad. It was designed to link Harrisburg to the back country and to create competition for Houston. Houstonians blocked this effort by building a "tap," which was joined to the main line in 1857 and drew traffic into Houston instead of into Harrisburg. The tap line inspired more Houstonians to develop other railroads. Courtesy, San Jacinto Museum of History

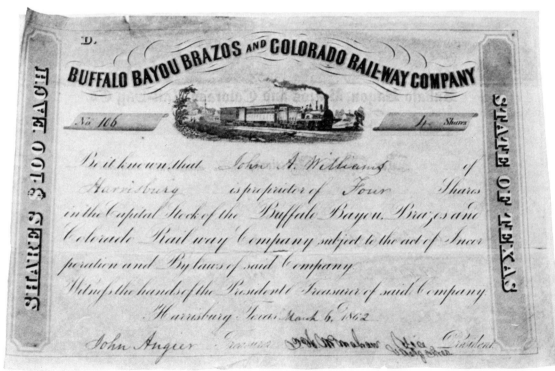

COMFORT, ECONOMY
AND SPEED!
Houston and Galveston!

THE HOUSTON NAVIGATION COMPANY'S
LINE OF STEAMERS

Consisting of the following first-class boats:

DIANA, Capt. Sterrett.
ISLAND CITY, Capt. Blakeman.
NEPTUNE.

All in the very best condit'on, leave Galveston for Houston, and Houston for Galveston, every day, making close connections, at Houston, with the Trains on the Texas Central and the Columbia Railroads, and at Galveston with the New Orleans Steamers.

On and after THURSDAY, MARCH 14, these steamers run by the following

SCHEDULE:

DIANA Leaves GALVESTON SUNDAYS and THURSDAYS, at 10 o'clock A. M., or on arrival of steamer from Berwick's Bay, reaching Houston at 8 P. M.; passengers taking dinner and supper on the boat. TUESDAYS at 4 P. M., arriving in Houston after midnight; passengers sleeping on board, and remaining at pleasure until the leaving of the morning trains for Hempstead, Navasota and Chappell Hill, for Richmond, Columbus and Columbia.

ISLAND CITY Leaves GALVESTON on MONDAYS, WEDNESDAYS, and FRIDAYS at 4 P. M., connecting, next morning, with all the trains from Houston for the interior of Texas.

DIANA Leaves Houston on MONDAYS, WEDNESDAYS, and FRIDAYS, and the **ISLAND CITY** On TUESDAYS, THURSDAYS and SATURDAYS, at 6 P. M., on arrival of the trains on the various railroads from the interior, reaching Galveston by 4 A. M., next morning. Passengers for the New Orleans boats leaving same morning, taking breakfast, if they desire it, on board.

☞ The advantages afforded by these boats to the traveler, are the saving of expense, securing comfort, and no time lost in making the connections, either inward or outward.

☞ The Company refer to the testimony of all travelers as to the accommodations of the boats, and the attentiveness of the officers to the safety of the passengers.

FARE EACH WAY, $3
For Passage apply on Board.

Houston Telegraph Printing Establishment.

Thomas W. House, a mayor of Houston during the Civil War, was one of the business leaders who helped to make Houston a dominant mercantile community in the 19th century. An Englishman by birth and a baker by trade, House came to Houston in 1838. By 1840 he was both a baker and an ice cream maker. He eventually became a cotton factor, creating a great private bank out of the profits from this and his enterprises in transportation. Also a major shipper of cotton to Mexico during the Civil War, he tried to break the blockade off Galveston. Courtesy, Texas Room; Houston Public Library

Virginia Point and Galveston across Galveston Bay by the ferryboat *Texas*. It required four hours to complete the trip between Houston and Galveston, but early in 1860 the completion of a railroad bridge provided a direct connection from the island to the mainland.

The most ambitious pre-Civil War railroad scheme was the Texas and New Orleans Railroad, chartered in 1856 with the purpose of binding Louisiana and Texas closer together in the event of war with the North. By January 1861 tracks had been laid from Houston to Orange and all 110 miles of the Texas portion of the road had been completed. Due to various delays and financial stringency, the Louisiana section of track was not finished until after the Civil War. The Texas and New Orleans as well as the Buffalo Bayou, Brazos and Colorado Railway Company eventually became part of the Southern Pacific's trunk line to California.

What was it like to travel on the early railroads with Houston connections? On the Buffalo Bayou, Brazos and Colorado, the first passenger coaches had originally been built in Boston to serve as streetcars. Each coach, sitting on only four wheels, could hold about 20 passengers, but they were later replaced by much larger coaches that could accommodate as many as 50 travelers each. Both passenger and freight cars were pulled by the 13-ton locomotive engine, the *General Sherman.* A passenger on the line, the British writer A.S. Fremantle, recorded in his journal that the train gave a tremendous jolt when it started and, "every passenger is allowed to use his own discretion about breaking his arm, neck, or leg without interference by railway officials."

Houston had become the foremost railroad center in Texas by 1860. With the enthusiastic cooperation of the state in the form of loans and public lands, more than 450 miles of track had been laid in Texas by the time the state joined the Confederacy. Houstonians pointed with pride to the fact that of that figure more than 350 miles led to Houston. In 1860, 115,010 cotton bales came into the city, the great majority transported by rail. This count was just short of double what it had been only two years earlier in 1858 and almost four times what it had been in 1854. These statistics are eloquent proof of what the railroads meant for Houston in the period between the attainment of statehood and the outbreak of sectional warfare.

In addition to the growth of transportation, other business and commercial activity boosted the fortunes of Houston and its entrepreneurs at this time. An example of this can be found in the career of Thomas William House, whose son Colonel Edward M. House would become famous as Woodrow Wilson's close friend and advisor. An Englishman by birth and a baker by trade, Thomas came to Houston from New Orleans in 1838. In Houston he became an ice cream manufacturer, a grocery and dry-goods dealer, and a banker. As early as 1840 House began to function as a private bank, accepting deposits and lending money. To this activity he added cotton factoring, and with his grocery and dry-goods sales, he soon became the largest wholesaler in the state. Ox wagons could often be seen waiting half a day at the T.W. House Plantation Commissary and Wholesale Grocery at the corner of Main Street and Franklin Avenue for their turn to be loaded. During the Civil

War House became mayor of Houston. During the blockade of Galveston, he shipped cotton to England through the Mexican port of Matamoros and purchased desperately needed supplies for the Confederacy in return. In the postwar era House expanded his holdings by developing railroad, shipping, and banking interests, and when he died in 1880, he left an estate valued at more than one million dollars. As entrepreneurs like House experienced success in their commercial ventures, they also helped to make Houston an important mercantile community.

The Texas Telegraph Company, a commercial endeavor that advanced communications to Houston, was organized and founded in Louisiana. In 1853-1854 the company strung wire from Shreveport to a number of communities in East Texas and then to Houston. In 1854 the connection between Houston and Galveston was made by using a wire under Galveston Bay. Service and financial problems led to the ultimate failure of the company, which was finally consolidated into the Western Union system in 1869. Another financial enterprise that played a role in the city's economic development was the insurance business. The Houston Insurance Company, established in 1858, offered merchants fire and marine insurance. An out-of-state firm, Southern Mutual Life Insurance Company,

insured the lives of Harris County slaves as well as their masters. To facilitate these and other business ventures, a Board of Trade was created, mainly to regulate freight and storage rates.

Houston's commercial development was hampered by the lack of banking facilities. Because of lingering feelings concerning the causes of the Panic of 1837 in the United States and the fact that most Texans shared Jackson's prejudices against banks, the 1845 state constitution prohibited the establishment of public banks and the issuance of paper money entirely. This regulation remained in effect until the Civil War era and made possible the development of a limited number of private banks. In addition to T.W. House, cotton merchant B.A. Shepherd also engaged in banking activity in Houston. In fact, in 1854 Shepherd became the first Houstonian to engage exclusively in banking for a livelihood, and the B.A. Shepherd Exchange and Collection Office was the first real bank in the city.

While business development was on the rise, the faint stirrings of labor union interest in Houston were also taking place. In June 1837 the Houston Mechanics Association was organized, its purpose to "advance the interests of all workingmen." As its first priority, the Houston group sought to organize a similar movement in Galveston, but while a few joint meetings were held, the

Although Texas issued currency, banker Samuel May Williams of Galveston also issued currency during the period of the Republic and statehood. Operating the thriving Commercial and Agricultural Bank of Texas, Williams believed he could supply money to ease currency shortages. In 1848, however, the Texas legislature ended the right of local banks to issue such currency. The currency placed power in the hands of bankers, particularly those in Galveston. Houstonians opposed this activity, in part to protect their own trade position. Courtesy, San Jacinto Museum of History

Galveston laborers failed to organize. By the late 1840s and in the early years of the next decade, the Houston group was regularly represented in the annual Fourth of July parade. However, active unionism, complete with regular negotiations over salaries and working conditions as well as the threat of strikes, did not become a reality in the Bayou City until after 1870. Basically, there were two reasons for this lack of success: the slow pace of heavy industrial development in the city and the fact that no assistance was received from national union organizations until the post-Civil War era.

As the institutions of Houston's commercial life were being planted, the city's physical appearance took shape. Buffalo Bayou continued to flow at the foot of Main Street, and passengers arriving by boat from Galveston traveled by two-wheeled horse-drawn carts to the Capitol Hotel. On the site of what had been the capitol of the Republic, the hotel perched one story above most of the wooden storefronts flanking Main Street. Ferdinand Roemer, the German colonizer whose work *Texas* (1849) served as an inspiration for German migration to Texas, was a guest at the hotel and noted

with distaste, "a number of men, evidently farmers, clad mostly in coarse woolen blanket-coats of the brightest colors—mostly red, white and green—stood around the stove, engaged in lively conversation." Roemer also observed that while the hotel did not compare favorably with similar establishments in Europe, one phase of its operations was impressive:

The numerous saloons . . . drew my attention. Some of them (considering the size of the City) were really magnificent when compared to their surroundings. After passing through large folding doors, one slipped immediately from the streets into a spacious room in which stood long rows of crystal bottles on a beautifully decorated bar. These were filled with divers kinds of firewater—among which, however, cognac or brandy were chiefly in demand. Here also stood an experienced barkeeper, in white shirt sleeves alert to serve the patrons the various plain as well as mixed drinks (of which latter the American concocts many) . . . the saloons were always filled.

Not all approved of saloons, however, for

In the 19th century, waterborne trade along Buffalo Bayou and through Galveston Bay was dominated by Charles Morgan's steamship line. Sidewheelers ran from his headquarters on the Galveston Wharf to Houston and New Orleans. In the 1870s he developed a near monopoly on trade along Buffalo Bayou by taking control of the Buffalo Bayou Ship Channel Company and dredging the channel to a 12-foot depth. Courtesy, Rosenberg Library

a municipal ordinance enacted in May 1855 closed saloons, billiard parlors, and bowling alleys on Sunday.

The cultural life of the city was improved by the organization in 1854 of the Houston Lyceum, located at 419 Main Street, which presented debates, lectures, occasional music concerts, and a free library for its members. Although for brief periods of time there were no recorded Lyceum activities, the group was strong enough to assist in the establishment of Houston's first free public library in the first years of the 20th century.

Since Houston's birth in 1836, the *Telegraph and Texas Register* had been the leading newspaper in the city. This was so because of the journalistic talents of its editor, Francis W. Moore, Jr. A brilliant man who had been an army surgeon during the War for Texas Independence, Moore also taught school and practiced law. He served as mayor of Houston in 1838, again in 1843, and from 1849-1852, and he was far from bashful in using his position as mayor to advance the fortunes of his newspaper. Neither the *National Intelligencer* nor the Houston *Morning Star* could rival Moore's creation in popularity or subscriptions.

In the pages of their favorite newspaper, Houstonians followed the politics of the day. Whereas politics in the Republic era had been essentially a question of personalities, national political parties now began to take root in Texas. Symbolically, the *Telegraph and Texas Register* affixed the word "Democratic" to its masthead, and commented, "the great principles that distinguish the Democratic party of the Union are the best calculated to advance the true interests of the people of Texas." Not only did the state become more involved in national political parties; it also became entangled in the crisis developing between the country's Northern and Southern states.

The annexation of Texas, coming as it did after nine years of sectional controversy, must be regarded as a major cause of the Civil War. Northerners saw the annexation of Texas as the extension and perpetuation of slavery, while Southern Congressmen openly threatened to abandon the Union if Texas were not admitted. Representing the Lone Star State in the United States Senate after annexation, Sam Houston had been a force for moderation on sectional issues and had voted to admit the free states of Oregon and California. Houston voted against the 1854 Kansas-Nebraska Act, which would have bypassed the Missouri Compromise, allowing slavery in Kansas and Nebraska territories. He was the only Southern Senator courageous enough to do so.

In Texas Senator Houston was pilloried and denounced as an apostate and traitor to the South. Twenty-two county conventions, among them Harris, demanded his resignation from the United States Senate. The state legislature adopted a resolution against virtually no opposition condemning his recent vote and notifying him that he would not be returned to Washington at the expiration of his term; indeed, had there been a provision for recall in the state constitution, his Senate term would have ended immediately. Finally, while he had enjoyed great popularity in the city of Houston over the years, here, too, he fell into disfavor because of his Union advocacy.

The state convention of the Democratic party assembled in Austin in January 1856. A resolution was quickly approved that cri-

Samuel May Williams, mason, banker, and entrepreneur, was typical of the men who had come to the Gulf Coast seeking a fortune. As a leader of the entrepreneurial faction in Galveston, Williams was one who stood in the way of those who sought to make Houston the dominant economic force in Texas. Like his opponents, however, Williams owned land across Texas, including property just over the Harris County line in Fort Bend County. Courtesy, Rosenberg Library

Houston's second mayor, Francis Moore, Jr., was a dominant figure in Texas life during the period of the Republic and antebellum statehood. In addition to a political career, he was the owner and editor of the Telegraph and Texas Register, *one of the most influential papers in the state. As a politician, he served as a reformer, giving Houston its first charter, police force, and market. He opposed dueling and was eventually able to make it illegal. After selling his paper in 1854, Moore traveled, studied geology, and became the Texas state geologist in 1859. He went north during the Civil War and died while on a survey in 1864. Courtesy, Texas Room; Houston Public Library*

ticized Houston's action and demanded federal protection for slavery anywhere it might obtain. Rejected by his party, Houston decided to run as an independent in the 1857 race for governor. The "Old Hero" confessed his disappointment when the Harris County Democratic convention, meeting at the Houston Academy in February 1857, refused to nominate him but instead named Hardin R. Runnels, who went on to receive the state Democratic nomination at Waco.

A strong defender of states' rights, Runnels was prepared to consider the prospect of secession from the Union in order to protect those rights. His lieutenant governor, Francis R. Lubbock, had been active in Democratic party affairs and for several years had served as a district clerk of Harris County. Houston and his choice for lieutenant

governor, Jesse Grimes, campaigned as "old Democrats," a posture that placed them in opposition to the party's states' rights emphasis.

In the bitter campaign Houston put himself forward as the champion of the Union and a force for national harmony. However, his valiant efforts and past associations were not enough; for the first time in his Texas career, he suffered an election defeat. Runnels gained 32,552 votes and Houston 23,628, while Lubbock was also victorious by a substantial majority. Runnels was the popular choice in both Houston and Harris County.

The 1857 gubernatorial election destroyed existing political alignments in Texas. The two wings of the Democratic party stood for states' rights versus Union, or, expressing it another way, pro- and anti-

Houston. Sectionalism and the threat of secession were constant political themes and Houston newspapers joined in the debate over slavery. The institution was defended as a "positive good" and was justified on economic, religious, and social grounds. One Bayou City editor, Edward H. Cushing of the Houston *Telegraph and Texas Register*, insisted that slavery in Texas was a boon to the slave, considering his living conditions in Africa, and argued that the economic prosperity of the city was being retarded because of the lack of an adequate labor force. He concluded his editorial by urging the reopening of the African slave trade.

In reality, slavery was a significant factor in the economic life of Houston. By 1860 there were more than a thousand slaves working in both Houston and Galveston and the state's domestic slave trade was centered in the two communities. In the decade before the Civil War, a prime slave frequently sold for $1,500 in Houston. Also, Houston's economy was based mainly on the cotton trade and to a lesser degree on the sugar trade, and profitable cotton and sugar production depended on slave labor. Locally, slaves worked principally in domestic service, though occasionally a bondsman mastered a trade or worked on the wharves. Most urban masters retained two or three adult slaves and very few had more than six. The census figures of 1850 reveal that not a single master in Houston possessed 20; ten years later six owned more than that number.

At the fateful May 1859 state Democratic convention held at the Houston Academy the party nominated Runnels for reelection as governor and Francis Lubbock for lieutenant governor. Shortly after the convention adjourned, Sam Houston proclaimed that he would once again oppose Runnels for the state's highest office: "The constitution of the Union embraces the principles by which I will be governed, if elected." Edward Clark, a member of the state constitutional convention of 1845 and politically active since that time, announced as an independent candidate for lieutenant governor. Like Houston, Clark was running on a platform sympathetic to Unionism and opposed to secession.

In 1859 the "Hero of San Jacinto," now almost 66 years old and not in good health, decided upon one more race. As an independent, against the organized strength of the Democratic party, Houston made his position clear. As a slaveholder himself, he would not stand against the institution, but he would defend the Constitution and the Union come what may. After intensive campaigning Houston reversed the 1857 results and captured the governor's office in 1859 by a count of 36,357 to 27,500 for Runnels. The race between Clark and Lubbock was much closer; the former winning by about one thousand votes. In addition to the issues involved, the campaign demonstrated one constant in Lone Star politics; in times of crisis Texans turned to Sam Houston.

Governor Houston wished to interpret his election as a stand against disunion and secession, but such was not to be the case. The death of James Pinckney Henderson in Washington created a vacancy in the United States Senate and gave the state legislature an opportunity to appoint a moderate on the slavery question. However, the choice of Louis T. Wigfall, an ultra-secessionist and fierce foe of Governor Houston, indicated the political temper of the times.

When delegates met at the state Democratic convention in Galveston on April 2, 1860, they adopted an unrestrained secessionist platform. Houston lawyer Josiah F. Crosby was among eight delegates selected to attend the national Democratic convention at Charleston. Presided over by ex-Governor Hardin R. Runnels, the Texas delegation was committed to support only those candidates who would advance the Southern view on slavery and states' rights.

Two days before the Charleston convention met, a remarkable assemblage took place in the environs of Houston. Partisans of Sam Houston, a fair number of whom were veterans of the battle of San Jacinto, convened on the battlefield on April 21, 1860. Commemorating the 24th anniversary of the battle that marked Texas independence, they presented the name of Sam

Houston as "the people's candidate" for President of the United States. Thirteen delegates from Harris County urged "Old Sam" to accept the nomination and to contest for the nation's most prestigious office. In the official communication nofitying Houston of the action that had been taken, Harris Countians Andrew Daly and Jesse White stressed that the nation would turn to a candidate who was responsive to the interests of both North and South. Though he had few illusions about his election prospects, Houston did accept the nomination, observing once more: "The constitution and the Union embrace the principles by which I will be governed if elected . . . I have no new principles to announce."

At Charleston, amidst a growing atmosphere of crisis, Stephen Douglas remained committed to his "popular sovereignty" doctrine, which meant that slavery could be abolished if it was the desire of the local inhabitants. Douglas' position compromised too much to be accepted by many Southern delegations, including the united Texas delegation. Eight such groups bolted the Charleston meeting, repaired to Richmond, and nominated John C. Breckinridge of Kentucky as their candidate for President. Northern Democrats subsequently chose Douglas as their nominee, and the Republican party, anticipating victory because of the Democratic division, nominated former Congressman Abraham Lincoln of Illinois.

Threatened by the prospect of secession and war, some Texans joined other conservative Southerners in forming the Constitutional Union party, which adopted a platform advocating the abolition of slavery north of Missouri, essentially the restoration of the Missouri Compromise line. As one of the leading Unionists in the South, Sam Houston was a natural choice for the Presidential nomination. Houston did garner 57 votes on the first ballot, but John Bell of Tennessee received 68. In fact, Sam Houston had little chance of winning the Presidency in 1860, but he seems to have been heartened by the interest shown in his possible candidacy.

As national election day approached, General George Bickley, national commander of the Knights of the Golden Circle, arrived in Houston and organized a number of local units. A secret fraternal group, the purpose of the Knights was to perpetuate slavery and defend the way of life based on that institution. Founded in 1854, the organization was poorly financed and equally poorly led. In 1860 General Bickley planned a filibustering conquest of Mexico as an alternative to sectional strife. A filibustering expedition to Mexico could lead to war with that nation, and such a war could unite North and South against a common enemy. Two separate attempts, both financed and plotted in Houston, were made to invade Mexico. In each case when the expectant bands reached the Rio Grande, they scattered without crossing over into Mexico. Nevertheless, the Knights were a sign of the fanaticism of the times.

In the national election, which was conducted in Houston and Harris County without violence of any kind, Breckinridge received a handsome majority of the votes tallied. He also won the state with 47,561 votes to 15,402 for Bell; Douglas and Lincoln earned but a few votes between them. The almost one in four votes cast for Bell and thus against disunion have intrigued students of Texas history. Certainly slavery counted for little in West Texas, and federal military protection against Indian harassment was significant in that section. Sam Houston's popularity was also a factor, and pockets of Unionism existed wherever there were populous German settlements. Opposed to slavery and attracted to the political freedom of the United States, Texas Germans stood for the Union; that was particularly true of the German immigrant community in Houston.

Shortly after the results of the Presidential election came in on December 20, 1860, South Carolina formally seceded from the United States. In quick succession Alabama, Louisiana, Florida, Georgia, and Mississippi followed. Despite opposition by Governor Houston, a Texas secession convention was called.

The special convention began its deliberations on January 28 and unanimously chose Texas Supreme Court Justice Oran M. Roberts as its presiding officer. The convention delegates repealed the annexation resolution and drafted a secession ordinance. An interim Committee of Public Safety was organized, and February 23 was set as the date for popular statewide ratification of the convention's measures. The delegates themselves approved the secession resolution and the work of the convention generally, 166 to 8. All members of the Harris County delegation voted to secede, and anticipating approval in the upcoming popular election, the convention named seven delegates to attend the organizing sessions of the Confederacy. At Montgomery they witnessed the inauguration of Jefferson Davis as president of the new Southern nation. On February 23, 1861, the convention's action in favor of secession won the approval of the people, 46,129 to 14,697. Houston and Harris County went solidly for ratification of the convention's action. Just about all Houstonians of voting age wore the symbol of secession on their hats—a blue rosette with a silver star in the center. Prior to the vote, a mass meeting of Harris County citizens was held at the Market House in Houston and a resolution was drafted urging the resignation of all federal officers and recognition of the Confederacy.

Its actions ratified by the people, the secession convention reassembled in Austin on Saturday, March 2, and Texas was declared out of the Union as of that date. Memories were stirred, for exactly 25 years earlier Texas had proclaimed its independence as a Republic. On March 5 the convention approved and joined the provisional government of the Confederate States of America. The convention proceeded to modify the state constitution to make it conform to the Confederacy and called upon state officials to take a loyalty oath to that government. All consented to do so except Governor Houston and Secretary of State E.W. Cave. Houston refused to recognize the authority of the convention. At noon on March 16, the convention declared the office of governor vacant and swore in Lieutenant Governor Edward Clark as governor, a selection that was ratified at the legislature's next regular session.

In the interim, Houston received a letter from President Lincoln offering him 5,000 troops to keep Texas in the Union. This proposition Houston curtly rejected, noting that, "I love Texas too well to bring strife and bloodshed upon her." Still, another scheme was attractive to him. If the Republic of Texas were proclaimed once again, perhaps the conquest of Mexico would absorb the energies of the Confederacy rather than a fatal internal war. In Houston the old flag of the Republic was raised on a 100-foot liberty pole in Courthouse Square amidst the firing of cannons and a display of fireworks—a scene that was repeated in Galveston and other Texas cities. When it became apparent that the independent Republic could not be resurrected, Houston delivered one more bitter protest against the "usurpations" of the convention and resigned. Two years later at Huntsville, in the midst of the terrible war that he predicted would stem from disunion, Sam Houston passed away.

John C. Breckinridge (1821-1875) was supported by Southern Democrats, including the Texas delegation, in protest against the nomination of Stephen A. Douglas during the 1860 Presidential campaign. Engraved by John C. Buttre from a daguerreotype by Mathew Brady. From Cirker, Dictionary of American Portraits, *Dover, 1967*

The turning point in the battle
of Galveston was the capture of
the Federal steamer Harriet
Lane and the destruction of the
Westfield (pictured here). With
the loss of the major naval
vessels, the Federal forces called
for a truce and eventually
surrendered, giving control of
Galveston back to the
Confederate forces after a short
period of occupation. From
Harper's Pictorial History of
the Civil War, 1866

CHAPTER III

CIVIL WAR AND AFTERMATH

In April 14, 1861, Fort Sumter in Charleston harbor was captured by the Confederacy. Two days later Houstonians read of that fateful encounter in the local newspapers. On the Courthouse Square a salute was fired to mark the Union surrender and a public meeting was called by Mayor William J. Hutchins. At that meeting a committee was named to recruit a battalion for the defense of Houston, a finance committee was authorized to raise $5,000 to finance military purchases, and a training camp for volunteers was set up beyond the city limits near Harrisburg. By the end of April, more than 500 Houstonians had enlisted in the Confederate Guards, the Bayou City Guards, and the Turner Rifles. An artillery company was also recruited locally and all involved pronounced themselves "ready for immediate campaign service." The Turner Rifles became the first unit recruited in Houston to engage the enemy. On duty in Galveston, they exchanged fire with Union troops on August 3 in response to shelling by the Federal gunboat *South Carolina*.

Any possibility of compromise between North and South was destroyed after the engagement at Sumter. President Lincoln then issued a call for 75,000 volunteers to suppress "isolated rebellions in isolated parts of these United States," and with that

action, Virginia seceded. That state's decision was greeted with cheers and rebel yells in Houston, where recruiting activities intensified. By the end of the summer the Sumter Guards and the Houston Artillery were stationed in the Bayou City as well as the Texas Grays, the Home Guards, and the Houston Cavalry. Peter W. Gray, Captain D. McGregor, and Captain A.D. Morse organized and led these groups respectively.

Captain F.O. Odlum's Davis Guards were also enlisted locally. Recruited mainly among the city's Irish population, the company saw action in the battle of Galveston on January 1, 1863, and also later in the critical defense of Sabine Pass on September 8, 1863. The soldiers of the Davis Guards spent the first summer of the war in training and caught the fancy of the local citizenry. The Houston Ladies Aid Association provided them with clothing and blankets, and even after the company was transferred to Galveston in the fall, Houstonians followed their fortunes with great interest and concern.

Before the war was over, Terry's Texas Rangers became the most famous Texas cavalry force to fight under the Confederate banner. Benjamin F. Terry and Thomas S. Lubbock, both of whom had seen action at Bull Run, returned to Houston and issued a

By 1860 Galveston had become the major port on the Texas Gulf Coast. Although Houston could be reached by shallow draft vessels, the center of commercial activity was on Galveston Island. The handsome houses, shops, and churches seen in this 1860 view testify to the prosperity of the island city. Courtesy, Rosenberg Library

call for volunteers to serve in Virginia. Enlistment was for the duration of the fighting and each man was required to furnish his own arms and equipment for his horse. Ten companies of 100 men each were needed and by far the great majority of the volunteers came from Houston and Harris County. When Colonel Terry accepted Captain J.G. Walker's company as part of his cavalry arm, nine companies from Harris County had joined the Confederate army. This prompted Edward Cushing, the feisty editor of the *Telegraph and Texas Register*, to comment:

We now think Harris County has done enough. The balance of her population is needed for home service . . . We think, under all the circumstances, it will be but right to ask the remainder of our volunteer forces to stay at home and give the rest of the State a chance.

The Rangers left Houston on September 11, 1861, and traveled by railroad and riverboat to New Orleans. There Terry was invited to meet General Albert Sidney Johnston at Bowling Green, Kentucky, where Johnston was recruiting an army for the defense of Tennessee and Kentucky. At Bowling Green the company was formally activated as the Eighth Texas Cavalry, but they continued to be known as Terry's Texas Rangers. On December 17, 1861, the Texans were engaged for the first time in battle at Woodsonville, Kentucky, and here Terry was killed while leading a charge. With Terry's death, Lubbock was advanced to command, but he was ill at the time and died in Memphis on January 9, 1862. The unit remained intact, however, and thereafter participated in many engagements, including Shiloh, Murfreesboro, Chickamauga, and Knoxville. At the conclusion of the war, they were placed under the command of General Joseph Wheeler and formally surrendered to General William Tecumseh Sherman at Greensboro, North Carolina, on April 28, 1865.

When Texas seceded from the Union, 400 miles of the state's coastline between

General John Bankhead Magruder (1810-1871) distinguished himself in the eyes of Texans when he recaptured Galveston for the Confederates. By the end of the Civil War, Galveston was the only major Confederate port not in Federal hands. From Cirker, Dictionary of American Portraits, *Dover, 1967*

the Sabine River and the Rio Grande were virtually defenseless. Realizing that this constituted a tempting invasion route, the Texas Secession Convention had voted sorely needed funds to fortify Sabine Pass, Galveston, Matagorda Island, Aransas Pass, and Port Isabell. As a commercial center and still the leading natural port in Texas, Galveston was of particular importance to the Confederacy. By midsummer of 1861 the Federal blockade had reached the Texas coast, and Major Joseph J. Cook, a graduate of Annapolis, assumed responsibility for Galveston's defense. A delegation of the island's leading citizens journeyed to Richmond and requested additional heavy ordnance for the protection of the community, but already the South had little to spare.

During the summer of 1862 there were minor skirmishes at Corpus Christi and Sabine Pass, but these were but feints in preparation for the concerted assault against Galveston. On October 4 Union Commander William B. Renshaw, with eight warships at his disposal, knocked out the only heavy gun defending the channel and demanded the surrender of the city. A truce was arranged, but it was not until Christmas Day that 300 Union soldiers landed at the harbor, occupied Kuhn's Wharf, and prepared to resist a Confederate counterattack.

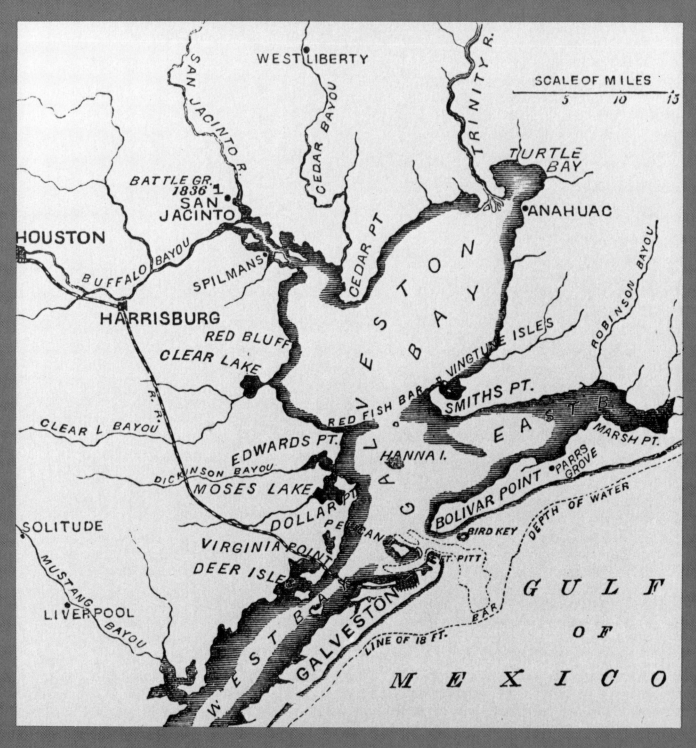

Before its capture by a Federal navy force led by Commodore Renshaw, Galveston had served as an important Confederate port. It was the main entrepôt for the commerce of a large portion of Texas. When the island was recaptured by the Confederates, it once again opened the way for the export of cotton and the import of munitions. From Harper's Pictorial History of The Civil War, 1866

Brigadier General Paul O. Hebert, a Mexican War veteran and former governor of Louisiana, had been named by President Jefferson Davis to the command of all Confederate troops in Texas. However, Hebert created a great deal of antipathy in the Lone Star State by his indifferent defense of Galveston and his arbitrary action in placing all of Texas under martial law. Consequently, when General John Bankhead ("Prince John") Magruder was named to replace Hebert, the appointment was viewed with enthusiasm by the citizens of Galveston and Houston. Magruder, a West Point graduate who had distinguished himself in the Virginia Peninsular Campaign, vowed to recapture Galveston. He also pledged that under no circumstances would he permit Houston to fall to Union forces. He believed the city to be in a class with New Orleans as a vital commercial and railroad center; it must be held at all costs.

Shortly after General Magruder replaced Hebert, he began to formulate his strategy for the recapture of Galveston. He determined to launch an attack both by land and sea, and river steamers figured prominently in the plans. At the foot of Main Street in Houston, the *Bayou City* and the *Neptune* were being transformed into gunboats. While stevedores lined the decks with cotton, sharpshooters crouched behind the bales. When the boats set sail from Houston, they looked like nothing more than Galveston-bound freighters. In their wake plodded two other Houston ships, the *Lucy Gwinn* and the *John F. Carr*, packed with veteran infantry troops prepared to storm the island.

Magruder decided to attack Galveston on New Year's Eve, anticipating that after an evening of celebration, the enemy's guard would be down. Details of the battle reached Houston on New Year's Day, and occasioned much joy. The *Bayou City* and the *Neptune* had engaged the Union gunboat, *Harriet Lane;* the *Neptune* went down but the *Bayou City* rammed and captured the United States cruiser. Both commanding officers of the *Harriet Lane* were killed in the fighting. The battle ended when the Federal

flagship *Westfield* ran aground and was blown up by its own crew. Four other Union ships escaped, but the ground forces, most of them recruited in Houston, captured the Union garrison. The North attempted to conquer the island city again in 1863, but the endeavor failed, and at the end of the war, Galveston was the only major Confederate port not in Union hands.

The significance of the campaign was not lost on the citizens of Houston. Had Galveston been taken, a gun would literally have been pointed at their heads. The reality of the encounter was brought home when about 350 Union prisoners were marched through the streets of the city before their internment in a local prison camp. On January 21 General Magruder and his officers were honored with ceremonies that included a ball at Perkins Hall and a victor's parade down Main Street. Given the joy of the moment, perhaps editor Edward Cushing of the Houston *Tri-Weekly Telegraph* could be forgiven a slight degree of exaggeration when he insisted, "this action will take place as the most brilliant, all things considered, of this war."

In September 1863 the Union once again attempted to gain a foothold in Texas. New Orleans had already been captured by the North and from there an army of 5,000 men was dispatched by sea to invade at Sabine

On October 4, 1862, Federal forces steamed into Galveston Bay and demanded the surrender of the city, thus denying the Buffalo Bayou trading network access to the sea. Waiting until December 25, 1862, to come ashore, the Federals landed on the island and occupied Kuhn's Wharf on the waterfront. Operating from Houston, General John B. Magruder marshalled his forces and struck back on December 31, 1862. The battle shifted along the wharf, although the Federals held on with support from their ships. Confederate vessels appeared, breaking the Union squadron and the defense of the wharf. Courtesy, San Jacinto Museum of History

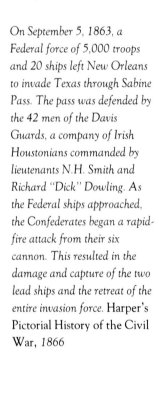

On September 5, 1863, a Federal force of 5,000 troops and 20 ships left New Orleans to invade Texas through Sabine Pass. The pass was defended by the 42 men of the Davis Guards, a company of Irish Houstonians commanded by lieutenants N.H. Smith and Richard "Dick" Dowling. As the Federal ships approached, the Confederates began a rapid-fire attack from their six cannon. This resulted in the damage and capture of the two lead ships and the retreat of the entire invasion force. Harper's Pictorial History of the Civil War, 1866

Pass. The overall Federal strategy contemplated a successful landing and then an advance on Beaumont and Houston. If the campaign proceeded as planned, then Galveston would capitulate as a matter of course. The Union leader Major General William B. Franklin, set out with four gunboats and 17 transport craft carrying about 1,500 men for the initial attack.

The defense of the Texas side of Sabine Pass had been entrusted to the Davis Guards, who were holed up at Fort Griffin, an unfinished earthwork consisting of mud fortifications 100 yards wide and ringed by swamps. Although commanded by Captain Frederick H. Odlum, the defenders were inspired by the leadership of Lieutenant Richard Dowling. A genuine folk hero among his Irish compatriots, "Dick" Dowling had owned the Bank of Bacchus Saloon on Congress Avenue in downtown Houston. Anticipating an attack, Dowling encouraged his men to practice shooting at stakes in the narrow channels, which the attacking Federal armada would have to cross.

On September 8, 1863, the Federal vessels entered the harbor at Sabine Pass. The gunboats *Clifton* and *Granite City* steamed up the Texas side of the channel, defended by Fort Griffin, and the *Sachem* and *Arizona* proceeded along the Louisiana channel to attack the defenders from the rear. One of the Union transports prepared to land 500 infantry who would storm the fort when it had been reduced by the gunboats. The complete operation was thought to be easy work since Fort Griffin was defended by only 47 men, among them the intrepid Dick Dowling. Exercising great patience, Dowling waited until the Union ships came within close range and then opened fire. Dowling later claimed that in 35 minutes he fired his cannon 107 times, certainly a record for heavy artillery. In a few minutes the United States ships *Sachem* and *Clifton* were rendered helpless, and the others fled the harbor. The two disabled boats mounting 13 guns and their crews, consisting of 350 men, were captured by the victorious Dowling.

The battle of Sabine Pass spared Texas a successful Yankee invasion and a sustained campaign. Most certainly, Houston would have been captured and railroad communication between the city and the remainder of the Confederacy would have been cut. Desperate for a victory of any kind, President Jefferson Davis optimistically wrote, "Sabine Pass will stand, perhaps for all time to come, the greatest military victory in the world." In accordance with a personal order by Davis, one of the two war decorations officially granted by the Confederacy was especially struck for the Davis Guards. As for Dowling, a statue in his honor stands in Hermann Park today. Each year on St. Patrick's day, ceremonies are held commemorating his great triumph. Still a young man at the time of his death in 1867, Dowling was buried in St. Vincent's Cemetery.

A third effort to invade Texas also failed to endanger Houston and the more thickly populated portions of the state. Fearing that the South would receive aid from the French through Mexico, Union troops attempted to occupy the Texas coast near the Mexican border. On November 5, 1863, six thousand Federal troops led by General Nathaniel Banks captured Brownsville. Over the next 60 days, Banks strengthened his position by successfully investing Corpus Christi, Aransas Pass, Mustang Island, Indianola, and Lavaca. However, as the prospect of French inter-

vention lessened, most of the U.S. troops along the Texas coast were withdrawn, except a small contingent in Brownsville. The withdrawn troops constituted the bulk of a new Union army, which, led by General Banks, attempted to invade East Texas from Louisiana. But, on April 8, 1864, the hastily assembled Confederate troops commanded by General Richard Taylor routed the Yankees at Mansfield, Louisiana, less than 50 miles from the Texas boundary. Once again, a threat to the city of Houston and the interior of Texas had been subverted.

Compared to other cities of the Confederacy during the Civil War, Houston endured very little hardship and, in fact,

TO THE CITIZENS

OF

HARRIS COUNTY.

At the request of the Board of Aldermen, the undersigned have been appointed by the Mayor of the City of Houston, a Committee to solicit contributions of Warm Clothing &c., for the troops of the Confederate States, and particularly for the sons and brothers of Harris county, who have gone into the service of their country.

Those who are enjoying the comforts and safety of their homes, must not forget that they owe these things to the brave soldiers now in the field.

Harris County has responded nobly to the call for men: It remains to be seen whether all the patriots of the County have gone into the Army.

Our brave defenders will soon be exposed to the rigors of a cold climate, and to other hardships to which they are entirely unaccustomed. The Government is young, and has not been able to provide the soldiers with clothing. It remains for the people to supply the want by voluntary subscription.

What is most wanted is Woolen Socks, Blankets, new and old, Under Shirts and Drawers, Overcoats, Yarn, Flannel. Donations in money will also be received.

Depot at Wilson's Building, for Ladies' Committee; At the respective places of business of the Gentlemen's Committee.

A list of all articles furnished will be kept, with the names of those by whom they are furnished. The articles will be handed to the Agent of the State, and when appraised it is expected the value of them will be returned in Treasury Notes of the Confederate States.

Confidently believing that Harris County will cheerfully clothe her own soldiers, we submit this appeal to our fellow citizens.

Mrs. T. B. J. Hadley.	C. S. Longcope.
" A. C. Allen.	T. M. Bagby.
" Jane Young.	F. A. Rice.

The following named persons are requested to act in concert with the Committee, and forward the donations to the Committee.

At Lynchburg,	Capt. J. C. Walker.
" Baker & Thompson's Mill,	Theo. W. McComb.
" Baytown,	Dr. J. L. Bryan.
" Harrisburg,	John B. Harris.
" Huffman's Settlement,	E. Dunk.
" West's Precinct,	R. D. Wescott.
" Cypress,	C. H. Baker.
" Spring Branch,	W. Tentdler.
" Mrs. Wheaton's Settlement,	Dr. A. J. Hay.
" Hockley,	— Abbot.
" Rose Hill,	C. F. Duer.

continued to grow and prosper. Although the bulk of the able-bodied male population was stationed on various fronts, thousands of slaves were sent to Texas from Arkansas, Louisiana, and other Southern states to prevent their liberation by advancing Union troops. They provided a work force for the successful crop harvests between 1861 and 1864, and also for stepped-up railroad construction.

When the Federal blockade of Galveston pinched off trade and commercial activity in the island city, business increased in Houston, accompanied by inflation. In the Bayou City flour sold for $50 a hundred-pound sack, milk for $1 a quart, and beef for 25 cents a pound. Whiskey, which had been 50 cents a gallon before the war, went up to $8 per gallon, and coffee, when it could be obtained, cost $3 a pound. Barbers raised their price for haircuts, and with starch at $1 per pound, laundresses increased their fees for washings. The increased prices angered Houston's newspaper editors, who lashed out at speculators and those who reaped exorbitant profits during "perilous times."

Houstonians also suffered minor food shortages during the war years. Coffee and tea were always in short supply, as were salt, flour, and soap. Beef, cornbread, and barley water became standard fare in steamboat dining rooms where before the war elegant dinners had been served. Non-food items, such as firewood, candles, and iron and brass products were also difficult to come by. Nevertheless, the people of Houston never experienced serious want during this time. However, as the problem of inflation increased, many creditors proved more reluctant to accept Confederate money in satisfaction of debts. Of course, this posture contributed to the decline of the value of the currency and in turn forced prices to escalate still higher.

While the Lone Star State was further removed from the locale of battles and less prone to invasion than other Southern states, proportionately more men were recruited for military service in Texas than any other Confederate state. As has been noted, Houston and Harris County con-

tributed more than their share of men. The Bayou City also contributed matériel and supplies for the war effort. Flour mills provided food for Confederate troops, while iron and brass foundries forged cannon and shot. A setback was sustained in June 1862, when fire destroyed the Alexander McGowen Foundry on Preston Avenue, which was attempting to fill two large Confederate government contracts. The Cushman Foundry and Machine Shop on the south bank of Buffalo Bayou filled the orders instead. In addition to the sinews of war, the foundries also manufactured cooking utensils and agricultural tools for use on

Facing page:
Although little action took place along the Texas Gulf Coast during the Civil War, the war was felt by the citizens through the shortages that developed and the needs of the troops. Early in the war volunteer committees of ladies were already at work soliciting aid for the soldiers. Courtesy, San Jacinto Museum of History

Left:
Houston has always been a city that uses social events to benefit worthwhile causes. In 1862 the ladies of Houston and Harrisburg organized a musical and tableaux vivant to benefit the hospital for Confederate troops established by Dr. Bryan. Courtesy, Special Collections; Houston Public Library

the home front. Spurred by the emergency nature of the times, small, primitive factories sprang up and produced wagons, ambulances, furniture, shoes, tents, and blankets. Also, the leather industry prospered from the increased demand for large shipments of harnesses and saddles. Finally, in 1869 the Houston City Mills, a textile factory on the south bank of the bayou near the eastern limits of the city, began production and employed 80 people.

In the year 1840 scarcely 1,000 bales of cotton entered Houston; by 1860 that figure had reached 115,854 bales. Then during the war years Houston continued to augment its stature as one of the principal cotton-trading centers of the Confederacy. This was due to a number of factors: the capture of New Orleans and temporary control of Galveston by the Union, and the trade that subsequently developed with Mexico. Furthermore, the northern Mexican states were on friendly terms with Confederate and Texas authorities and stood to profit from the wartime trade with Texas, so transporting cotton into Mexico and guns, ammunition, and other matériel out was a relatively easy matter.

With the Union blockade, Matamoros, previously a minor port, became a place of frenzied activity. Riverboats carried cotton

to the Gulf and at that point it was transferred to oceangoing vessels bound for international markets. A number of Houston merchants, among them William Marsh Rice, made fortunes by taking up residence in Matamoros and acting as cotton factors.

In January 1862 the state legislature approved a statute to consolidate and amend the various acts incorporating the City of Houston. Essentially nine square miles, with the Harris County Courthouse at the center, were set out as the city limits. The act also spelled out the qualifications for holding office in Houston. In order to qualify as an alderman, a candidate had to own real estate valued at least at $1,000; a candidate for mayor had to be worth twice that amount. The City Council was composed of eight aldermen, two from each of the four wards, and a polling place was situated in each ward. Geographically, the wards were defined as follows: First Ward, north of Congress Street and west of Main Street; Second Ward, north of Congress and east of Main; Third Ward, south of Congress and east of Main; Fourth Ward, south of Congress and west of Main. Then in 1867 the Fifth Ward was established north of Buffalo Bayou and White Oak Bayou.

While not sharply defined, the principal powers enjoyed by the City Council were

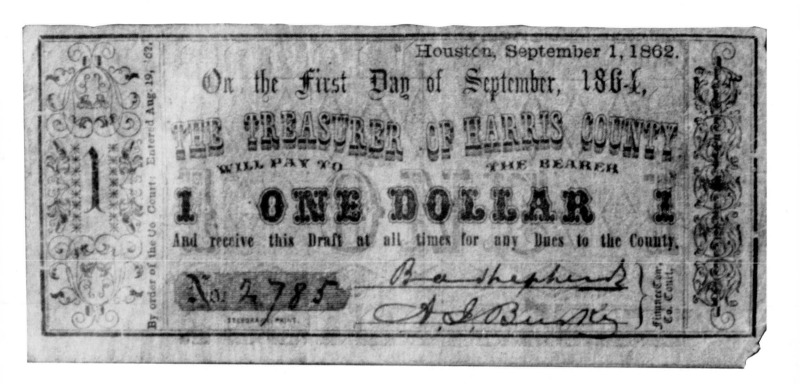

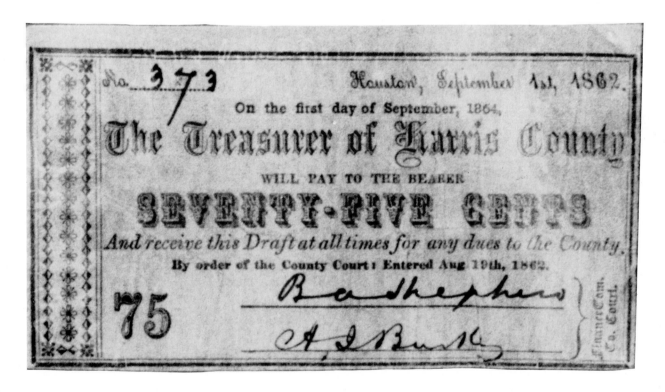

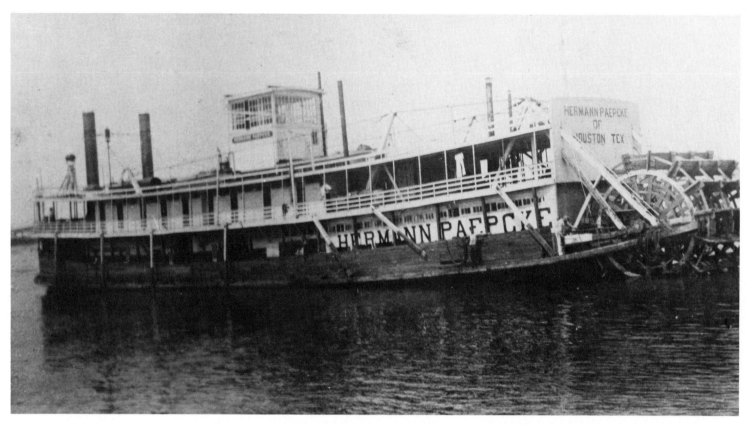

In the second half of the 19th century, Buffalo Bayou was filled with shallow-draft steamboats, such as the stern-wheeler Herman Paepcke, *carrying cotton, hides, wool, other agricultural products, and passengers from Houston to the Gulf for transfer to oceangoing steamers off Galveston Island. Courtesy, Rosenberg Library*

the right to grant or withhold licenses and the right to mandate taxes. When the periodic attempts by the Council to collect back taxes failed, tax collector and assessor G.S. Hardcastle promptly offered the uncleared property for sale. As with the houses, so with hogs. The City Council passed an ordinance providing that stray hogs be sold at auction after being impounded for three days. Also, in an effort to do something about unsanitary conditions in the city, the Council created Houston's first Board of Health on June 21, 1862.

From the time of its founding, the leadership abilities of Houston's mayors had varied. In the first race for mayor, held on August 14, 1837, James S. Holman, a business associate of the Allen brothers, beat Francis R. Lubbock and Thomas W. Ward. The turnout in this contest was very low, partially because to qualify to vote for a mayor or alderman a Houstonian had to be free, white, a citizen of Texas, a resident of Houston for at least six months, and the owner of at least $100 worth of city real estate for at least three months prior to the election. The city's first dynamic mayor was Francis W. Moore, Jr., an editor of the

Telegraph and Texas Register, who served on and off during the period of the Republic and early statehood. A crusader against lawlessness, Moore saw one of his objectives realized when dueling was abolished within the city limits. Thomas W. House, a successful businessman, became mayor of Houston in 1862 and served with honor during the Civil War.

The first regular wartime state election was held in Texas in August 1861. Confidence in and enthusiasm for the Confederacy was still running high and Francis R. Lubbock defeated the incumbent, Edward Clark, on a platform pledging loyalty to the South and the energetic prosecution of the war. A merchant and planter, Lubbock began his business career in Houston, where he claimed to have sold the first bag of flour in the city for $30 and the first sack of coffee for 25 cents a pound. He was Sam Houston's comptroller of the Republic and in 1841 was elected district clerk of Harris County. Lubbock had been a delegate to the Democratic National Convention at Charleston in 1860 as a proponent of secession. Once installed at Austin as governor, he sought close ties with the

Confederacy and announced himself an admirer of Jefferson Davis.

In November 1861 the state legislature appointed Louis T. Wigfall and W.S. Oldham to represent Texas in the Confederate Senate. Judge Peter W. Gray of Houston was elected a member of the House of Representatives in the First Congress of the Confederacy.

As the Texas gubernatorial campaign of 1863 drew near, Governor Lubbock announced that he had been offered a place on the staff of Jefferson Davis and thus would not be a candidate for reelection. He was succeeded by Pendleton Murrah, and locally Judge Grey was defeated for reelection to the Confederate House by A.M. Branch because of his support for conscription laws and the draft exemption for overseers.

The Confederacy was doomed: New Orleans had fallen to the Union on April 24, 1862; Vicksburg had been captured by Grant on July 4, 1863; and Lee's invasion of the North had been halted at Gettysburg in that same month of July. Financial and supply problems contributed to the internal collapse of the South as did increasing internal condemnation of the war. Union sentiment, present in Texas and other Southern states before the war, increased in intensity as the military campaigns wound down.

In January 1864 General E. Kirby Smith assumed control of the Trans-Mississippi department of the Confederacy, which included Texas, Arkansas, Louisiana, and Mississippi. Smith set up headquarters in Shreveport and then devised the strategy that frustated the Union invasion of East Texas in 1864. However, although Smith wished to continue the war after General Lee's surrender at Appomattox, his troops were not of the same mind. The desertion rate was high and many were fleeing to Mexico. In the middle of May some 400 soldiers at Galveston attempted to desert, but were held in check by their commanding officer, Colonel Ashbel Smith. However, a week later Smith acknowledged the desperate nature of the situation and ordered the evacuation of Galveston. Conditions

throughout the state were chaotic, made worse by Governor Murrah's departure; he, along with many other public officials and military men, left Texas for Mexico, where he died within a month.

Although the city of Houston had not been invaded during the war, it was not spared at the war's end. On May 23, 1865, about 2,000 Confederate soldiers from Galveston looted the Confederate Ordnance Building and the Clothing Bureau of the Confederate army. Six-shooters and muskets as well as clothing and blankets were taken, but there was little personal violence committed. Mayor William Anders ordered all saloons closed, and a military guard of 1,000 men was hastily recruited to patrol the streets and ensure order. Civilians apparently did not loot or plunder military stores in Houston, though such conduct did take place at San Antonio and Huntsville.

General Kirby Smith departed Houston for Galveston accompanied by the wartime hero of the island city, General John Bankhead Magruder. On June 2, aboard the U.S. warship *Port Jackson* in Galveston Bay, Smith formally surrendered the territory of the Trans-Mississippi department to Brigadier General Edmund J. Davis. Shortly thereafter the Union standard flew over the Harris County Courthouse, replacing the old Confederate emblem. Federal occupation troops were not long in taking up a position in Houston. On June 20, 1865, five

When the war ended in defeat
for the Confederacy, General
Gordon Granger was sent to
Texas by the Federal
government to establish a
provisional government. From
Harper's Pictorial History of
the Civil War, 1866

companies of the 114th Ohio Regiment and the entire 34th Iowa Regiment arrived by special train from Galveston and marched through the city. The orderly transfer of power was marred by the death of a black cook with the Union troops, stabbed by a local citizen whom he had threatened with a brick. In general, however, calm prevailed, and when the Amnesty Office of the provost marshal opened on June 25, Mayor William Anders was the first Houstonian to swear allegiance to the United States and be readmitted to citizenship. On July 4, 1865, American flags were displayed throughout the city and salutes fired in honor of Independence Day.

General Gordon Granger, a compassionate man and understanding of the defeated Confederacy, was sent to Texas to maintain order and to establish a provisional government anticipating the ultimate return of Texas to the Union. His first act upon landing at Galveston was to issue an order emancipating all Texas slaves and declaring illegal all laws enacted since secession. On June 19, 1865, General Granger carefully read a copy of the Emancipation Proclamation, which

had taken effect on January 1, 1863, and was now operative in Texas. That day, called "Juneteenth," has since been celebrated by Texas blacks as Emancipation Day. Because thousands of slaves had been sent further south to Texas by frightened masters in Louisiana, Arkansas, and Missouri, there were more than 200,000 blacks in Texas when the 13th Amendment took effect. Appraised of their new status and cast adrift, many ex-slaves wandered into Houston from the plantation bottomlands of the Trinity and Brazos rivers. Their situation occasioned sympathy on the part of many Houstonians, as the editor of the *Tri-Weekly Telegraph* wrote:

We cannot help but pity the poor freedmen and women that have left comfortable and happy homes in the country and come to the city in search of what they call freedom. Nearly all the old buildings that were not occupied . . . serve as homes for these people. Many of these buildings are not fit for stables.

In January 1866 the crowds of blacks that gathered downtown were viewed with alarm by many white Houstonians. A 9 p.m. curfew for black people was enacted by occupation authorities along with a threat to compel the unemployed to work for the army without pay. However, some ex-slaves were able to find employment on a sharecropping basis for area planters.

It was not all discord between the races following the Confederate surrender. Old ties were renewed when many ex-slaves returned to their former plantations to work for wages or on a sharecropping arrangement. Blacks and whites mingled socially when at Houston's first "Juneteenth" celebration in 1866 a banquet was tendered by the ex-slaves and their families with their former masters as guests of honor. In the city of Houston there was no deliberate segregation of housing and the wards were fairly well balanced between white and black inhabitants. As an example, the Fifth Ward, which by 1920 was almost exclusively black, had a ratio of 561 white families to 578

Houston's schools began as small private institutions, such as Miss Brown's Young Ladies Seminary (pictured here) and Mrs. Noble's Seminary for Girls. Classes in these girls' schools consisted mostly of the basic "three R's" and instruction in skills such as dancing, sewing, and sometimes French. In the 1870s the schools were absorbed into the public school system. Courtesy, Harris County Heritage Society

black families in 1870. Yet aldermen were elected on a ward basis, which made it difficult for blacks to secure representation on the City Council. Later, when residential segregation was a fact of Houston city life, aldermen were elected at large.

On March 3, 1865, President Lincoln signed into law the bill creating the Bureau of Refugees, Freedmen, and Abandoned Lands, more commonly known as the Freedmen's Bureau. General Edgar Gregory was placed in charge of the Texas District, with headquarters at Galveston, and arrived in Houston in December. Gregory began his assignment by making a 700-mile tour of the state during the course of which he spoke to some 25,000 freedmen and their employers. He called for understanding on the part of both blacks and whites and stressed that his first task would be to secure employment for former slaves roaming the countryside or milling about in the cities. He appointed 12 local agents to assist him in this work, one of whom was based in Houston. To improve the labor situation, he sought to promote the contract system of employment between blacks and their old masters. All agents of the Freedmen's Bureau were required to furnish copies of the Emancipation Proclamation to all employers and state officials and to make certain that it was read to all working freedmen. The agents were also required

to instruct the freedmen to make written contracts with employers and to register the contracts with officials of the bureau.

One of the statutory responsibilities of the Freedmen's Bureau was to "maintain schools for freedmen until a system of public schools could be established." With encouragement from bureau personnel, a Negro school began to hold classes at the African Methodist Church on Dowling Street in Houston. However, attendance was irregular and the content of instruction was disturbing to some whites, since it stressed the importance of the Union army in achieving black freedom. But the mere presence of a school for blacks acted as a spur to the movement for free public instruction in Houston. In February 1870 a public meeting was held and a committee drafted a bill for legislative consideration that would enable the city to begin free public education. Although this particular request was denied, a free county public school system, aided by state funds, did become a reality. By 1873 Harris County maintained 24 public schools in which 1,561 students were enrolled. A full term was rarely completed, however; in 1874 the county schools were in session for only four months and in 1876 for only two or three.

In 1876 the state legislature granted to Texas cities local control over the schools and the right to claim a pro-rata share of state educational funds. While the local election generated little interest and the turnout was very light, Houstonians did vote in favor of local control. Then, in 1877, the City Council passed legislation that mandated free public schools for all children 8 to 14 years old. It was stipulated that three trustees and a superintendent, appointed by the mayor and approved by the Council, would be responsible for the maintenance of the public school system in the city. Without a dissenting vote, and certainly reflecting the prevailing sentiment of the day, the schools were deliberately segregated.

The appointment of Andrew Jackson Hamilton as provisional governor of Texas on July 21, 1865, introduced the official period of Reconstruction in Texas. Since the state had officially seceded from the Union when it joined the Confederacy, Texas had to repeal the act of secession, repudiate all debts incurred in the cause of the Confederacy, and draft a new constitution excluding slavery to legally regain its proper status within the national government. These steps were accomplished at a constitutional convention at Austin on February 7, 1866, and the new state constitution was ratified by the people of Texas. Houston's delegates at the convention were G.W. Whitmore, J.W. Flanagan, F.A. Vaughan, and C.W. Bryant. The convention's presiding officer, J.W. Throckmorton, was elected governor. A good start had been made; it appeared that Texas would rejoin the Union and moderation would prevail.

In the elections of 1866, Radical Republicans gained control of Congress and swiftly moved to impose their view that the ex-Confederate states were not repentant enough and that there was little genuine concern for blacks' rights in the South. Texas, which had elected former Confederate leaders to state and national offices and also passed a series of "Black Codes" restricting the status of freedmen, seemed to suggest the truth of their accusation. Governor Throckmorton was replaced by ex-governor Elisha M. Pease, and, as a result of federal prodding, still another constitution was adopted in 1869. The constitution of the United States was declared to be the supreme law of the land and the eventual ratification of the 15th Amendment enfranchised black males. Finally, in 1869, in a contest monitored by the military, Edmund J. Davis bested Andrew J. Hamilton in the election for governor.

In 1866 former Confederates who wished to participate in the government of the United States were required to sign an amnesty oath to establish their loyalty to the government in Washington. This oath, however, applied only to the period of Presidential Reconstruction. In 1867 the reconstruction of Congress limited the amnesty of 1866. Courtesy, Special Collections; Houston Public Library

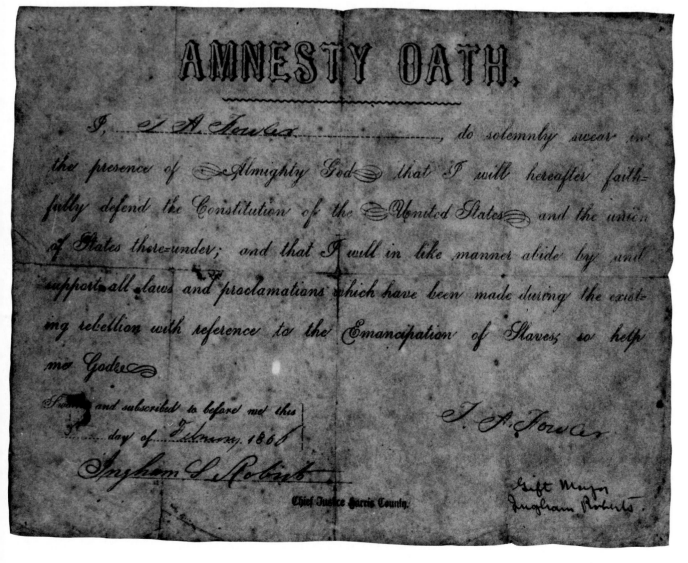

Right:
Dry goods merchants such as William Clark and Sam Sterne were still relying on family networks to expand their business in the late 1860s. Although Sterne was based in Houston, he used a relative in his operation at Millican. This was a traditional practice in the 19th century and reflected the continuing uncertainty regarding communications in trade and the need that many merchants felt to have kin taking care of their business interests. Courtesy, Harris County Heritage Society

Far Right:
Simpson, Branard and Company's 1866 advertisement emphasized productivity and labor-saving machinery for both the farm and the home, including the reaper, grain mills, a washer, and sewing machines. Through this advertisement the firm demonstrates its ability to serve a modernizing city, particularly one that had been cut off from such products during the war. Also, by emphasizing equipment used in the production of grain, the company suggests that the range of agricultural products for export was growing beyond textiles and hides. Courtesy, Harris County Heritage Society

Facing page, bottom left:
In the years after the Civil War, the trade rivalry between Galveston and Houston, which had been suspended, was renewed. Agents such as Arnold and Brothers made every effort to develop special services to bring trade to them and to their community. Courtesy, Harris County Heritage Society

Facing page, bottom right:
In the years after the Civil War, Houston continued to develop as a center for trade. Firms such as Peel and Dumble took advantage of the communication center to develop a trade in cotton, hides, and wool. All three were available along the coast. In addition, these firms distributed machinery and farm equipment to their customers. Courtesy, Harris County Heritage Society

This page:
Although Houston had been isolated from the East by the Civil War, merchants reformed their trade networks quickly in late 1865 and in 1866. Peel and Dumble, who were able to reform connections for trade to the East, were working to reestablish the cotton trade by importing the equipment necessary for ginning the cotton grown on the Gulf Coast. Courtesy, Harris County Heritage Society

The last phase of Reconstruction in Texas encompassed the administration of Edmund J. Davis from January 8, 1870, to January 17, 1874. Enjoying the complete backing of the military in Texas and President Grant in Washington, Davis reigned as a near dictator for four years. With the assistance of the "State Police," organized by Davis in July 1870, the governor sought to implement his radical beliefs. Democratic party meetings were frequently disrupted and martial law declared in order to ensure Republican victories at the polls. Often those who opposed Davis were falsely arrested and held on the flimsiest of charges. By the "Carpetbag Constitution" of 1869, Davis was empowered to appoint more than 8,000 state, county, and local officials, which left little power in the hands of the Texas electorate. In the gubernatorial race of 1873, Davis was opposed by Richard Coke. Coke won the 1873 campaign and, after a power struggle with Davis, became the governor of Texas.

Meanwhile, politics on a local level in Houston reflected statewide trends and developments. In 1867 Alexander McGowen was elected mayor in a contest that generated so little interest that not a single fight at the polls was noted. Perhaps with a trace of disappointment, the editor of the *Telegraph* commented: "What a quiet and peaceable city Houston has become. But few cities of the size and population of Houston can boast such a record the day after a city election." However, in 1869 the city could not meet its municipal payroll and military authorities ordered the removal of the mayor, recorder, and marshall. Joseph R. Morris was named mayor and, though a "carpetbagger" from Connecticut, turned in a credible performance; during his term the wages of city employees increased, as did the city's trade and general prosperity.

The local political situation changed rapidly in 1870. Radical Thomas H. Scanlan, who had served for two years as an alderman prior to that date, was appointed mayor of Houston by Governor Davis. Born in Ireland, Scanlan came to Houston in 1853 and quickly began business as a general merchant. After the war he declared for the

From January 1870 to January 1874, Edmund J. Davis served as governor of Texas. Davis had come to Texas in 1848 from Florida and had served as deputy collector of customs on the Rio Grande, district attorney, and district judge. During the Civil War he rose to the rank of brigadier general in the Union army. Later he was elected to the first Reconstruction Convention and served as president of the second Reconstruction Convention. From Thrall, Texas 1879

Radical Republican cause and, enjoying the backing of the occupation forces, rose rapidly in municipal politics. He was honestly dedicated to improving the lot of freedmen and it was during his years in office (1870-1873) that blacks first served on the police force and black councilmen, Richard Allen and James Snowball, were elected in Houston for the first time.

Scanlan was a somewhat typical mayor of the times in that there were persistent charges of financial mismanagement and personal graft during his tenure of office. A report ordered by Governor Coke after Scanlan left office in 1873 placed Houston's indebtedness at $1,414,000 as against the approximately $200,000 to $300,000 it had been when Scanlan took office. Yet, the mayor's critics had to admit that he had improved roads and bridges, constructed a markethouse, and extended the sidewalks. In November 1872, in the first campaign in six years where local officials were freely elected, Scanlan triumphed along with the two black aldermen. Predictably, cases of fraud were heard along with the particular allegation that large numbers of nonresident blacks came into Houston from the countryside to register and vote. However,

this contention was doubtful at best; Houstonians apparently believed that Scanlan's accomplishments and virtues outweighed his faults.

The 1872 municipal election was noteworthy in another way. The Ku Klux Klan, founded at Pulaski, Tennessee, in 1866, existed in many parts of Texas. The ultra-secret, terrorist organization committed to the maintenance of white supremacy and Southern sovereignty was most popular in East Texas. In Houston the Klan warned blacks not to vote in the 1872 race and implored white voters to refuse to elect any blacks to the City Council. The 1870 census count indicates that there were 793 male Negroes 21 years of age or older living in Houston and thus eligible to vote. It is impossible to say how many actually voted in the 1872 election, but the black turnout was heavy and two blacks were elected to the City Council. Always more popular in rural areas than in the city, the Klan in Houston was unable to muster much influence in municipal politics during the Reconstuction period.

Segregation of blacks and whites, begun in the public schools at this time, also extended to sports. On July 14, 1868, the *Daily Telegraph* informed its readers that a black baseball team had been organized in the city. Known as the Six Shooter Jims, the team offered to play a "match game with any other colored club in the state." During the Civil War there had been a complete lack of organized sports in Houston, but interest picked up in the period after the fighting ceased. On April 21, 1868, to commemorate San Jacinto Day, a baseball game between the Houston "Stonewalls" and the Galveston "Robert E. Lees" was played out at the battleground. With a number of veterans of the battle of San Jacinto in attendance, the reporter for the Houston *Daily Telegraph* caught the spirit of the occasion:

The contest now commenced in good earnest . . . but from the first innings it was apparent to the most disinterested that the Lees (although the vaunted champions of the state) had at last met more than their

Thomas J. Scanlan, Houston's Reconstruction mayor, may have been the most controversial mayor in the city's history. Although his administration was active in expanding the city's facilities, it was tainted with charges of corruption and building the public debt, which violated the traditional approach to public funding. In many ways Scanlan was typical of his era, but the traditional leaders of Houston were not ready to accept Scanlan's standards of administration and his term ended in 1874. Courtesy, Texas Room; Houston Public Library

match. . . . At the conclusion of the eighth inning, the Lees, disheartened by the success of their antagonists, gave up the game and acknowledged themselves beaten fairly and squarely. The runs being counted, it was found that the score stood Stonewall's 34, the Lee's 5. Mr. McKernan, the umpire, then declared the Stonewalls the Champions of the State of Texas. Three cheers were then given for the Lee Club, three for the Stonewall, three for the umpire and scorers, and three for San Jacinto, when the bases were taken up, everything gathered together, and all started for Lynchburg, for the ball.

As it had in the past, horse racing also engaged the attention of Houstonians. The Houston Post Oak Jockey Club had been organized in 1839 and had promoted a few races before it disbanded in 1846, and racing flourished thereafter from time to time on an informal basis. Then in May 1868 work was completed on the Houston Racing and Trotting Park, adjacent to Main Street and two miles from the Courthouse. October 13, 1868, was proclaimed "Derby Day" and almost 3,000 fans witnessed the event. Because of the Houston climate, racing continued into the winter months, attracting enthusiasts from all over the Gulf South. Also in the late 1860s, the Houston Turnverein, a society of German citizens, established the first bowling center in Houston. Amateur boxing also gained in popularity, but professional boxing and cockfighting were frowned upon by some and railed against by Houston's clergymen. Nevertheless, such events did take place.

Fairs provided another source of amusement for the city dweller. Again, Houston's German population was in the forefront, staging a celebration early in the summer called the "Volkfest." Out at the fairgrounds "King Gambrinus," the German Bacchus, presided over a series of floats and decorations. Speeches, gymnastics, music, and dancing were the order of the day and annually attracted thousands of spectators. Also, the state fair of the Agricultural, Mechanical, and Blood Stock Association of Texas was often held in Houston. With financial backing from the local business community, farm machinery and products were displayed and prizes awarded. With its emphasis on rural values and farm animals, this meeting was certainly a precursor of the famous Houston Rodeo and Fat Stock Show of modern times.

After a dormant period occasioned by the war, culture and the arts began to flourish again in Houston. Theater groups and opera companies that had earlier come to the city from New Orleans and Mobile reappeared. To accommodate them, in 1873 a new theater, the Opera House, was completed at the southwest corner of Main and Franklin

and opened to large crowds. A smaller variety theater on Fannin Street, Canterbury Hall was generally used for local amateur productions and minstrel shows. Various opera companies offered *Il Trovatore*, *La Traviata*, *Fra Diavolo*, *The Magic Flute*, and *Martha*. Finally, rave reviews greeted the performance of the famous Croatian soprano, Ilma di Murska, whose voice boasted a range of three octaves and who triumphed as the lead in *Norma* at the Opera House in 1878.

Literary societies continued to grow and develop, among them the Houston Literary Society (1875), the Horticultural and Pomological Society (1876), and the Houston Economics and Debating Club (1875). Also, as they had been doing since its inception, members of the Houston Lyceum continued to work for the establish-

ment of a public library system. While the realization of that particular dream still remained in the future, Houstonians never wavered in their interest in and appreciation of cultural refinements.

As life in Houston began to normalize after the Civil War, its inhabitants were faced with yet another challenge. Because of its tropical, humid climate and its proximity to the Gulf, Houston had always been subject to the dread disease of yellow fever. Epidemics were recorded by city authorities in 1839, 1844, 1847-1848, 1854-1855, 1858, 1862, and 1867. The scourge in 1867 was among the worst in the city's history and was made even harder to bear by the negligence of local officials. When manifestations of the disease appeared in neighboring towns in January 1867, no quarantine was declared locally. By Septem-

Galveston gradually became ascendant as the entertainment and vacation spot for many Houstonians in the years after the Civil War. Bathers staying at such establishments as the Beach Hotel would change their clothes in the small portable cabins in front of the structure before going for a refreshing swim in the Gulf. Courtesy, Rosenberg Library

ber the plague had claimed hundreds of lives and numbered among its victims the only physician in Harrisburg and the still youthful Dick Dowling, hero of the battle of Sabine Pass. Perhaps hardest hit were unacclimated Northern soldiers on occupation duty. As a preventative measure, large vats of tar were burned in army camps, but the disease continued to ravage officers and men, blacks and whites alike. Extra grave diggers and additional carpenters were hired by sexton H.G. Pannell to bury the Union dead, but the work did not go fast enough. In his book *True Stories of Old Houston and Houstonians*, Dr. S.O. Young recorded an amusing incident. An angry Federal commander sent for the sexton, who was well known for his pro-Southern feelings:

He was taken before the commander who said to him: "Mr. Pannell they tell me you dislike to bury my soldiers!" "General!" said Pannell, "whoever told you that told you a damned lie. It's the pleasantest thing I've had to do in years and I can't get enough of it. I would like to bury every damned one of you."

Sexton Pennell was ordered imprisoned by the Union commander, but he did not remain in jail for long because his services were in too great a demand.

By November the crisis had abated. Frost and cold weather had killed the plague-bearing mosquitoes, and more rigid quarantine methods had also proven helpful. Interestingly enough, a number of Houston physicians, including Dr. Ashbel Smith, Dr. Louis A. Bryan, and Dr. Alva Connel, suspected that the mosquito was the chief culprit in yellow fever cases, but none had been able to adduce scientific proof. Although the city suffered a mild epidemic in 1873, it did not begin to approach the terrible ordeal endured in 1867.

The city had endured the travail of the Civil War and Reconstruction periods and emerged with its growth still constant. Unlike other major cities of the South, it had not been compelled to rebuild from the ashes of physical ruin. The questions of slavery and secession had been resolved on the battlefields of the vanquished Confederacy. Optimistic, perhaps to a fault, Houstonians looked to the future.

Although the 20th-century storms are better known, the Gulf Coast has been the target of many storms over the years. Evidence of the strength of the 1867 storm is to be found in this image of Galveston's waterfront. Damage inland caused by winds, heavy rains, and flooding from fast-rising streams was almost as severe. Courtesy, Rosenberg Library

Houston and all of Texas were subjects of great discussion in Europe in the 1840s and 1850s. Land speculators, such as those responsible for this 1855 French illustration of Houston, sometimes created views that never existed. Courtesy, Bayou Bend Collection, Gift of Miss Ima Hogg; Houston Museum of Fine Arts

Texans have a special fondness for the traditional music played for the reels and other dances that were once part of annual celebrations and dances in Houston and elsewhere. Recreating the dinner and dance that Mrs. William Marsh Rice held every Christmas for 48 people, these musicians bring back 19th-century memories for 20th-century Houstonians. Photo by Story J. Sloane III, Harris County Heritage Society

During the days of the Republic and soon after, one of the most popular recreations was formal dancing. Photo by Story J. Sloane III, Harris County Heritage Society and the Texas Army

The Nichols-Rice-Cherry House, built opposite the Harris County Courthouse at the corner of San Jacinto and Congress by 1850, is a part of the fabric of Houston. The house served as an elegant home for the merchant Ebenezer Nichols and then was sold to William Marsh Rice in 1856. Later the house became rental property, but was saved in 1897 by Mrs. Emma Richardson Cherry who moved it to the far prairie in the Montrose area. The house has been associated with enterprise, education, and through Mrs. Cherry, with the arts. Courtesy, Harris County Heritage Society

In 1954 the oldest surviving residence in Houston was threatened with destruction by the city, which had used it as park headquarters, zoo building, and storehouse. Interested citizens began a formal preservation movement in Houston by uniting to save the structure. It had been the home of both Nathaniel Kelley Kellum, an early industrialist, and Zerviah Noble, an early teacher. Preservation of the house led to the creation of the Harris County Heritage Society, an active museum and preservation organization for Houston. Courtesy, Harris County Heritage Society

Built on the southeastern edge of Harris County on Clear Creek, the "Old Place" is the oldest standing structure in the county. Erected by John Williams, an early member of the Austin colony, the structure served as a line camp for many years before being expanded as a residence in the 1850s. In 1971 it was moved to Sam Houston Park and restored to its original condition as a tribute to the settlers who came to the county more than a decade before Houston was founded. Courtesy, Harris County Heritage Society

Left:
This residence built by Houston entrepreneur and lumberman Eugene Pillot in 1868 was perhaps the first major domestic building erected after the Civil War in Houston. Equipped with running water fed by a tank, with gas lighting, and with what may well have been the first attached kitchen in Houston, the home was both fashionable and modern, reflecting Pillot's position as a leader in the community. Courtesy, Harris County Heritage Society

Bottom left:
Throughout the 19th century, gentlemen of Houston would retire for an evening of brandy, cigars, and cards. The Pillot House smoking room is furnished for a game of cards that might have been played on an evening in the 1870s.

Bottom right:
Festivities in the home of Eugene Pillot were characterized by a French elegance captured in the home's restored interior. Photos by Story J. Sloane III, Harris County Heritage Society

The San Felipe Cottage, built in 1868 and remodeled in 1883, represents the modest homes of the Houston middle class in the late 19th century. In its six small rooms it housed small to middle-sized families, including those of two of Houston's fire chiefs. Courtesy, Harris County Heritage Society

In Houston's German homes of the 19th century tables at Christmas time were laden with cakes, cookies, and other sweets made with recipes brought from Germany. The Germans appear to have brought many Christmas customs to Houston. Courtesy, Story J. Sloane III, Harris County Heritage Society

Above:
Born near Rusk in 1851, James Stephen Hogg, a progressive Democrat, served as the first native-born governor of Texas between 1891 to 1895. Moving to Houston in 1904, Hogg had already played an important role in developing the Texas Company following the Spindletop discovery. Hurt in a railroad accident, Hogg maintained a limited schedule of activity until his death in March 1906. Courtesy, Bayou Bend Collection, Gift of Miss Ima Hogg; Houston Museum of Fine Arts

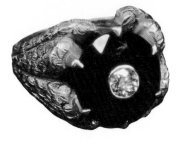

Left:
Presented to Governor James Stephen Hogg, this diamond ring with the stone set into tar from the Spindletop oil field captures the pride of Texans in their newly found natural resource. Courtesy, San Jacinto Monument

*By about 1880 Houston had
grown from a village to a city
and was on its way to becoming
a mercantile and transportation
center. From Thrall,*
Texas 1879

CHAPTER IV

THE BAYOU CITY IN THE GILDED AGE

1209, 1211, 1213, 1215 Congress Ave Houston, Texas

In his widely read novel, *The Gilded Age,* Mark Twain lamented some of the "boom or bust" features of American life in the last quarter of the 19th century. Houstonians who purchased Twain's book at one of the city's growing number of bookstores or borrowed it from the Houston Lyceum would have found much with which to agree. No longer a placid village astride a picturesque bayou, Houston was fast becoming a noisy, bustling, mercantile and transportation center. Unmarked by the type of Civil War devastation visited upon Richmond and Atlanta, Houston had continued to grow and prosper during the era of Reconstruction. The city was now poised for a period of expansion unlike anything it had known before.

Railroad construction played a significant part in facilitating this growth. One important railroad emanating from the Bayou City, the Houston & Texas Central, had been chartered in 1848 with the Allen brothers among the original stockholders. Some 55 miles of track had been completed before secession, and it was the first railroad to resume building after the Civil War. Connections were made with Bryan in 1867, Corsicana in 1871, and Dallas in 1872. When the line extended even farther northward to Denison in 1873, its linkage with the Missouri, Kansas & Texas at that site gave the Lone Star State a through con-

nection to St. Louis. The first Pullman service in Texas was established on this line between Houston and St. Louis in 1873. However, some costly mistakes were made in the purchase of other Texas railroad properties, and the Houston & Texas Central was forced into receivership. In 1893 it was incorporated into the Southern Pacific system.

In 1875 three prominent Houstonians, Paul Bremond, Colonel T.W. House, and Eugene Pillot, joined other enterprising capitalists in chartering the Houston East & West Texas Narrow Gauge Railroad. Bremond, an imaginative man, had come to Houston in 1842 and prospered as a merchant and investor. Before work began on his railroad venture, he visited the Centennial at Philadelphia in 1876 and viewed an exhibit of a narrow gauge railroad. A subsequent trip to Colorado to observe the actual operation of another such road, the Denver & Rio Grande, confirmed his belief in that type of construction. He then purchased the two engines in the Centennial exhibit, the *Giraud* and the *Centennial,* and shipped them to Texas. After resolving some financial problems, work began on the projected road in 1876, and within four years it connected with Livingston and Moscow.

Nicknamed "Hell Either Way Taken," Bremond's road, designed to reach the Piney Woods region of northeast Texas, was projected in two parts. One trunk would run

Facing page, left:
Although Houston was still a market for the traditional self-taught builder who had not studied building in a formal manner, it also began to attract trained designers, such as Eugene T. Heiner, who could build commercial structures for the growing city. Courtesy, Harris County Heritage Society

Facing page right, top:
As Houston began to prosper, the city itself became a market for fashionable goods. While A.C. Morin, a carpenter, represented the traditional way of building houses, other firms, such as the Bayou City Marble Works, were importing fine architectural elements and building a taste for sophisticated design. Courtesy, Harris County Heritage Society

Facing page right, bottom:
In the mid-19th century, George E. Dickey was the leading force in Houston architecture, trading on his experience throughout Texas and his experience with both domestic and commercial architecture. Though clearly an important regional architect who grew with Houston, Dickey aspired to national status. Courtesy, Harris County Heritage Society

This page:
In the late 19th century, medical practice was changing. Broadsides and advertising, however, were still in use and M. Kahen's advertisement reflects the character of practice and knowledge in the community during the years after the Civil War and Reconstruction. Courtesy, Special Collections; Houston Public Library

WONDERFUL DISCOVERY
OF THE TINTED GLASSES,
M. KAHEN, Optician, Houston, Texas.

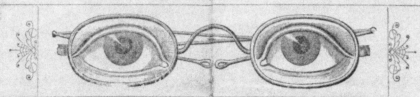

The eye being a rather delicate organ, great care should be exercised in the selection of proper spectacles. Many believe that spectacles should be resorted to only when the sight becomes so defective as not to be able to do without them. This is a great mistake, which must be combatted. Whenever there are unmistakable evidences of the need of their aid, they should be used; a neglect of this rule sometimes produces mischief which results in serious disease if this course be persisted in.

WHEN TINTED GLASSES SHOULD BE USED.

When the eyes water, or become so fatigued by short exercise as to be obliged to be frequently closed, or relieved by viewing different objects.

When the letters of a book appear to blend with one another, or become double and treble.

When more light is requisite than formerly; for example, when the light must be placed between the eye and the object.

When objects cannot be seen without removing to an increased distance.

When much difficulty is found in threading a needle.

When the eye becomes confused, as if they had a mist before them.

When black specks seem to be floating in the sight.

When any of the above indications arise, these Glasses should be used at once.

The Advantages to be Derived from the Use of Tinted Spectacles and Eye Glasses.

Are: Being of a perfect construction they assist and preserve the sight, rendering frequent changes quite unnecessary. They confer a brilliancy and distinctness of vision with an amount of ease and comfort not hitherto enjoyed by spectacle wearers. The lenses are ground on the most scientific principles, rendering the sight as clear as when in its full strength of youth.

Am manufacturing spectacles for near and far-sighted; Cataract and Shooting Glasses; Frameless Eye Glasses; Patent Double Vision Spectacles, Coquilles and Colored Glasses for weak eyes.

MR. M. KAHEN respectfully refers to the following residents of Houston, as to the merits of the Tinted Glasses:

Houston, January 22, 1884.
MR. M. KAHEN, Optician.
Dear Sir: "Having used a pair of your Tinted Glasses, I take pleasure in recommending them. I find them better suited to the eye than any I have used for eight years. The magnifying power which is usually harsh to the eyes is softened by the Tinted Glass, and is also beneficial to the sight."
Yours respectfully, JAMES MURISON.

Houston, January 22, 1884.
MR. M. KAHEN, Optician.
Dear Sir: "Having bought two pair of your Tinted Glasses, one for myself and the other for my wife, I take pleasure in saying to you that we are pleased with them."
W. HARRAL.

Houston, January 23, 1884.
MR. M. KAHEN, Optician.
Dear Sir: "Your Tinted Glasses give the best satisfaction, I believe they are all you recommend for superior quality and well suited for the eye."
Z. EMMICH.

Houston, January 23, 1884.
M. KAHEN, Optician.
Dear Sir: "I have been wearing glasses for the last thirty years, and I find the Tinted Glasses I have from you to please me in every particular better than any glasses I ever wore."
SAMUEL SAM.

Houston, January 23, 1884.
M. KAHEN, Optician.
Dear Sir: "Having bought the first pair of glasses I ever used of you, being tinted I use them only for night use, and find them better suited to the eye than any glasses I ever tried. The magnifying power which is usually harsh to the eyes is softened by the Tinted Glasses, and is also beneficial to the sight."
Yours truly, JOHN D. USENER.

Houston, January 24, 1884.
M. KAHEN, Optician.
Dear Sir: "I have used your Tinted Glasses and I have been using glasses for the last six years, and have used different kinds of glasses, and I found that the Tinted Glasses give me more satisfaction than any glass I have ever used. I recommend them to be a fine, soft glass for the eyes."
Respectfully, W. C. WAGLEY.

Houston, January 24, 1884.
M. KAHEN, Optician.
Dear Sir: "From personal use of your Tinted Glasses, I take pleasure in assuring you of great benefit and relief to the eye experienced by me, and freely recommend their use."
J. R. MORRIS.

Houston, January 24, 1884.
M. KAHEN, Optician.
"I know they are good."
E. BROWN.

Houston, January 25, 1884.
M. KAHEN, Optician.
Dear Sir: "I have used your Tinted Glasses, and they have given me convenient satisfaction since I have used them, and any one wearing glasses, I recommend them to be softer to the eye than any clear glass." Yours respectfully, A. T. AUTRY.

Houston, January 25, 1884.
"I take pleasure in recommending the use of the Tinted Eye Glass, now used by my wife, sold by Mr. M. KAHEN, Optician. They afford much relief to her, therefore, improved her eyesight."
A. GROESBEECK.

Houston, January 25, 1884.
"This is to certify that I have been using spectacles for the past seven years, and during that time have tried a great many different kinds of glasses, but none have proved so satisfactory as the pair of Tinted Glasses sold me, by Mr. KAHEN, Optician, and I recommend them to every one using eye glasses."
Very respectfully, Mrs. E. ADAMS.

Houston, January 25, 1884.
M. KAHEN, Optician.
"I have used your glasses now for the last four months, and found them to do me more good than any I had before. I can recommend them to any of my friends." Respectfully yours, A. CRAMER.

Houston, January 25, 1884.
"I have examined the Tinted Glasses, sold by Mr. KAHEN, and believe them to be very superior glasses, and possessing qualities in advance of ordinary glasses."
E. P. TURNER.

Houston, January 25, 1884.
"After having tried all kinds of glasses, I find none so good as the Tinted Glasses sold by M. KAHEN, Optician."
N. ALLTMONT.

Houston, January 29, 1884.
Mr. M. KAHEN, Optician.
Dear Sir: "Have been wearing glasses for three years, and lately purchased a pair of your Tinted Glasses, which I claim to be better than any I have ever used, and would freely recommend them to the public."
E. PILLOT.

Houston, January 29, 1884.
M. KAHEN, Optician.
Dear Sir: "Your Tinted Glasses are the best I have ever used." GEO. T. KENDALL.

OFFICE HOURS: 9 A. M. to 12 M., and from 2 to 5 P. M.
When desired will call at residence. Address

M. KAHEN, Optician,
No. 54 Main St., HOUSTON.

FRANKLIN PRINTING HOUSE

As the railroad net spreading from Houston grew, connections to other trade centers became increasingly important. The emphasis on connections to the rest of the nation, combined with Pullman Palace sleeping cars, shows the standard of service that Houstonians had come to expect. Courtesy, Harris County Heritage Society

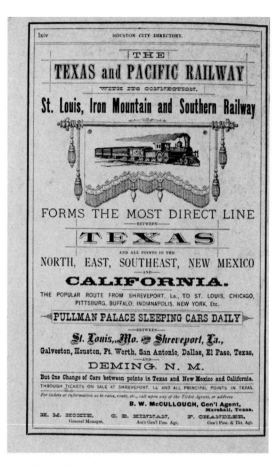

Tickets to ride the International and Great Northern Railway's "Lone Star" route could be purchased at the Union Depot at the head of Congress Street in 1881. From the collections of the Dallas Historical Society

northeast from Houston through Marshall to Texarkana, with branches from Goodrich and Jasper to the Sabine. This route would link up with the timber-producing belt of East Texas, while the other trunk would run in a southwesterly direction to Laredo through Victoria and Goliad. However, this latter road was never constructed.

By 1883 the Houston East & West Texas had reached Nacogdoches, providing access to the Piney Woods timber forests, and by 1885 its ultimate destination, the Sabine River. In the last quarter of the 19th century, Houston became the hub of the state's lumber industry, and at the height of its operations, the three-foot gauge road transported 20 carloads of lumber to the city daily. Houston was ideally situated; the timberlands were to her east, and the vast market for lumber supplies lay to her west. Of course, as additional lines radiated out of the city, the market was proportionately increased. In 1899, 420 million feet of lumber passed through Houston railroad terminals destined for other parts of the state as well as national and international markets.

Bremond had invested his entire personal fortune, reputed to be $500,000, in the railroad that opened the timber forests, and his death in May 1885 forced the road into receivership. The property was acquired in 1894 by Blair & Company Bankers of New York City, who placed it under the direction of Norman S. Meldrum as president. Meldrum, who played a prominent role in Houston civic and cultural affairs, operated the road with efficiency until October 1899, when it, too, became part of the Southern Pacific.

Another career closely tied to the opening of the timber forests was that of John Henry Kirby. Born near Peachtree Village in East Texas, he attended Southwestern University for a brief time, but failed to graduate because of lack of funds. Returning to the Piney Woods, he took up residence at Woodville, read law, and was admitted to the state bar. Backed by Eastern capitalists, Kirby was instrumental in the formation of the Texas and Louisiana Land and Lumber Company and also the Texas Pine Land As-

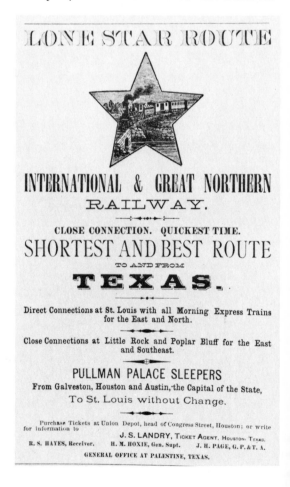

sociation. Kirby, by now the dominant force in two of the largest timber companies in Texas, moved to Houston in 1890 to join the law firm of Hobby and Lanier.

For better logging of his vast lumber holdings, Kirby, in 1893, began construction of the Gulf, Beaumont & Kansas City Railroad between the Neches and Sabine rivers. He continued to buy up timberlands and extend the railroad, and in 1896 he erected his first sawmill at Silsbee. In 1901 he founded the Houston-based Kirby Lumber Company and was reputed to be the "wealthiest man in town." The company's headquarters were located in a seven-story building erected by Kirby at the corner of Main Street and Rusk Avenue. Known chiefly as a lumberman, Kirby continued to practice law while branching out into banking and related interests. Still later, he became active in the oil industry, serving as president of the Southwestern Oil Company of Houston and then founding the Kirby Petroleum Company in 1920. During a lengthy and active business career, he found time to represent his district in the Texas state legislature and serve as a member of the War Industries Board during World War I. Kirby, whose initiative helped build the Bayou City's fortunes, died at his home in Houston on November 9, 1940.

By 1890 almost 8,500 miles of railroad track had been laid in Texas, substantially improving transportation to and from Houston and contributing significantly to the city's expansion. Houston businessmen and transportation leaders had long cherished another prospect, that of bypassing Galveston and achieving direct access to the sea. On October 9, 1866, the Houston Direct Navigation Company was chartered to improve navigation conditions on Buffalo Bayou. Among the company's founders were Eugene Pillot, Timothy H. Scanlan, Joseph Jones Reynolds, and Peter Gabel. While the founders of the company were prohibited from exercising exclusive navigation rights on the bayou, they were authorized to have, "a sufficient number of steamers, barges, and propellers, to meet the demands of commerce."

The Houston Direct Navigation Company prospered from the time of its incor-

The long leaf pines of East Texas were logged and brought to many different mills for processing. Here we see the Weir Long Leaf Lumber Company's mill pond in 1900. Courtesy, Barker Texas History Center; University of Texas

The Weir Long Leaf Lumber Company was one of a number of Houston-based firms that owned vast stands of timber in the pine forests of East Texas. Taking advantage of the rail network, which focused on Houston, such firms made the lumber industry one of the bases of the Houston economy. Courtesy, Barker Texas History Center; University of Texas

Built to house Samuel E. Carter's Lumberman's National Bank, the S.E. Carter Building was the first tall building in Houston. Complete with a walnut-paneled boardroom, the structure marked the beginning of the growth of Houston's skyline. Carter, who had made his fortune in lumber, was one of those who brought the timber trade of East Texas to Houston. Courtesy, Texas Room; Houston Public Library

poration. Exorbitant Galveston wharfage costs and obstructions placed in that city's harbor during the Civil War worked to Houston's advantage. Oceangoing vessels bound for Galveston adopted the practice of unloading in mid-channel and transferring a portion of their cargoes to smaller barges that could navigate to Houston. This neatly avoided the payment of fees in Galveston. In addition to running barges carrying freight, the Direct Navigation Company also awarded contracts for the construction of four bayou passenger steamers to travel between Houston and Galveston. The trip aboard the *T.M. Bagby*, the *Diana*, the *Lizzie*, or the *Charles Fowler* was popular with both businessmen and honeymoon couples, who traveled in accommodations that rivaled any Mississippi River steamer of the era.

The same year that the Direct Navigation Company was chartered, the Buffalo Bayou Ship Channel Company was also chartered, with former Texas Secretary of State E.W. Cave as president. This company set about the task of deepening the channel but quickly expended its available funds. Ten thousand dollars was secured from the federal government, but by 1873 the company's financial resources were once again exhausted. Denied any further federal assistance, the principal stockholders, many of whom also held an interest in the Direct Navigation Company, turned to Charles Morgan of the Morgan Steamship line for assistance. Morgan, whose holdings at one time totaled more than 100 ships, had long chafed under the Galveston wharfage monopoly and was anxious to boost Houston as a rival port. Accordingly, in 1874 he entered into an agreement to purchase both companies and also to construct a nine-foot channel, not less than 120 feet wide, from Galveston Bay to the vicinity of Houston.

By mid-1875 eight dredges, six tugs, and a number of derricks and barges were at work clearing the channel day and night. Despite major storm damage and a hurricane in September, the channel was finished on April 21, 1876—San Jacinto Day. The western terminus of this channel lay seven miles

below Houston, and Morgan completed his larger scheme by building a railroad, the Texas Transportation Company, from that site into Houston's Fifth Ward. Morgan's steamers were thus linked with railroad connections to Houston and therefore with any connecting road in Texas.

This represented just the early beginnings of the Bayou City's future as a deep-water port. Two other developments aided this process: on July 14, 1870, the United States Congress designated Houston as an official "port of delivery" and authorized a federal survey of Houston's proposed channel; and in May 1874 a number of prominent cotton factors and local merchants organized the Houston Board of Trade. This organization was later joined in the task of municipal promotion by the Houston Commercial League, founded in 1890, and the Houston Business League, established in 1895. The present Houston Chamber of Commerce, organized in 1910, can trace its ancestry directly back only to the creation of the Houston Business League in 1895.

The Houston Board of Trade, established principally to encourage the cotton trade, soon changed its name to the Houston Board of Trade and Cotton Exchange. Almost from the time of its founding, cotton had been important to the economy of Houston. Plantations upriver on the muddy Brazos had sent their crop to Houston for shipment to Galveston, other parts of the United States, and Europe as well. Profits earned during the Civil War and after had bolstered the fortunes of such early Houston millionaires as Colonel T.W. House, William Marsh Rice, and others. To compress the cotton for easier shipment, a number of compress companies were founded. The Houston Cotton Compress (1860), Bayou City Compress (1875), and International Compress (1882) were among the most important of these concerns. Cottonseed-oil factories and cotton warehouses also dotted the Houston industrial scene. Since cotton was a major export from Houston at the time, the Cotton Exchange was vitally interested in reasonable transportation rates to foreign and domestic markets and thus enthusiastically supported the ship channel project.

In addition to the ship channel project and further railroad expansion, improvement of the city's roads and streets was also necessary to Houston's transportation network. Complaints about the dusty and muddy condition of Houston's streets finally resulted in some action. Conditions became so intolerable that in 1882 the Fifth Ward, a largely black area, petitioned the City Council for the right to secede and found the "City of North Houston." Faced with this threat, utility connections were extended to the area and some promises were made regarding the improvement of streets. In the heart of the city, Preston Avenue east of Main Street was topped with shell and Chenevert Street was ditched and graded. In the summer of 1882, two blocks of Main Street were paved with limestone squares over a gravel base, financed by owners of adjacent property. Other Houston merchants subsidized street improvement using planking, brick, and asphalt. In 1892 the Magnolia Cycling Club was able to conduct its first annual bicycle race over paved streets in the Houston Heights neighborhood. Perhaps the most significant statistic was that by the turn of the century the city

In the 19th century, lumber factories began to shape the lifestyles and homes of each community. Producing standardized sashes, doors, blinds, and trim, dealers such as H. House provided materials for the builders of the community and began to provide an elegance not previously available. Courtesy, Special Collections; Houston Public Library

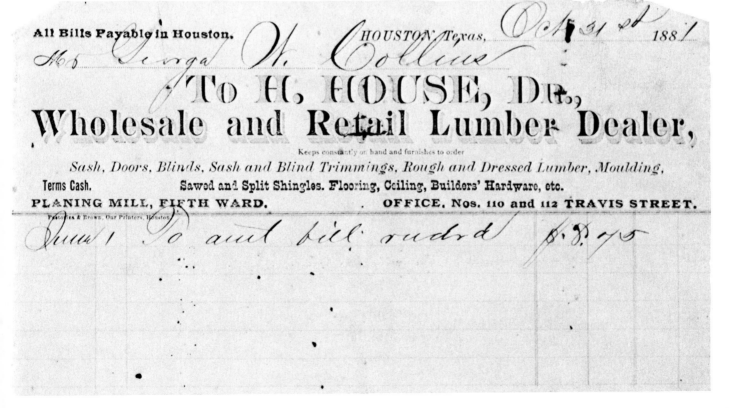

could boast of 26 miles of paved road.

Municipal improvements and business expansion were not accomplished without an increase in labor agitation and strikes. In 1878 the Houston City Council authorized the local street commissioner to pay his workers in scrip. The men were excused from their duties for a two-hour period during which time they had to find someone to purchase the paper. Thirty cents on the dollar was the highest offer for the vouchers, and the workers returned to inform the commissioner that they were unwilling to work at that rate. They removed their tools from the city's streets, as requested, and an alderman took their case to the Council, which decided against the strikers and ordered them back to work. Another situation in which public employees displayed new militancy occurred in 1880, when the city was unable to meet its December payroll and the Houston policemen threatened to strike. Efforts to hurriedly borrow the money proved unsuccessful, but the police officers stayed on the job and were eventually compensated.

Employees of private concerns also developed labor unions, such as the Texas Typographical Association, which maintained a chapter in Houston since 1838. In September 1880 printers employed by the Houston *Post* demanded a raise from 35 to

40 cents per thousand copies. Management struck back by pointing out that *Post* printers received a higher wage than those employed by any other newspaper in the city and threatened to discharge those who did not immediately return to work. In less than a week the strike was broken, and the printers resumed their employment at the old rate of 35 cents. However, the organizers of the strike, John Wilson and George Fortney, were denied their jobs back.

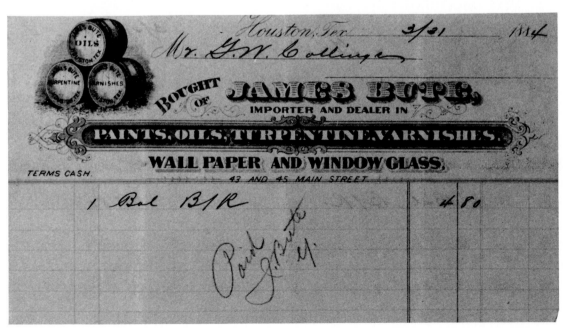

In 1885 a local chapter of the Knights of Labor was established, but two years earlier the organization's activities touched the Bayou City. In 1883, primarily because the Mallory Line at its New York pier discharged white union laborers and replaced them with black nonunion labor, the Knights of Labor called a general strike at Galveston. The Knights demanded that the company cease its discriminatory practices against union labor and reinstate the workers who had been discharged. Upon the Mallory Line's rejection of the union demand, some 2,000 Galveston longshoremen walked off their jobs. In less than a week, the strike spread to Houston, where local dockworkers refused to handle any shipments billed for Galveston. Although this strike ended unsuccessfully, it did aid in the establishment of the Negro Longshoremen's Association in 1884 with membership in Galveston and Houston.

Black involvement in politics in general increased after Reconstruction. Adoption of the Texas State Constitution of 1876 marked an official end to the decade of Reconstruction. The document called for

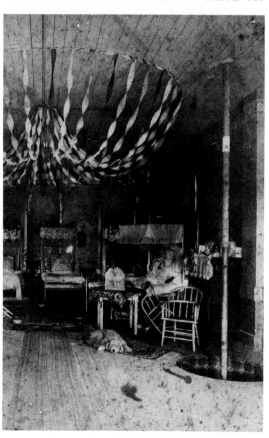

acceptance of the 13th and 14th amendments to the federal Constitution and outlawed discrimination on grounds of race where voting rights were at issue. Although many in Houston and Harris County were opposed to these and other features of the document, it was overwhelmingly ratified on a statewide basis. Amended countless times, this constitution, written more than one hundred years ago, serves the Lone Star State to this day as fundamental law.

Now that the Federal troops had been removed, Houstonians and residents of Harris County returned to their former political allegiance. Democratic candidates for the national Presidency were unfailingly supported as were nominees for the state's highest elective office at Austin. Perhaps the most popular political figure in Houston during this time was James Stephen Hogg. As state attorney general (1886-1890), he fought for effective legislation to regulate abusive railroad practices and also achieved more stringent control of out-of-state insurance companies doing business in Texas.

Campaigning as a reform candidate, he was elected for two terms as governor (1891-1895). His most significant contribution in that office was to champion the creation of the Texas Railroad Commission, which in time became the most effective state regulatory body in the nation. He also endeared himself to the Houston business community by his frequent trips to New York, Boston, and Philadelphia, seeking capital for local business development and stressing the opportunities that awaited the enterprising businessman in Texas. Hogg returned to private practice as an attorney and prospered through oil investments after the Spindletop boom. He continued to play a prominent role in national Democratic politics until his death in 1906, and important contributions later were made to the city of Houston by his son, Will Hogg, and his daughter, Ima Hogg.

The Democratic party also dominated politics on a municipal level. James T.D. Wilson was appointed mayor of the city in 1874 by Governor Richard Coke to replace

William R. Baker, Houston's mayor during the 1880-1885 period, had come to Texas as a young man in 1841 from New York. Baker had served as county clerk, but later became involved in the development of Houston's business community. He served as a member of a number of corporate boards, as owner of the Houston Post, and as president of the City Bank of Houston, helping to found one of the great banking institutions of the city. Courtesy, Texas Room; Houston Public Library

the local carpetbag administration of T.H. Scanlan, and a few months later he was elected in a popular contest. He also served as mayor for another term (1877-1878). Formerly engaged in real estate and banking, Wilson was a confident spokesmen for the city's business community. Another popular politician with a strong business background was William R. Baker, mayor in 1880-1886. A former director of the Houston & Texas Central Railroad, he was also for a time president of the City Bank of Houston. Other Houston chief executives of this era were Andrew J. Burke, Daniel C. Smith, and Samuel H. Brashear.

It was at this time, the last quarter of the 19th century, that blacks in Houston moved more into the political mainstream. Grateful to President Lincoln for their liberation and encouraged by the Freedmen's Bureau in that direction, most Texas blacks tended to identify with the Republican party. However, in their attempt to return to local ascendancy, Texas Democrats sought black support on fusion tickets. Generally, however, blacks resented such proposals in which they were granted only token representation on the ticket. As a case in point, the black vice-president of the Harris County Republican Convention commented on the county ticket selected in 1876: "You seem to think because a man says he is an independent Democrat he is better than a Republican. What good is it for us to . . . help independent Democrats instead of trying to help some of our own sort." However, the situation did not show much improvement in Harris County, for in 1880 only one black candidate was included on the ticket. Fusionism was also attempted on a local level when Houston Greenbackers selected a city ticket that included token representation. A black, Milton Baker, was nominated for street commissioner, but the entire ticket failed of election.

In an effort to discourage black participation in politics, Democrats proposed payment of a poll tax as a requirement for suffrage. This proposal, which had been voted down at the constitutional convention, came up several times during the late-

19th century but was always defeated. Although the purpose of the proposed tax was to eliminate black voters, many Democrats believed that it would fall just as heavily on poor whites. However, after a number of unsuccessful attempts, the state legislature, in 1903, passed a constitutional amendment sanctioning a poll tax for voting. The amendment was ratified by a two-to-one vote and it did reduce the number of voters in Texas elections. Houston and other cities then adopted a municipal poll tax for local elections, which acted to keep some blacks and Mexican-Americans away from the polls. One perhaps unexpected development was the formation of "poll tax associations" in which local politicians purchased poll taxes for minority voters to assure their casting a ballot for the party in power. One such "association" appeared in Houston at this time.

Not content with quasi-legal methods to keep blacks from the voting booth, so-called "white men's parties" sprung up in Waller, Harris, Matagorda, and Washington counties. Physical intimidation was used by these groups, sometimes ending in serious violence. Frustrated in their political ambitions

and suffering economic deprivation as well, blacks in Houston sought other means to advance their cause. In addition to joining such organizations as the Knights of Labor and the Farmers Improvement Society, they attended national protest conventions in Nashville, Tennessee, in 1876 and 1879. In order to publicize their achievements and encourage individual initiative on the part of blacks, fairs, most of them connected with agriculture, were frequently sponsored. Both the Colored Lone Star State Fair Association and the Afro-American Fair were often held in Houston. In 1890 Houstonians Richard Allen and Samuel J. Dixon attended the National Afro-American League meeting in Chicago, which was called to condemn the conditions under which blacks were compelled to live.

Richard Allen, who also attended the 1879 convention at Nashville, was among the most politically active members of the Houston black community. Elected to the state legislature in 1871, he also served as customs collector for the Port of Houston and as a city alderman. He became the first grand master of the Colored Masons in Texas and was a Presidential elector in 1904. As a leading exponent of black migration, he organized a statewide meeting where plans were drawn up calling for the organization of emigration clubs to facilitate the exodus from Texas. A mistaken impression circulated that lands could be had for almost nothing in Kansas and Oklahoma. Some interest was generated in an ultimately unsuccessful Mexican colonization scheme and in an imaginative proposal to establish a separate colony for Texas blacks in the northwestern corner of the state. A "back to Africa" movement also had its partisans, and in 1881 black Houstonians organized an ultimately unsuccessful society to encourage emigration to Liberia. Authorities differ on the exact number of blacks who left the state at this time, but the total was insignificant.

As blacks had to struggle to achieve political representation, they also had to fight for adequate educational facilities. The landmark Texas Constitution of 1876 abolished

James T.D. Wilson, a Houston banker, was the man selected to end the rule of the Scanlan administration. Appointed mayor in 1874 by the governor, he was elected for the 1875 term and then again from 1877 to 1878. Wilson rebuilt the market house, which had burned in an 1876 fire. Courtesy, Texas Room; Houston Public Library

the office of state superintendent of schools and provided for virtual autonomy on the part of local school boards. The statute also provided in generous fashion for the support of local schools. Any incorporated city or town, by a majority vote of the property taxpayers, could assume exclusive control of the public schools within its limits.

The City of Houston became among the first in the state to take control of its schools. However, this was not the first instance of free public education in Houston. A free county school system supported by state funds was already operative in Harris County. In 1873 Harris County operated some 24 schools with slightly more than 1,500 students in attendance. In 1874 Ashbel Smith, whose major contributions to education in Texas still lay in the future founding of the University of Texas, was named superintendent of county schools. A physician whose medical skills were much in demand, Smith found time to screen each applicant for a teaching position in the county and to become an active advocate of educational reform, including the improvement of black education.

Based on the results of the local election, the City Council in 1877 established free

The design of the 1895 Central High School building reflected the latest taste in school planning. The tall windows provided light for the students in the different classrooms. The building also included modern facilities such as a gymnasium. However, the school served only a small portion of the youth of high school age in Houston and the majority did not complete high school. Courtesy, Harris County Heritage Society; Litterst-Dixon Collection

public schools for all children from the ages of eight to fourteen. Three trustees and a superintendent, appointed by the mayor and approved by the Council, would manage the system. From the very beginning the schools and teaching staffs were segregated by order of the City Council. Attendance was not compulsory and the school year lasted only six months. Finally, in order to be certified to teach in the Houston public schools, an instructor must pass examinations in "orthography, reading, writing, English grammar, composition, geography, and arithmetic." Still, because of the paucity of applicants, the records indicate that most applicants were deemed qualified. The average monthly wage for a teacher in the Houston public schools at this time was just under $50.

Segregation in the local public schools

meant that from the beginning black schools would be poorly funded. The Slater and Peabody funds, created by Northern philanthropists, did provide some money for urban black institutions, but not enough to redress the imbalance. Spokesmen for the black community protested against a worsening situation and 13 black educational and political leaders, some from Houston, organized the Colored Teachers State Association in 1884. This organization called upon the state to provide college training for blacks and also sought help from the private sector. Colleges and universities for black students were established by the Methodist, Roman Catholic, and Baptist churches, but few of the educational attempts proved lasting. For example, the Baptist Missionary and Education Association of Texas founded Houston College in 1885 with 100 students, but within a few years classes ceased to meet.

No single individual did more for the cause of education in Texas than Ashbel Smith. Although he maintained a home at Evergreen Plantation on Galveston Bay, his medical practice rooted him in Houston as well. In 1876 Smith published an article in the *Texas Christian Advocate* entitled "Education of the Negro," which urged the state legislature to increase its appropriation for black education. Shortly thereafter, Governor Richard Coke appointed Smith one of three commissioners charged with locating a site for the Agricultural and Mechanical College for Colored Youths, later Prairie View University. However, the chief labor of the last years of Smith's life was the founding of the University of Texas. As president of the first Board of Regents, Smith was instrumental in designing the initial curriculum at the university and assembling its first faculty. Although a statewide referendum resulted in the location of the university in Austin, Smith was successful in locating the medical department of the university at Galveston. Smith was the principal speaker on November 16, 1882, the day the cornerstone of the first building on the campus at Austin was laid. Prophetically, he told his audience, "Texas holds embedded in its earth rocks and minerals which now lie idle, because unknown, resources of incalculable industrial utility, of wealth and power. Smite the earth, smite the rocks with the rod of knowledge and fountains of unstinted wealth will gush forth." How could Smith know that his promise would be fulfilled beyond his wildest dreams in 1923, when oil was discovered on university-owned property?

In late-19th-century Houston, another great personality embarked on an eventually outstanding career. William Sydney Porter, born in Greensboro, North Carolina, came to Texas in 1882 and worked in Austin as a bank teller and as a draftsman in the General Land Office. In 1894 he resigned his position at the bank to devote all his time to editing a humorous weekly magazine, *Rolling Stone*. When this venture failed,

he moved to Houston in 1895 and began to write editorials and short stories for the *Post*. Ordered to stand trial for alleged embezzlement of funds at the First National Bank of Austin, he fled to Honduras, but later returned and was imprisoned. While in the federal penitentiary at Columbus, Ohio, Porter began to write short stories under the pseudonym "O. Henry." In 1902, upon his release from prison, he went to New York, where he died in 1910. His reputation as perhaps America's greatest short-story writer is undimmed to this day.

The Houston *Post*, which published Porter's work before he was "O. Henry," was founded in 1880 by Gail Borden Johnson, who in 1881 combined it with the old Houston *Telegraph and Texas Register*. Financial difficulties caused the paper to suspend publication briefly in 1884, and the next year a merger of the *Morning Chronicle* and *Evening Journal* resulted in the present Houston *Post*. Edited by R.M. Johnson, the newspaper employed a number of writers just commencing their careers who later became justly famous. Among this group was Marcellus E. Foster, later associated with the Houston *Chronicle*, and William Cowper Brann. Brann was briefly an editorial columnist for the *Post* before moving to Waco, where he founded the monthly *Iconoclast*,

Dr. Ashbel Smith (1805-1886) was made superintendent of the Harris County schools in 1874. Among his various accomplishments, Dr. Smith had been minister to France, president of the board of examiners at West Point, and a legislator from Harris County. From Cirker, Dictionary of American Portraits, *Dover, 1967*

which sought to combat "hypocricy, intolerance, and other evils." Brann, a bitter, sarcastic critic of the Baptist faith, was shot to death in Waco in 1898 as he prepared to depart on a lecture tour.

As well as being a time of initiative in the literary realm, the last quarter of the century was also a time of expansion for theater and opera in Houston. Shakespeare was represented by *Romeo and Juliet, Julius Caeser,* and *Othello,* but certainly the highlight was the appearance of Edwin Booth in *Hamlet* at Pillott's Opera House. Playing in Houston on February 23, 1883, the engagement had been sold out for months before Booth's arrival. On the day of the performance, disappointed ticket-seekers were offering as high as $20 for seats that had originally sold for $2. The drama critic for the Houston *Post* noticed that Booth's diction was "clear and incisive . . . moreover, he invested the role with an air of fascinating wildness and awe-inspiring mystery." Two women with somewhat lively reputations also adorned the Houston stage at this time. On April 19, 1888, Mrs. Lilly Langtry appeared in a one-night presentation of *A Wife's Peril* at Pillott's Opera House. The local reviews

were hardly complimentary both as regards her acting ability and her much-heralded beauty. On February 4, 1891, Sarah Bernhardt graced the stage before an audience of almost 2,000 in *La Tosca,* but once again Houstonians professed themselves disappointed. Many patrons left before the play was half over, and the ubiquitous *Post* critic observed that while her performance drew generous applause, there was nothing "wild and uncontrollable" about her actions.

In 1901 the famed Metropolitan Opera paid its first visit to Houston and performed *Lohengrin,* featuring Ernestine Schumann Heink as Ortrud. The company appeared in the Winnie Davis Auditorium, a hall located on the southern edge of town at the corner of Main and McGowen that opened in 1895 and was named for a daughter of the former Confederate President. Other famous personalities who entertained Houstonians at this time included the celebrated Oscar Wilde, who lectured on "aestheticism" at Gray's Opera House on Fannin Street on June 23, 1881. The Young Polish pianist and future president of his nation, Ignace Paderewski, was wildly cheered by his Houston audience on January 31, 1896. Paid the then remarkable sum of $2,500 for one night's concert at the auditorium on McGowen Street, the "wizard of the piano" did not disappoint his listeners.

One more person of note came to the city at this time, though not in the entertainment field. On March 29, 1880, some 5,000 residents of the Bayou City turned out to welcome ex-President Grant. The bitter memories of the Civil War must have been at least temporarily forgotten, because the former Union commander received a tumultuous reception when he arrived on the first train to enter the new Union Station. A large crowd followed Grant's party to the Hutchins House on Franklin Street, where the balcony almost collapsed under the weight of those who sought to shake hands with the distinguished guest. At a reception held later in the day, Grant, who seemed genuinely affected by the obvious good will of the crowd, said:

In regard to the receptions which have been tendered me elsewhere throughout the circle of the globe, I can assure you that none go nearer to my heart than those given me by my own countrymen. Especially is this gratifying in a section of the country that was so recently in conflict with us. I agree in the sentiment that we are a happy and united people, and it would take a stronger power than any one man now in existence to separate us. United as we are, we are the strongest nation on earth.

The "strongest nation on earth" would again become embroiled in war before the century's end. The controversy with Spain that culminated in the Spanish-American War at first occasioned little interest on the part of Houstonians. However, all of that changed when the USS *Maine* sank in Havana harbor on the evening of February 15, 1898. Two days later flags atop the post office and City Hall were flown at half-mast in honor of those who had lost their lives when the ship blew up. Within a week, a 30-ton cannon intended for the protection of Galveston was being closely guarded at the Congress Avenue depot of the Interna-

tional & Great Northern Railroad.

On San Jacinto Day, April 21, a pyrotechnical representation of the sinking of the *Maine* was staged, and four days later, when Congress declared war against Spain, the Bayou City was prepared to contribute to the war effort. Adjunct General W.H. Mabry of the Texas Volunteer Guard ordered all military companies in Houston to prepare for service and on May 4 the Light Guards and the Emmet Rifles departed for Austin. A recruiting station was opened at 209 Main Street and Camp Tom

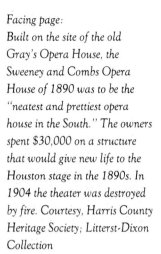

Facing page:
Built on the site of the old Gray's Opera House, the Sweeney and Combs Opera House of 1890 was to be the "neatest and prettiest opera house in the South." The owners spent $30,000 on a structure that would give new life to the Houston stage in the 1890s. In 1904 the theater was destroyed by fire. Courtesy, Harris County Heritage Society; Litterst-Dixon Collection

Above left:
This vision of Houston 50 years in the future was published in the Houston Chronicle *of October 14, 1902. It represented the view based on the best available understanding of technology. The artist saw a city with 20-story skyscrapers and a bayou that had been widened to allow visits from ocean liners. Transit would be either by rail or omnibus. In some respects the city did parallel the artist's vision, for the tall buildings were not built until some years after 1902, and liners did come up the bayou. Transit did not exist in 1952, however. Courtesy, Harris County Heritage Society; Litterst-Dixon Collection*

Left:
In the late 19th century, prominent Houstonians often joined military units, particularly the Houston Light Guard. During its 1888 summer camp, the group assembled for its photograph. Missing people and leaders caught in certain distinct positions were added after the fact in this unique image of the group in dress uniform. Courtesy, Texas Room; Houston Public Library

Texas German Gazette,

(DAILY AND WEEKLY.)

69 Main Street.   Houston, Texas.

HUGO LEHMAN, Propr.

CIRCULATES EXTENSIVELY IN THE CITIES OF HOUSTON, GALVESTON, AND IN THE GERMAN SETTLEMENTS OF THE WHOLE STATE.

IN COMPARISON TO CIRCULATIONS OUR ADVERTISING RATES ARE THE MOST REASONABLE OF ANY PAPER IN THE STATE.

SPECIMEN NUMBERS SENT ON APPLICATION.

For Advertising, Subscription and Club Rates, address

Texas German Gazette,

HOUSTON TEXAS

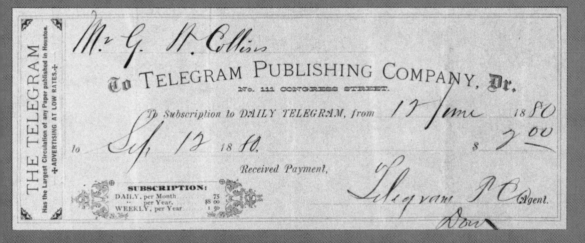

THE TELEGRAM
Has the Largest Circulation of any Paper published in Houston.
ADVERTISING AT LOW RATES.

Mr. G. W. Collins
To TELEGRAM PUBLISHING COMPANY, Dr.
No. 111 CONGRESS STREET.

To Subscription to DAILY TELEGRAM, from 17 June 1880
to Sep 17 18 80. $ 2.00

Received Payment,
Telegram P C Agent.

SUBSCRIPTION:
DAILY, per Month   75
"   per Year $8.00
WEEKLY, per Year   1.50

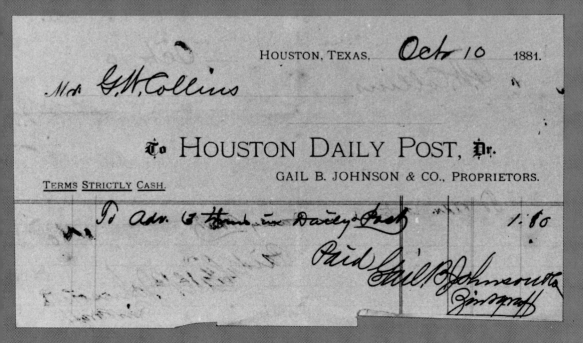

HOUSTON, TEXAS, Oct 10 1881.

Mr. G. W. Collins

To HOUSTON DAILY POST, Dr.

GAIL B. JOHNSON & CO., PROPRIETORS.

TERMS STRICTLY CASH.

To Adv. 6 time in Daily Post   1.60

Paid Gail B Johnson & Co

Ball was established at Forest Park, just east of Heights Boulevard. Perhaps the high point for the city was reached when on the night of May 30, Colonel Theodore Roosevelt and a trainload of his "Rough Riders" stopped over in Houston for six hours. Queried by a reporter for the *Post*, the future President confessed his impatience at the indefinite state of hostilities and his desire to "get some action." The "splendid little war" was concluded so rapidly that few Houstonians were actually able to serve.

From the time of its founding in 1836, the history of the city of Houston had been shaped by its rivalry with Galveston. In fact, the Allen brothers turned their attention to Houston only after first failing to secure title to a tract of land that later became the center of the settlement at Galveston. Although Galveston enjoyed natural advantages as a port and harbor, interest in a ship channel to give Houston direct access to the sea had begun even before the Civil War. During that conflict Galveston was captured and temporarily occupied by the Union, while Houston escaped unscathed. In the period after the war, Houston began to develop its potential as a port and to forge ahead as a railroad and trading center and, at

the turn of the century, Houston was beginning to emerge as a lumber and oil distribution center as well. The vision and foresight of Houston businessmen would have assured dominance for Houston in this intercity rivalry, but the terrible Galveston flood of 1900 hastened that process.

As early as September 4, 1900, the United States Weather Bureau at Galveston posted telegraphic bulletins to the effect that a "tropical cyclone" was moving westward in the Gulf of Mexico. Such warnings at that time of year were hardly novel and, unfor-

Facing page:
The blocks around Houston's city hall were the center of commercial life in the city at the turn of the century. Stude's Bakery and Confectionery was directly across the street from the city hall and served the entire community with its delivery wagons. Courtesy, Harris County Heritage Society; Litterst-Dixon Collection

Right:
Major hotels had become palaces by the late 19th century. The group of men posing in the lobby of what may have been the first Rice Hotel were surrounded by the classical elegance of the interior architecture. Courtesy, Harris County Heritage Society; Litterst-Dixon Collection

tunately, little attention was paid to them. By September 7, the surf had become too dangerous for bathing and the full fury of the storm hit on September 8. The entire city was under from one to five feet of water by 4 p.m. and by 5:30 all connections with the mainland had been destroyed. The climax of the storm was reached about 8 p.m. when the wind, blowing at an estimated 120 miles per hour, shifted from east to southeast and a tidal wave about six feet high swept across the city. After midnight the wind died down, although in the interim an estimated 6,000 persons had died and half of Galveston had been destroyed.

In the wake of Galveston's disaster, the tendency that had begun in the period after the Civil War whereby Houston emerged as the leading city in the Gulf Coast area was now complete.

As the 19th century drew to a close, Houston could boast electric lights, telephones, paved streets, and many other "wonders." It had 210 manufacturing plants, one stock-and-bonds house, and a population of almost 45,000. The 200-room Rice Hotel, a five-story structure, was still the tallest building in town and the largest hotel. The mayor and City Council pointed with pride to the fact that Houston was the

largest railroad center in the country south of St. Louis, the second-largest manufacturing center in Texas, and the second-largest city in bank clearings in the South, exceeded only by New Orleans. Now a major factor in the cotton, lumber, and rice industries in Texas, Houston was on the verge of realizing two principal reasons for its phenominal growth in the 20th century—the discovery of oil and the attainment of a deep-water port.

For many Houstonians, the leading hotels of the city were also the best dining spots. At the Christmas season, many residents and visitors alike found their way to dining rooms such as this one for the Christmas celebration. Courtesy, Harris County Heritage Society; Litterst-Dixon Collection

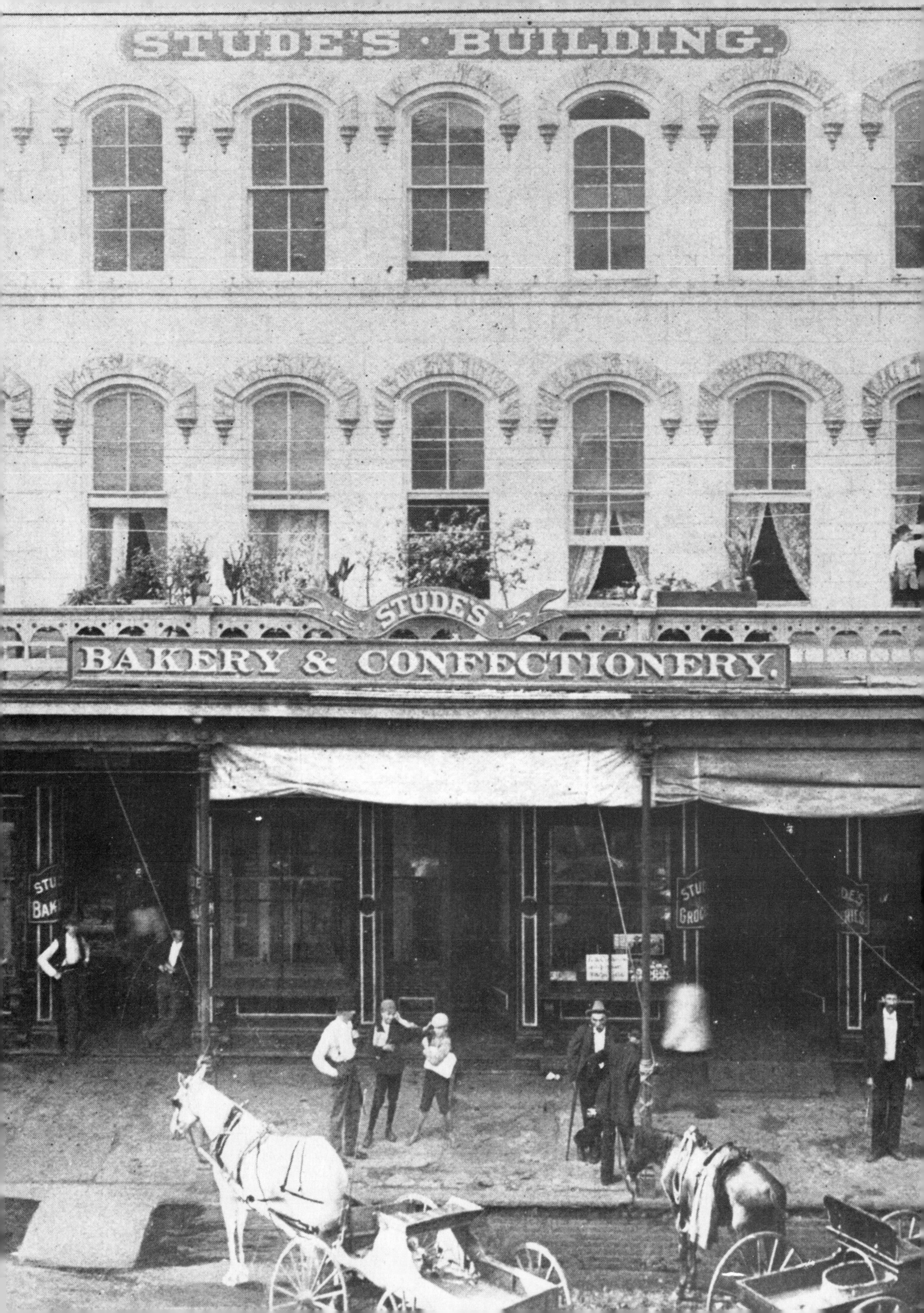
STUDE'S · BUILDING.
STUDE'S
BAKERY & CONFECTIONERY.

In the years before World War I, a number of notable breweries flourished in Houston. Locals such as these two delighted in the products of the Magnolia and Southern Select breweries, which helped to keep one cool on a hot summer day. Courtesy, Harris County Heritage Society; Litterst-Dixon Collection

Houston took many years to develop a professional police force. Beginning with constables in 1838, the force had an inconsistent tradition until the post-Civil War period, when it became professionalized. By the early 20th century, the officers of the force had begun to develop into a professional body that could protect the growing city. Courtesy, Harris County Heritage Society; Litterst-Dixon Collection

Above:
Houston was served by a volunteer fire unit from 1836 until 1895, at which time civic leaders instituted a professional fire service. The Central Fire Station housed both motorized and horse-drawn equipment during the era of World War I. As the city changed, however, the horse-drawn equipment was phased out. Courtesy, Harris County Heritage Society

Left:
For Houstonians in the years before World War I, literary, musical, and artistic societies were an important part of life. At a 1915 meeting, members of the Jewish Literary Society fete a visiting author. Courtesy, Harris County Heritage Society; Litterst-Dixon Collection

Although oil was first developed in the Spindletop fields, drilling moved closer to Houston as oil was discovered in Harris County at sites such as Humble and Pierce Junction. In the 1920s the derricks of the Pierce Junction Field could be seen from downtown Houston. Courtesy, Texas Room; Houston Public Library

CHAPTER V

ENERGY CAPITAL AND DEEP-WATER PORT

The earliest written account of the use of petroleum in North America dates from a stormy day in July 1543, when Spanish ships, returning the few survivors of the unlucky De Soto expedition back to Mexico, sought shelter along the Texas Gulf Coast. In the area of Sabine Pass the travelers sighted a dark, thick liquid floating on the water, and they used this substance to reinforce the bottoms of their ships. In fact, the Indians already knew of the existence of petroleum. The Karankawas visited oil springs along the Texas coast seeking their curative powers. The Indians immersed themselves in the springs to combat rheumatic pains and also applied the oil as a salve to cuts, burns, and sores. The narratives of the French and Spanish explorers in Texas touch on the location of various oil springs, and in the early colonial period of Texas history American settlers recorded oil "seeps" in Sabine, Shelby, Nacogdoches, Anderson, and Bexar counties.

Attempts had been made to drill an oil well in Texas before and during the Civil War, all of which resulted in failure. However, the Pennsylvania oil discoveries in the postwar era stimulated interest in further Texas exploration. Perhaps the mystique and allure of the search for oil has never been so graphically stated as in this letter to George W. O'Brian of Beaumont from a former Confederate comrade-in-arms, writing from Liberty, Texas. The letter is particularly in point since oil would ultimately be found in both the environs of Liberty and Beaumont:

... if we are prepared for the excitement, we will make our fortune. What is the use of toiling with aching brains and weary hands for bread, when gold so temptingly invites you to reach out and clutch it?

There were some minor wells drilled in Central Texas at Brownwood in 1878 and Greenvine, Washington County, in 1879. Rumored strikes in the neighborhood of San Antonio and Corpus Christi intensified the search for oil, which culminated in the first significant discoveries at Corsicana

in 1894. In his landmark work, *Oil! Titan of the Southwest,* Carl Coke Rister refers to the Corsicana field as the "curtain raiser" of the oil boom in the Southwest. Certainly drilling techniques and marketing strategies employed there for the first time were later utilized at the oil strike that ushered in the modern age of petroleum. In 1894 an artesian well company engaged in drilling for water at Corsicana hit an oil sand at 1,030 feet. Although located almost 200 miles north of Houston, what transpired at the Corsicana field was to be of vital concern to the Bayou City. In its first year of production, output from five wells constituting the Corsicana field totaled 1,450 barrels of oil; by 1900, 836,000 barrels were produced annually. However important the Corsicana discovery was, though, it served primarily as the forerunner of the Spindletop field at Beaumont.

Whereas at Corsicana oil was discovered accidentally while drilling a water well, Spindletop at Beaumont derived from the expertise of a trained mining engineer working with the theory that petroleum should accumulate around a salt dome. In 1892 Patillo Higgins, a young Beaumont businessman, had abandoned a projected well near that city at 300 feet because he was unable to drill through quicksand. Near despair and virtually at the end of his financial resources, in 1899 Higgins accepted Captain Anthony F. Lucas as a partner in the Gladys City Oil, Gas, and Manufacturing Company. For some years Lucas had worked with salt domes in Louisiana, and his experience persuaded him that oil would be found in the vicinity of the large salt dome known as "Spindletop." Also, Lucas was familiar with the problems of drilling in quicksand, an asset that proved invaluable at Spindletop. By now Higgins had sold all his drilling rights to Lucas, retaining only a small royalty percentage on the land.

Raising the necessary capital to finance the exploration proved an almost insurmountable task. The popular geological wisdom was that Lucas would fail. Virtually all available capital was depleted in an unsuccessful well abandoned at 575 feet,

but Lucas was determined to persevere. He took a small bottle of oil from the unsuccessful well and headed east seeking assistance. In Pittsburgh he convinced the wildcatting firm of Guffey & Galey, in fact a front for the Mellon interests, to take an interest and provide the working capital.

Drilling commenced on the Lucas lease in the fall of 1900, and as the year closed success still seemed far away. However, on the cold, clear, midmorning of January 10, 1901, the fantastic "Lucas gusher" at Spindletop blew in. Caldwell Reines described the famous event in *Year Book for Texas, 1901*:

At exactly 10:30 a.m., the well that made Beaumont famous burst upon the astonished view of those engaged in boring it, with such a volume of water, sand, rocks, gas and oil that sped upward with such tremendous force as to tear the crossbars of the derrick to pieces, and scattered the mixed properties from its bowels, together with timbers, pieces of well casing, etc., for hundreds of feet in all directions.

For nine days the phenomenon was the wonder and puzzle of the world. It flowed unceasingly and with ever increasing force

and volume until when it was finally controlled it was shooting upward a tower of pure crude oil, of the first quality, quite two hundred feet, and spouting in wanton waste 70,000 barrels of oil per day.

In fact, for nine days Spindletop drenched the surrounding countryside with 70,000 to 100,000 barrels of oil daily; the largest flow from any previous well drilled in the United States had 6,000 barrels. Also, Spindletop was then the largest producing well in the world outside the Baku field in Russia. Certainly no single event in the first half of the 20th century gave such a prod to the modern industrial development of Texas and Houston as did Spindletop. Three major companies that were founded in Beaumont shortly after the Spindletop discovery—the Texas Company (later Texaco), Gulf, and Humble—later relocated their principal offices in Houston.

The original architect of the Texas Company, Joseph S. Cullinan, had been active in the Corsicana discovery. There he had organized J.S. Cullinan and Company, the first pipeline and refinery company in Texas, and in order to increase local consumption, introduced two new applications for oil: as a dust-settling device for streets and as a fuel for locomotives. He moved to Beaumont in 1902 and organized a $50,000 corporation named the Texas Fuel Company. Then, with financial backing from ex-Governor James Hogg, the notorious Wall Street speculator John W. "Bet-A-Million" Gates, and others, the Texas Company was chartered with assets of $3 million on May 1, 1902. The new corporation succeeded to the properties of the original Texas Fuel Company, among which were a number of leases secured near the original site of Spindletop. Almost immediately after its reorganization the Texas Company began to expand its operations. Subsidiary companies were utilized for production, and pipelines were laid to Port Arthur, Houston, and New Orleans. New leases were actively pursued, and in 1901 the Sour Lake discovery, 25 miles northwest of Beaumont, provided the corporation with its first bonanza.

Joseph Cullinan, who had learned the oil business in Pennsylvania, moved to Texas in 1897 to organize the first pipeline and refinery in Corsicana. Organizing the Texas Company in Beaumont in 1902, he brought his firm's headquarters to Houston in 1905 and in the process he established Houston as the executive headquarters of the American oil industry. Courtesy, Texas Room; Houston Public Library

This was followed in 1905 by a major strike at the Humble field, just northeast of Houston in Harris County. Early in 1905 the first refinery was built at Port Arthur, and in 1908 the headquarters of the Texas Company were moved from Beaumont to Houston. The Sour Lake and Humble discoveries in the environs of Houston and the Bayou City's access to tidewater within the pipeline system of the Texas Company made such a move sensible. In February 1905 Cullinan wrote to a business associate, "Houston seems to me to be the coming center of the oil business for the Southwest." Relocating the main office of the company in Houston marked the beginning of the city's place as the executive headquarters of the oil industry in the Southwest. (The Texas Company moved its headquarters to New York in 1913 and its name was changed to Texaco in 1959.)

The modern-day Gulf Oil Corporation also stems from the discovery at Spindletop. An outgrowth of the J.M. Guffey Petroleum Company, which was organized in May 1901, the company has conducted operations in Houston since 1916. With financing provided by the Mellon interests in Pittsburgh, the Gulf Refining Company of Texas was created with interests acquired from Captain Lucas of the Spindletop field. In January 1907 the Gulf Oil Company was formed with A.W. Mellon as president and Guffey's interest was purchased for some $3 million. A 400-mile pipeline was then constructed from Port Arthur to the Glen Pool field in Oklahoma, discovered in 1906, and the refining of Oklahoma crude began the next year. By 1928 the company's assets had grown to an estimated $232 million, while crude production rose to 78 million barrels annually from operations throughout the U.S. and in several other countries.

Another corporation, the Humble Oil and Refining Company, was founded by William Stamps Farish and Robert Lee Blaffer, who met in an oilmen's boardinghouse in Beaumont in 1902. Farish, an attorney, and Blaffer, then working for the Southern Pacific Railroad, joined forces in 1904 to form a drilling partnership. The

next year they moved to Houston in order to concentrate on the nearby Humble field, where oil had been discovered in January 1905. Suddenly the little village to the northeast of Houston with a population of less then 800 was experiencing the same "boom" conditions that had characterized Beaumont after Spindletop. Real estate that had been selling at $6,400 per acre at Humble leaped to $16,000 per acre within a week's time. In three months the output of the Humble field was two million barrels and by 1906 it had produced 15,594,000 barrels of oil. Robert L. Blaffer and William S. Farish were among the most successful of the oilmen active in Humble.

In 1911 Blaffer and Farish were joined by Ross S. Sterling, a future governor of Texas, and Walter Fondren as the original founders of the Humble Oil Company. During 1911 and 1912 the company operated almost exclusively in the Humble field, which by now had begun to decline in production. In 1912 the headquarters of the company were

Facing page:
Tri-Fin Oil Company's Moers No. 1 Well on Chocolate Bayou in Brazoria County is typical of the wells drilled in the Houston area after the Spindletop field came in. These wells produced oil that was shipped to Houston and the refineries and docks along the ship channel to the rest of the world. Courtesy, Rosenberg Library

Left:
Andrew William Mellon (1855-1937) served as president of the Gulf Oil Company upon its formation in 1907. Painting by Oswald Birley. Courtesy, National Gallery of Art. Gift of Ailsa Mellon Bruce. From Cirker, Dictionary of American Portraits, Dover, 1967

moved to Houston and drilling operations were started in Oklahoma. By 1917 producing properties had been added at the Sour Lake and Goose Creek fields between Houston and Beaumont. On March 1, 1917, the company was reorganized and given a new charter as the Humble Oil and Refining Company with a capitalization of one million dollars. In the new organization Blaffer and Farish merged with Schulz Oil Company, Ardmore Oil Company, Globe Refining Company, and Parrafine Oil Company, founded by Harry Weiss. In 1918 Humble received $17 million from Standard Oil of New Jersey in exchange for a half-interest in a deal that brought Humble the capital for the construction of pipelines and refineries and brought Standard Oil a reliable source of crude oil.

At its inception the Humble Oil and Refining Company represented a combination of very successful but relatively small oil producers with an ambition to form a large, "integrated company" that would produce, transport, refine, purchase, and market oil. The new company was launched at a time when the demand for oil products was on the rise, which seemed to augur success in the future. However, just a few months after its incorporation, Humble was involved in a general strike of workers in the Gulf Coast oil industry.

In the summer of 1916, prodded by the Texas State Federation of Labor and the Houston Trades Council, a local union was formed at the Goose Creek oil field. Other locals were then organized in neighboring fields and discussions were held in Houston to coordinate an overall strategy. However, the producers, among them Humble, refused to recognize the oil workers or enter into negotiations of any kind. Therefore, on October 31, 1917, some 10,000 production workers struck the Gulf Coast Texas and Louisiana fields, seeking a minimum wage of four dollars a day. Federal mediation efforts were undertaken in Houston and Washington and the strike was settled to the detriment of the workers. There was no immediate improvement in wages and hours, but the continued demand for oil and increased

prices did indirectly benefit those working in the field.

One of the most interesting developments to flow from Spindletop was the creation, in 1901, of the Houston Oil Company. Capitalized at $30 million, the company was the largest in Texas at the time of its incorporation. The Houston Oil Company acquired more than 80,000 acres of pine and timber lands in an area just north of the Beaumont-Spindletop location from attorney John Henry Kirby. A long-term timber agreement was signed between Kirby's corporation and the oil firm whereby the Kirby Lumber Company would purchase and cut timber on lands possessed by the Houston Oil Company, thus providing the Houston Oil Company with a guaranteed income from timber sales and generating additional capital for petroleum exploration.

The financing required for this complicated venture was beyond Kirby's own resources and thus he sought the assistance of Eastern capitalists. In this connection he was put in touch with a New York City corporation lawyer, Patrick C. Calhoun, grandson of the famous Senator from South Carolina. However, potential investors were wary of oil explorations in unproved locales, and adequate financing could not be secured. Then in 1913 Joseph S. Cullinan resigned from the Texas Company because of major policy differences and turned his attention to the prospects of the Houston Oil Company.

Finally, after almost three years of persuasion, an agreement was concluded in November 1916 between the Houston Oil Company and Cullinan's Republic Production Company. The deal gave Republic Production sole rights to petroleum exploration on Houston Oil Company lands. Further, Houston Oil accepted a half-interest in any oil drilled, while conveying to Republic Production a half-interest in the 800,000 acres owned by the oil company. The arrangement was good for both companies: for Houston Oil it meant diversification and for Republic Production, capital in the form of lands in East Texas on which to seek oil.

In July 1918 Republic Production successfully drilled a well at the Hull field in Liberty County. Other discoveries were recorded at the Spurger and Silsbee fields in the East Texas counties of Hardin and Tyler. The original timberlands of John Henry Kirby continued to produce oil until after World War II, vindicating the faith of

Joseph S. Cullinan.

The coming of the oil age to Houston spawned a number of related industries. By the mid-1920s the Houston Gulf Gas Company and the Houston Gas and Fuel Company supplied the needs of homeowners and business consumers. James Abercrombie, who began as an oil field hand and then functioned as a driller-contractor at the Spindletop and Humble fields, invented a device to prevent well blowouts caused by excessive pressure. Shortly thereafter Abercrombie's old roustabout buddy, H.S. Cameron, began to mass produce the invention. In this fashion, in 1922, Cameron Iron Works, today one of the largest suppliers of heavy duty oil field equipment in the world, began operations.

The career of Howard Robard Hughes, Sr., father of the eccentric millionaire, Howard Hughes, Jr., illustrates the significance of the many oil-related industries spawned in the wake of the great boom at the turn of the century. Hughes was born at Lancaster, Missouri, on September 9, 1869. He entered Harvard in 1893, but withdrew after two years to begin the study of law at

As the public utility companies developed, so did activities that they sponsored for their employees. Baseball teams were fielded by the Houston Gas and Fuel Company and the Houston Lighting and Power Company early in the 20th century to provide recreation for employees and status for the firms. Courtesy, Harris County Heritage Society; Litterst-Dixon Collection

As the center of the Texas oil industry, Houston was home to many firms such as the Mission Manufacturing Company, which supplied the pipe, gauges, valves, and machinery necessary to pump oil from the fields of East Texas and the Gulf Coast. Courtesy, Harris County Heritage Society; Litterst-Dixon Collection

the University of Iowa. When Spindletop was brought in at the turn of the century, he was practicing with his father at Keokuk, Iowa, and had the foresight to recognize the event as the beginning of a major new industry. He immediately came to Beaumont, entered the drilling and contracting business, and for seven years moved from one field to another experiencing the peaks and valleys of oil exploration at that time.

In 1907 Hughes was active in the Pierce Junction and Goose Creek fields, but failed to complete the wells because of the inordinately hard rock formations he encountered. For some time Hughes had been aware of the industry's need for a specially designed bit that could penetrate the surface of very hard rock. Hughes, with the encouragement of his drilling partner, Walter B. Sharp, determined to design a successful rock bit. He returned to Keokuk, and within two weeks he had designed a bit with cone-shaped revolving cutters laced with rigid steel teeth. Under a heavy weight of pipe, the bit would roll on the rock at the bottom of the well, grinding and pulverizing it, rather than merely scraping the surface of the rock. In its initial test at the Goose Creek field, the bit penetrated 14 initial test feet of hard rock, which no prior equipment had been able to accomplish. This was done in the then remarkable time of 11 hours—the Hughes bit penetrated medium and hard rock surfaces with 10 times the speed of any equipment previously employed.

In 1909 Hughes and Walter Sharp organized the Sharp-Hughes Tool Company to manufacture the bit on a large scale. Sharp died in 1912 and Hughes then assumed management of the company. Later improvements of the hard rock bit and the development of bits of different design appropriate to different formations have also been patented and manufactured by the company.

By the end of 1901, more than 50 Houston industrial plants had changed over from coal to oil usage, and the first local freight train utilizing oil rather than coal was run by the Houston & Texas Central Railroad. Although few Houston attorneys had specialized in oil and gas law prior to this time, they were able to draw articles of incorporation for fledgling young firms. In rapid fashion, the Peoples Oil & Gas Company, Florence Oil Company of Houston, Southwest Texas Oil & Mineral Company, and the Twentieth Century Oil Company of Texas, among others, were chartered with high expectations. On June 6, 1901, the Houston Oil and Stock Exchange was created, one of its purposes being to protect credulous investors from sharp promoters.

With the development of the Humble field, pipelines came to Houston. The Spindletop, Goose Creek, and Humble strikes were all within a short distance of Houston. The Bayou City enjoyed certain advantages that other potential refining and wholesale centers did not—great expanses of uncommitted land, fresh water, and, once the ship channel was built, an inland waterway secure from devastating storms like those that had crippled Galveston and Texas City.

In her definitive study, *The Port of Houston: A History*, Marilyn McAdams Sibley notes that in 1914 when deep water was finally realized, Houston became the "perennial boom town of twentieth century Texas." Already a leading cotton-trading center, the combination of the beginning of the oil age and the completion of the ship channel coalesced to shape the destiny of the city.

Like so much in the history of the Bayou City, the ever-present rivalry with Galveston acted as the spur to completion of the ship channel. In 1890 the U.S. Congress appropriated $6.2 million for the construction of jetties at Galveston. By 1896 the jetties were completed, and Galveston became a true deep-water port with a channel 25 feet deep. This constituted a threat to the operation of barges on Buffalo Bayou. As long as oceangoing ships must anchor beyond the Galveston bar to discharge or take on cargo, barges could go to Houston as well as Galveston. However, if such vessels could load and unload at the Galveston wharves, the barges would quickly be put out of business. Also, once Galveston achieved deep water, Houston's primacy as a railroad center was also threatened. If a spur to Galveston were built, Houston could effectively be bypassed.

Just before he resigned from the United States House of Representatives in 1896, Joseph C. Hutcheson submitted a bill requesting a federal survey for a 25-foot channel to Houston. With little comment the bill carried in the House and was shepherded through the Senate by Roger Q. Mills of Texas. Then, as Congress was about to adjourn, Hutcheson set up a visit to Houston by members of the Rivers and Harbors Committee to inspect and appraise Buffalo Bayou. At this juncture, Thomas H. Ball, an attorney from Huntsville, was elected to the seat that Hutcheson had held and after meeting with a number of Houston's leading businessmen, including Thomas W. House, became an ardent spokesman for the proposed waterway.

The membership of the Rivers and Harbors Committee inspected Buffalo Bayou in February 1897. Fortunately for the city, heavy rains for almost two weeks before the inspection caused Buffalo Bayou to rise to its banks and then overflow, giving the appearance of a substantial waterway. In quick order the Rivers and Harbors Committee submitted a favorable recommenda-

In the days before the ship channel was dredged, boats of all sizes lined the banks of Buffalo Bayou.

In August of 1915 a storm ripped across the Gulf and into Galveston Island. Although the island was protected behind the sea wall, storm damage was still substantial, as the wreckage of the Mosquito Fleet along the Galveston wharves testifies. This storm, combined with the opening of the ship channel, played a major role in the decline of Galveston and the rise of Houston as a great port. Courtesy, Rosenberg Library

127

tion, with the agreement of a federal board of engineers. Colonel Henry Martyn Robert, chairman of the committee of engineers and better known as the author of *Robert's Rules of Order*, estimated that the initial construction cost of the waterway would be $4 million and that the annual maintenance would be approximately $100,000.

Selected as one of the minority Democratic members of the Rivers and Harbors Committee, Congressman Ball undertook the task of securing an appropriation for the proposed ship channel. The Republican administration of President William McKinley saw little political advantage to be gained by the appropriation and spokesmen for Galveston interests were also not encouraging. However, the terrible Galveston storm of September 1900 strengthened Ball's case and worked to the advantage of Houston by pointing up the desirability of an inland port protected from the sea. Thus in the same bill that allotted funds to restore Galveston to its pre-storm condition, an appropriation of one million dollars was granted to begin work on the waterway from Houston to the Gulf of Mexico. The plan was finalized on June 13, 1902, when President Theodore Roosevelt signed the bill making the appropriation.

A nephew of William Marsh Rice, Horace Baldwin Rice was one of the mayors who led the way to Houston's development in the early 20th century. Serving from 1896 to 1898 and then from 1905 to 1913, Rice played a role in developing the city parks and encouraging city planning. During his term the city acquired the waterworks. Rice also helped to develop the ship channel. He had served as mayor under the alderman system and then became the first commission mayor of Houston. Courtesy, Texas Room; Houston Public Library

Work on the channel began almost immediately but proceeded at a snail's pace. Continued funds proved hard to come by, and in March 1905 Congress modified the project by locating the turning basin of the channel at Long Reach, just above Harrisburg. The turning basin was almost five miles away from the foot of Main Street, where the Allen brothers had originally planned the head of navigation, but the Long Reach site was incorporated into the City of Houston in 1926. By 1907 the channel had been dredged to 18.5 feet, but the work languished once again as appropriations from the federal government were reduced.

The year 1910 proved critical to the ultimate completion of the project. In December of that year a delegation headed by Mayor Horace Baldwin Rice journeyed to Washington and requested an appearance before the Rivers and Harbors Committee. There they unveiled the Houston Plan by which the city consented to pay half the cost of a 25-foot channel from Bolivar Road to the Turning Basin. The proposal was accepted on the basis of a cost estimate of $2.5 million and the new terms were approved by Congress on June 25, 1910. The Bayou City's offer was unique, since before this time no substantial sharing contributions had ever been made by local interests. However, since that time no major project has been consented to by the federal government without assurances of local participation and guarantees that waterfronts would be publicly owned.

A bill was then introduced and passed in the state legislature enabling Harris County to create a navigation district encompassing the entire county and to put to a vote a bond issue of $1.25 million. Governor Thomas M. Campbell enthusiastically signed the bill and on January 10, 1910, the citizens of Harris County authorized the bond issue providing for the creation of the Harris County, Houston Ship Channel Navigation District. The bonds, which proved difficult to market, were eventually purchased by a number of Houston banks. Jesse H. Jones, by now a leading Houston

Wharves at the foot of Main Street comprised the Port of Houston before dredging moved most cargo downstream to the Turning Basin.

businessman, was influential in convincing the bankers to purchase the bonds and thus guarantee completion of the project. In 1913 the citizens of Harris County sanctioned another $3 million in bonds for port improvements and the City Council created a harbor board to administer the affairs of the port. In 1922 the city group was merged with a district board to establish a Port Commission with authority to acquire wharves and other properties for the improvement of the ship channel.

The 1910 and 1913 bond issues assured completion of the 51-mile ship channel. Twenty-four dredges were at work in the Turning Basin section by January 1913, and a year later the channel was dredged to a depth of 25 feet, with a bottom width of 100 feet. Houston now truly could boast of a link to the sea. In September 1914 the *William C. May*, a four-masted sailing ship, touched at the Clinton docks with a cargo of iron pipe. The next month the *Dorothy*, drawing almost 20 feet of water, delivered 3,000 tons of anthracite coal, also at Clinton.

The Houston Ship Channel was completed according to its prescribed width and depth on September 7, 1914. Although in use almost continuously from that time on, the formal dedication of the channel was on Tuesday morning, November 10. In addition to Mayor Benjamin Campbell and other city and county officials, Governor Oscar B. Colquitt, Governor-elect James E. Ferguson, and Lieutenant Governor-elect William P. Hobby were also present. Then President Woodrow Wilson, employing remote control, fired the cannon that heralded the opening of the new port. A few seconds later Sue Campbell, daughter of the mayor, threw a wreath of white rose petals into the waters of the Turning Basin, and the Port of Houston was christened. To complete the ceremonies, a band played the "Star-Spangled Banner" from a barge floating in

The mayor's daughter, Sue Campbell, participated in the dedication of the Houston Ship Channel on November 10, 1914.

the center of the Turning Basin, and a 21-gun salute was fired by the United States revenue cutter *Windom*. In the evening the celebration was continued downtown with a "Ships of All Nations" parade; an exact replica of the battleship *Texas*, escorted by a company of sailors and marines, was the demonstration's highlight. The completion of the ship channel assured Houston's continued and increasing economic growth. Before the end of 1915, a number of ships were sailing regularly between Houston and North Atlantic ports and in the first year of the port's operation, almost 87,000 tons of freight passed through the city's docks.

There was certainly much cause for celebration in 1914. Two other major projects were finished in that year: the Gulf Intracoastal Waterway and the Panama Canal. The Gulf Intracoastal Waterway had been envisioned by Texans even earlier than the ship channel and was first approved by the federal government in 1873. It linked the Houston Ship Channel with a canal that ran some 200 miles below Galveston, thus further boosting Houston as a port city. The Panama Canal gave Gulf ports access to the Pacific and entree to the markets of the Far East.

However, at the start of World War I in Europe, Houston experienced a decline in trade, as did the rest of the nation. In late September 1914 the Houston *Post* noted that the crisis had caused more than a $58-million decrease in United States exports. At the outset of the fighting, Great Britain had placed cotton on the contraband list with negative results for Houston's economy. Since 1914 was the year that the city obtained deep-water status and the ship channel was completed, the new figures were all the more disappointing. Actually, the amount of overall trade through the Port of Houston declined by almost one-half, while cotton fell off by one-third. However, in response to political pressure exerted by Texan and other Southern Congressmen, and their own need for cotton, the British soon took the commodity off the contraband list. When the United States declared war against Germany on April 6, 1917, cotton was selling at $21.25 a bale, close to an all-time high. Prices of other staple products also rose dramatically.

While some discontent was expressed with the amount of business transacted by the Port of Houston early in the war, its future growth and development were

In the years before Prohibition, Houstonians found opportunities to enjoy the products of local breweries such as the Magnolia Brewery. These party-goers were photographed about 1900. Courtesy, Texas Room; Houston Public Library

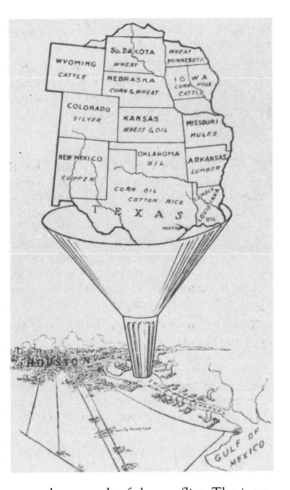

assured as a result of the conflict. The internal-combustion engine proved essential to the functions of a modern army and thus a greater demand for petroleum was created. The ship channel was a perfect location for oil refineries since it was inland and pro-

tected from storms. Abundant land and deep water made the area desirable, and refineries were assured of ample crude oil supplies from nearby fields. Because of these advantages, Humble Oil and Refining Company, Sinclair Oil Company, Empire Oil and Gas Company, and the Petroleum Refining Company either had plants in operation or purchased land along the channel route to construct refineries before the conclusion of the war in Europe.

The building of refineries and other industries along the channel led to a fundamental change in the character of business activity in Houston. From its inception in 1836, the city acted as a funnel, dealing with commodities ultimately bound for other locations. The improvement of roads and the construction of railroads that had marked the middle and late 19th century only acted to rivet this function as an intermediate trade center more closely on Houston. However, by 1918 some 22 industries had purchased sites for development below the Turning Basin and 16 above. Astute observers of Houston's economy now realized that the city would develop as an industrial as well as a distribution center. In an economic sense, the completion of the ship channel and the increased demand for petroleum fashioned the course of 20th-century Houston.

As Houston boomed in the 1920s, it became the focal point for produce throughout the middle United States. Groups such as the Young Men's Business League of Houston boosted this image with flyers and brochures encouraging everyone to share their vision of Houston. Courtesy, Special Collections; Houston Public Library

As Houston's port grew, so did the industries along the ship channel. Seventeen different railroads brought produce and raw materials to Houston and the leaders saw the community becoming a major industrial center on the Gulf. Courtesy, Special Collections; Houston Public Library

As the United States began to prepare for World War I, it was still defended by a small professional army and national guard units of the type seen here marching down Main Street in 1915. Within two years, these men would be fighting on the Western front. Courtesy, Harris County Heritage Society; Litterst-Dixon Collection

CHAPTER VI

BETWEEN THE WARS: THE BOOM CONTINUES

The assassination of the Austrian Arch-Duke Franz Ferdinand at Sarajevo on June 28, 1914, plunged the major nations of Europe into war. In less than three years the United States, the state of Texas, and the city of Houston would be deeply involved in the "war to make the world safe for democracy." Although many Houstonians adopted President Wilson's advice and remained "neutral in thought as well as deed," others were very conscious of developments in Europe. Four Texans—Albert Sidney Burleson, David F. Houston, E.M. Gregory, and Thomas M. Love—served in the President's wartime cabinet. Houstonian Edward M. House acted as Wilson's principal private advisor and would later be his chief negotiator at the Versailles Peace Conference. In the period prior to America's entry into the war, preparedness was a popular issue with most Houstonians, and eventually Camp Logan in Houston would become one of the largest military posts and training centers in the state.

The Congressional declaration of war on April 6, 1917, was popular in Houston and throughout the Southwest. The movement of troops through the city became a common occurrence and local recruiting activities were also stepped up. The old Federal Building on Fannin Street was repaired and improved for use as army, navy, and marine corps recruiting offices. The city took pride in the results of this service; by June 1917 more than 12,000 men were enrolled in local selective service registration. Also, the citizens of Houston had not been found wanting in financial contributions; Liberty Loan subscriptions added up to more than $2.5 million.

The Port of Houston was clogged with war materials being shipped to England and France. Conscious of their importance to the economy, workers were determined to share in the profits generated by the struggle in Europe. On October 31, 1917, Texas Gulf Coast oil workers, along with their coworkers in Louisiana, went out on strike demanding a wage of four dollars a day. The U.S. government quickly stationed 2,000 troops in the fields and at refineries

and pumping stations to prevent sabotage. Just beyond Houston work was delayed on the construction of an airport at Ellington Field when laborers insisted on a more favorable federal government contract, and two companies of soldiers were required to restore order. There was no labor agitation on the docks during the war, but in 1920 a brief walkout against certain employers took place. In 1900 the Houston Labor Council claimed that there were 3,000 workers in the city who belonged to 41 different unions; the opportunities presented by the increased need for workers in 1917-1918 surely added to the number.

War-induced prosperity reigned in the city, and on the surface all seemed well. However, this was just the proverbial "calm before the storm."

Construction work had already begun on Camp Logan, a National Guard Training Camp situated about 3.5 miles from the center of town. The Third Battalion, 24th United States Infantry, consisting of 654 black soldiers and eight white officers, arrived in mid-July 1917 to take up guard duty at the camp. Mayor Dan M. Moody and members of the Houston Chamber of Commerce were apprehensive about these soldiers coming to Houston. They acquiesced after learning that only black troops could be spared for guard duty and that they would stay in Houston no more than seven weeks. Mayor Moody later recalled telling a friend, "the feeling that something was going to happen was in the air."

A Night of Violence: the Houston Riot of 1917, by Robert V. Haynes, is the definitive account of what followed. On Saturday evening, July 28, most of the black troops went into town for a night's diversion. A few incidents took place over the city ordinance requiring segregated seating on streetcars, but they were all peacefully resolved. However, on the following evening two platoons of the 24th, anxious to make bed check, piled on to a streetcar, only to be curtly ordered off by the conductor for violation of the segregation rule. A fight almost ensued, but cooler heads prevailed.

THE HOUSTON POST.

VOL. 33, NO. 142.   HOUSTON, TEXAS, FRIDAY, AUGUST 24, 1917.   PRICE FIVE CENTS.

NEGRO SOLDIERS LEFT TRAIL OF DEAD IN MARCH ON POLICE

Fourteen Killed and 18 Wounded in Riot Near Army Camp---Bayonets Used On Bodies of Some of Victims---Troops Mutinied, Firing on Their Own Officers---Trouble Due to Clash With Police. County Is Now Under Martial Law.

Fourteen are known dead—with possibly other bodies yet to be found—and 18 wounded as the result of a mutiny of a portion of the negro troops of the twenty-fourth infantry, regular army, sent to Houston to act as guards.

All citizens will remain in their homes or usual places of business at once.

THE DEAD.
At C. J. Wright's Morgue.
IRA D. RAINEY, mounted police officer, bayonet wound

Following these events local police authorities met with some of the white officers and agreed on some steps: soldiers who persisted in challenging segregation would be disciplined by the military, and sidearms would be withheld from black military police. The latter step was a virtually unprecedented action, and it exacerbated the sense of alarm felt by many of the black soldiers.

Friction between Houston police officers and the soldiers precipitated the riot of August 23, 1917. It had been inordinately hot for the previous week, and on that day the temperature hit 102 degrees, increasing irritability on the part of everyone concerned. Following the arrest and beating of two black soldiers in downtown Houston, ostensibly for interfering in the detention of one of their comrades, all passes and leaves from Camp Logan were cancelled. A rumor then spread among the black soldiers that they were being confined to their quarters because a white mob was forming to march on the camp. A number of them then broke into four company supply tents and seized arms and ammunition. Ordered to return the guns and repair to their quarters, some 100 to 125 men instead moved out of the camp. It was about nine o'clock at night when they started to march into the city. Firing at random as they proceeded on Washington Avenue, the soldiers gunned down four civilians, two of them children.

In the resulting battles with Houston police, five members of the force were killed and three black soldiers were seriously wounded. Two white soldiers were also killed while attempting to restore order. The acknowledged leader of the black troops, Vida Henry, acting first sergeant of Company I, urged the soldiers to attack the downtown police station. This they refused to do, and many returned to camp. Others sought safety in the homes of black Houstonians, where they were rounded up the next day. According to subsequent investigation, Henry refused to return to camp and took his own life; his body was discovered lying across the railroad tracks in Houston's Fourth Ward.

The cause of the Houston riot were many

On Friday, August 24, 1917, Houstonians were horrified to learn of the riot by troops at Camp Logan. Courtesy, Special Collections; Houston Public Library

and varied. City officials, anxious to secure federal contracts and not wishing to antagonize the War Department, had given little thought to protecting black troops in an alien, rigidly segregated setting. Undeniably, police brutality in enforcing segregation laws angered black soldiers. The trial records indicate that black soldiers frequently urged civilians to be more forceful in demanding their rights. It is also true that soldiers who were expected to give their lives in France to "make the world safe for democracy" would reasonably expect better treatment at home.

In the court-martial after the riot, 41 soldiers were sentenced to life imprisonment and 13 to death by hanging. The mass executions were carried out at Camp Travis, near San Antonio, in the early morning of December 11, 1917. The military authorities then conducted two more courts-martial in which 16 men were sentenced to death and 12 to life imprisonment. At this point President Wilson intervened and commuted the sentences of 10 men from death to imprisonment for life. With that action, a tragic chapter in Houston's history came to a close. As for Camp Logan, where the black troops had been stationed, it was used for hospitalization of wounded men in 1918. At the end of the war, the site was acquired by William C. Hogg and his

brother, Mike, who turned over more than 1,000 acres at cost to the City of Houston. Memorial Park, Houston's largest recreational area, is presently located on that site.

By the early spring of 1918, American troops were in action on the major battlefields of the Western Front. A number of Houstonians of the 12th Aerial Squadron, which had trained at Ellington, landed in England, and nine former members of the Houston Health Department were serving with the medical corps in France. The 33rd Division, which was made up of National Guardsmen from Illinois, was trained at Camp Logan before going to France, and in May 1918 Donald Gregg became the first Houstonian to die in action there. Before the war ended a tragic number of others were killed or seriously wounded in the carnage of Bellau Wood and Château Thierry. Thus, the news of the armistice was received with great joy and celebration in Houston. One day later, November 12, 1918, a writer on the staff of the Houston *Post* graphically described the local reaction:

At 4:15 the *Post* was on the street and then the city rubbed its eyes and awoke. First the cry of the newsboys, then the honking of automobile horns, then far out in the city came the rattle of the city's private arsenals of light pocket artillery. The locomotives then got into action and gradually all the factory whistles and sirens for miles around. No one able to get up remained in bed. Lights gleamed in every dwelling and people poured down into the business district. Until late in the day the revelry continued. Monday night it was renewed with greater vigor . . . at 6 o'clock the downtown streets were filled, at 7 they were crowded, at 8 they were jammed, at 9 they were choked and from then on it was one wriggling, squirming, squeezing mass of humanity, awakened rudely from sleep but joyously from a horrible nightmare which had lasted four years.

The racial tension that had plagued Houston during World War I did not completely dissipate at the war's end. The Ku

Although the San Jacinto Monument was yet to be built, the battlefield site was a popular spot for Houstonians. The waterfront area had been developed and many residents attended patriotic events at the site of San Jacinto. Many more visited the site for a picnic away from the city. Courtesy, Texas Room; Houston Public Library

Houstonians sought a variety of ways to escape the heat and humidity of Houston's summers. Sylvan Beach, with its pavilions, piers, parking lots, and other facilities was popular for many during the years after the turn of the century. Courtesy, Texas Room; Houston Public Library

Klux Klan, which had been active in the Reconstruction era but had since gone into eclipse, experienced a resurgence in Houston after the war. A local chapter was established again in 1920, and it directed its hatred against the city's foreign-born as well as against blacks. Oscar F. Holcombe, then a building contractor and real-estate investor, joined the group, but after a brief period he quit and sharply disavowed racial and religious bias.

In 1921 Holcombe was elected to succeed A.E. Amerman as mayor of Houston. The local Klan proposed not to campaign against Holcombe in his first bid for reelection if he would dismiss three Roman Catholics who held senior positions in his administration. When Holcombe refused, the Klan leadership tried to injure him with a false accusation of gambling, but that ploy also failed. From 1921 to 1957 the "Old Gray Fox," as Holcombe was called, served a total of 22 years as mayor.

The first full-time mayor in Houston's history was H. Baldwin Rice, who was elected in July 1905. The next year, after much citizen participation, a charter was adopted providing for a commission form of government. Referred to as "government by a board of directors," the system worked relatively well in Houston. The commis-

sioners and mayor successfully reduced the municipal debt and effected a gradual reduction in taxes. Houston's efficient form of government was praised throughout the nation as an example for the future. Rice, who served as mayor until 1913, found the new form of government particularly suited to his talents.

During Mayor Rice's tenure the subject of city planning was broached. In 1911 the Houston Chamber of Commerce called for a detailed master plan for the city's future development. A few years later the City Council funded a study of selected European communities in order to garner ideas.

By the mid-1920s, traffic had already become a problem for the city that was about to become the largest city in Texas. Houstonians were finding that oil coming through the city from the nearby fields and refineries was changing every aspect of daily life. Courtesy, Harris County Heritage Society; Litterst-Dixon Collection

Most of the resulting recommendations attempted to assure greater citizen participation in local political affairs. Accordingly, in 1913 Houstonians approved amendments providing for initiative, referendum, and recall.

In 1922 Mayor Holcombe sought to create a municipal planning commission, but other than the preparation of some studies, nothing was really accomplished until 1929. In that year William C. Hogg was chairman of the City Planning Commission, which drafted a master plan for consideration by the City Council. As the developer of the exclusive and thoroughly planned River Oaks residential district, Hogg could speak with authority. However, coming as it did at the beginning of the Depression, the report was subordinated to more pressing problems.

Other efforts to improve the city came from the private sector. The event of long-

range significance for the city was the donation by George H. Hermann, on May 30, 1914, of 278 acres of beautifully wooded land that constituted the nucleus of present-day Hermann Park. As a member of Company A of the 26th Cavalry during the Civil War, Hermann fought with distinction in Texas and Louisiana. After the war he returned to Houston, operated a sawmill, and then went into real estate. The discovery of oil at Humble in 1903 made him a millionaire and left him free to devote his life to charity. In addition to providing Hermann Park, the bulk of his almost $3-million estate was used to create a trust for the purpose of building and maintaining Hermann Hospital, which was opened on July 1, 1925, on the edge of the park.

Another successful Houstonian who left part of his vast fortune to the city was William Marsh Rice. Rice came to Texas from Massachusetts in 1839 and prospered greatly during the Civil War as a cotton merchant. During the Reconstruction era he expanded his interests into railroad, banking, and real-estate operations. In 1891 Rice, who married twice but had no children, decided to return to the Northeast. However, prior to this he established a trust of $200,000 for the creation of a university

"dedicated to the advancement of art, literature, and science"; enrollment was to be limited to the white residents of Houston.

By the time Rice left Houston, he had accumulated a fortune estimated at about $3 million. Some years later in New York City, he was murdered by his valet, Charles F. Jones, who placed a napkin drenched in chloroform over Rice's face. In the lurid trial that followed, Jones confessed and, in exchange for going free, implicated attorney Albert T. Patrick, who had conspired with the valet to forge Rice's will. Although Patrick was sentenced to death, he managed to secure a reduction of his sentence and ultimately a full pardon. Rice's will, which initially provided that tuition be absolutely free at the university, was involved in complicated litigation. But by 1912, all legal questions had been resolved, and Rice Institute began operations with an endowment of $10 million, then the seventh largest in the nation. In 1907 the Board of Trustees had unanimously chosen Princeton professor Dr. Edgar Odell Lovett as the first president of Rice, and Lovett embarked on a tour of illustrious European universities in order to incorporate their best features at Rice. The famous Boston architect Ralph Cram was engaged to design the distinctive campus, and an impressive faculty was recruited, among whom were Julian Huxley as professor of biology and Stockton Axon, brother-in-law of President Woodrow Wilson, as professor of English.

Fifty-eight students entered Rice with the first class in 1912 and 35 graduated in 1916. From the very start the school, located on virtual prairieland out South Main and opposite Hermann Park, attracted students of the highest calibre. A distinguished and productive faculty, particularly in the physical sciences, added luster to the institution over the years. Because of its academic reputation, students from throughout the nation have been attracted to Rice, and all racial barriers to admission have been eliminated. A charter member of the Southwest Conference, the Rice "Owls" have had a storied football tradition. Particularly under Coach Jess Neeley, Rice generally fared well against such gridiron powers as Texas A & M and the University of Texas. Rice has also been successful in track and field, sending a number of its athletes to Olympic competition.

Another institution of higher learning established in the first part of the 20th century was the University of Houston. In 1923 the citizens of Houston voted to relinquish control of the city's public schools and create an independent system with its own taxing authority. An elected school board

was sanctioned, and in 1924 the schools were organized as an independent system. After a comprehensive search, the man hired as superintendent of public schools was Dr. E.E. Oberholtzer. From the inception of his term, Dr. Oberholtzer envisioned a municipal university for students who wished to remain in Houston while pursuing a college education. In 1927 funding was provided for Houston Junior College, which commenced its operations with some 400 students. At first the college classrooms were located at San Jacinto High School and classes were held in the afternoon and early evening. In 1934 Oberholtzer's dream was finally realized when the school board mandated the University of Houston as a full-fledged, four-year school; fittingly, Dr. Oberholtzer was appointed its first president.

Profiting from Dr. Oberholtzer's steady leadership, the University of Houston continued to grow. In contrast to Rice University's somewhat elitist admission policies, the University of Houston sought to enroll the working student living at home. Land was donated for a campus in the southeast portion of town and a building fund campaign was launched. It was at this juncture that Hugh Roy Cullen began his life-long association with the university. One of the legendary "wildcatters" of his day, Cullen made a

At the end of the 19th century, Houston began to develop a park system. At the bottom of Sam Houston Park, acquired in 1899, the city converted a small watercourse feeding into Buffalo Bayou into a pond, complete with fountain. The community needed more recreation and park facilities and, as early as 1910, Mayor Rice was advocating expansion of these facilities. Courtesy, Harris County Heritage Society; Litterst-Dixon Collection

In the 1920s Rice University was still on the edge of downtown and neighborhoods such as West University Place were just opening up. West University had several advantages, including proximity to Rice and to the newly developed Hermann Park. It became a separate incorporated community, protected from the expanding Houston of the era with its different tax structure. Courtesy, Special Collections; Houston Public Library

fortune successfully drilling for oil in South Texas. While he was not a college graduate himself, he was passionately devoted to the cause of education. Until the time of his death he was the principal benefactor of the University of Houston and a strong supporter of its athletic teams as well. Often criticized for his conservative political views, he was at the same time a staunch defender of academic freedom.

As in the case of education, the arts in Houston were heightened by the contributions of civic-minded residents. More than any other single individual, Edna Saunders presided over artistic affairs in the city. As a booking agent, she brought many world-renowned artists to Houston, among them, in 1920, the great Enrico Caruso. The fabled Italian tenor performed before a full house and, at his urging, the outer doors of the City Auditorium were left ajar for the benefit of those who had been unable to purchase a ticket for the concert.

Until the Music Hall was built in the 1930s, the City Auditorium was the center of Houston's cultural life. During these years

the Boston and Chicago opera companies appeared somewhat regularly in the city, as did the San Carlo Opera Company, which staged an annual tour of the United States. There were also attempts at locally produced operatic performances. In the late 1920s and early 1930s, Mary Carson, a local soprano, and Mrs. John Wesley Graham, an exuberant voice teacher, staged a number of performances, among them a very well-received *Madame Butterfly*. In January 1941 the Southern School of Fine Arts, a Houston group, produced *Carmen* as a benefit for the British-American Ambulance Corporation. Although the United States was not yet in the Second World War, concern was already felt in Houston for the nation's eventual allies.

The Houston Symphony Orchestra was founded in 1913 principally by the aforementioned Mrs. Graham, D.D. Naman, and Ima Hogg. Under its early conductors, Julian Paul Blitz, Uriel Nespoli, Paul Berge, and Frank St. Leger, progress was slow, but the orchestra began to make giant strides with the appointment in 1936 of Ernst Hoffman.

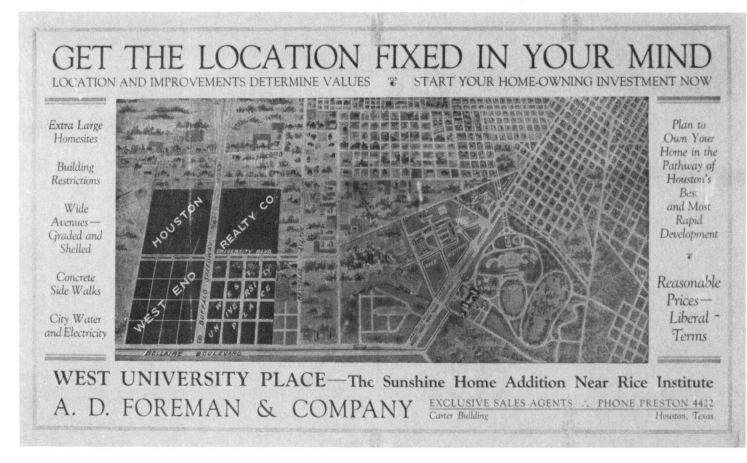

Funerals were an important part of life in Houston. Individuals whose life had been marked by achievement were often commemorated in an impressive manner as was the case in this 1920s funeral procession that combined the older traditions of the foot-escorted hearse with the modern traditions growing up around the automobile. Courtesy, Harris County Heritage Society; Litterst-Dixon Collection

Profiting from Hoffman's aggressive and inspired leadership, for the first time the Houston Symphony began to attract national interest. Another very popular innovation was the staging of free summer concerts in Hermann Park. On a beautiful summer's evening, an appreciative audience of more than 10,000 people became commonplace for these open-air concerts. Hoffman remained with the Houston Symphony until 1947 and had a decisive impact on the evolution of the organization.

In the field of visual arts, the Houston Museum of Fine Arts opened in 1924, becoming the first city museum in Texas. The trustees of the museum selected James Chillman, Jr., a professor of architecture at Rice Institute, as its original director. An energetic man, Chillman stressed the museum's availability to the public at large. He established the Junior Gallery with lectures, storytelling, and puppet shows, and the Art School where instruction was offered in both junior and adult divisions. Chillman was able to obtain some excellent

collections for the museum, including the "Annette Finnegan Collection of Ancient Art from Egypt, Greece, and Rome," and the "Edith A. and Percy S. Straus Collection of Renaissance Paintings and Bronzes." Certainly Houston artists of this era, such as Helen C. Davis, Frederic Browne, and Grace Spaulding John, must have been heartened by the museum's presence. Like his counterpart Ernst Hoffman at the symphony, Chillman was a cultural builder for the future.

In a physical sense, the "master builder" of Houston from 1910 to 1930 was Jesse Jones. Already wealthy from lumber and

real-estate investments, Jones in 1913 obtained a lease on the Rice Hotel from the William Marsh Rice estate. Then he purchased the land, demolished the old five-story building, and began the construction of an 18-story, 500-room modern hotel, which would be the largest hotel in the South. Jones himself drew the plans for the hotel and took pride in the fact that the edifice was located on the site of the first capitol of the Republic of Texas. At the front entrance of the hotel, Jones placed a tablet that read, "Site of the Capitol of the Republic of Texas, 1837-1838. Commemorating days when, after her glorious struggle, Texas stood an independent nation." For more than 40 years, the expanded "Rice" was the center of Houston's social and civic life.

In subsequent years Jones erected and managed the Kirby, Commerce, Milam, Electric, and many other buildings along Main Street and in downtown Houston. Although these buildings were often named for the structure's principal tenant, Jones refused to name a building after himself. He maintained his own private offices in the Bankers Mortgage Building, another one of his creations. In 1926 Jones widened his sphere of involvement when he purchased a

The Rice Hotel quickly became the center of many different kinds of social and recreational activities after it opened. During the World War I era, ladies would gather in the Crystal Ballroom of the Rice for a day of bridge. Courtesy, Harris County Heritage Society; Litterst-Dixon Collection

controlling interest in the Houston *Chronicle* and became its owner and president. By the mid-1920s Jones had personally supervised the construction of some 30 commercial sites and retained ownership of all of them. He topped off this burst of activity in 1927 with the completion of the 37-story Gulf Building, the tallest in Houston to that date.

A man of conservative instincts, Jones confined his political activity to Texas state politics during the national heyday of William Jennings Bryan. However, with Woodrow Wilson's nomination for the Presidency in 1912, Jones became an enthusiastic worker for the national Democratic party, and in 1924 he became the finance director of the Democratic National Committee.

On January 12, 1928, the Democratic National Committee convened in Washington, D.C., to select a site for the party's national convention. As finance director, Jones was named to a subcommittee to consider the money proposals and available convention facilities of the competing cities. Jones was particularly interested in the financial proposals, because he hoped to use the winning city's bid to satisfy the party's remaining debt from the 1924 campaign. Therefore, a few weeks prior to the Washington meeting, Jones had solicited offers from interested sites. Cleveland ($100,000), Detroit ($125,000), and Chicago ($130,000) had responded to his invitation and were in the running for the convention location. Jones later said that he felt the convention would not consider a Texas city because of the climate, and thus he had not invited a

During the 1920s and 1930s, Houston developed its own set of palaces for motion pictures and vaudeville, theaters designed in the classical manner with wonderful interiors, elaborate lobbies, and marble-fronted cashiers' booths. Courtesy, Texas Room; Houston Public Library

proposal from Houston.

Nevertheless, as he and the other two members of the subcommittee listened to the various proposals, Jones determined to enter a bid for Houston on his own. Reasoning that even if he failed, the city would at least receive some favorable publicity, Jones drafted a letter outlining his proposal and attached his personal check for $200,000, the highest bid to that point. No prior discussions had been held with Houston city officials; the action was entirely his own.

At this juncture in the subcommittee's deliberations, a $250,000 proposal was submitted on behalf of San Francisco, a city whose convention facilities were by far superior to Houston's. Jones admitted that Houston's convention hall would seat only 5,000, "but if you give us the convention we will build one to seat 25,000." That promise must have swayed a number of committee members, because on the first ballot Houston won 30 votes while San Francisco received only 25 (the remaining were scattered). In the final vote Houston was selected, with 54 votes to 48 for San Francisco.

The convention hall that Jones promised, the Sam Houston Coliseum at 810 Bagby Street, complete with 25,000 seats and all

modern facilities, was finished in mid-June, and two weeks later the delegates began to arrive. Yet however interesting the city of Houston proved, the delegates witnessed a relatively drab convention. Even for Houston the weather was hot and the proceedings needlessly dragged out for six days. Jones was nominated for the Vice-Presidency as a favorite son from Texas, but the Smith forces had marshalled their votes well in advance of the convention. Franklin D. Roosevelt nominated Smith, who won with relative ease.

For Houston the convention was a great success. Delegates from all over the nation came to the Bayou City and saw firsthand the remarkable progress that had been made since the commencement of the "Oil Age." Also, since Smith intended to make his anti-Prohibition stand an important part of the campaign, the fact that he was nominated in the midst of the Southern "Bible Belt" was widely commented on. The importance of the South to the party was further dramatized with the selection of Senator Joseph Robinson of Arkansas as the New Yorker's running mate.

The federal census of 1930 revealed that Houston had eclipsed both Dallas and San Antonio to become the most populous city in Texas. While its population of 292,352 left it considerably shy of New Orleans as the South's largest city, the growth of Houston since 1910 had been unparalleled. Fueled by oil and to a lesser degree cotton and lumber, the future seemed bright indeed. Then with little prior warning, the hard times struck. In May 1929 Buffalo Bayou flooded its banks causing damage estimated in the millions of dollars. Five months later, at brokerage houses throughout the city, the ticker tape told the story of "Black Friday," October 28, 1929.

The effects of the Great Depression soon struck the economy of Houston. Building permits dropped drastically, and in May 1931 unions affiliated with the Houston Building Trades Council went on strike.

In 1932 Houstonians voted overwhelmingly for Franklin D. Roosevelt and favorite son John Nance Garner, and soon began to benefit from New Deal legislation. They were grateful for the relief legislation sponsored by Franklin D. Roosevelt during the Depression, but were aware of the fact that the City of Houston discriminated against blacks and Mexicans in dispensing relief funds. Funds from the Reconstruction Finance Corporation, headed by Jesse Jones, the National Recovery Administration, and the Works Progress Administration were used for county road repair, slum clearance, and public building construction. The ship channel was improved with federal funds, and in September 1934 the Public Works Administration granted a loan of $1,219,-000 for the construction of a new City Hall. The PWA also funded the building of a new city-county hospital, the Jeff Davis Hospital. In 1935-1936 the Works Progress Administration employed almost 12,000 Harris Countians and spent more than $2 million financing some 70 projects in

The growth of the rail networks and the port saw Houston develop in many different areas during the 1920s. Sig Frucht was one of the leaders in the creation of a produce trade that linked the farms and orchards of the Rio Grande Valley to Houston and, through Houston, to the United States. Courtesy, Texas Room; Houston Public Library

Harris County.

Urban historians have argued that Houston was less affected by the Great Depression than many other major cities in the United States. This seems to have been true principally because of the continued worldwide demand for oil and related petroleum products. Houston was certainly unique in that there were no bank failures and thus no panicky rushes for deposits. Two major banks verged on collapse, but they were saved through the intervention of Jesse Jones and other business leaders who pooled their resources to offset the possibility of failure. Although Houston lost

out to Dallas as the host city of the 1936 Texas Centennial, that year the federal government granted one million dollars for the construction of the San Jacinto Monument. Designed by Houston architect Alfred C. Finn on the battlefield where Texas won its independence, the monument remains a testimony to liberty and freedom.

The Great Depression did result in a change in city government. Mayor Oscar Holcombe called for revisions in the city charter to grant more authority to the executive and less to the City Council. Holcombe argued that the precarious economic conditions of the period called for a forceful mayor, with powers akin to those enjoyed on the national level by President Roosevelt. The Council resisted this attack upon its privileges and insisted that the question be submitted to arbitration. In 1935 five attorneys constituting a board of arbitration ruled that councilmen could head specific departments only if appointed by the mayor. The controversy waxed and waned until 1942, when Houston adopted the city-manager form of government with eight Council members and a part-time mayor.

Oscar Holcombe took the mayor's oath for the seventh time on January 2, 1939.

Built in 1893, the Kiam Building was the first example of Richardsonian Romanesque design in Houston. It was also the first building to use electric elevators and one of the first to include plate glass windows for display. By 1918 the Sakowitz Brothers had moved their department store into the structure. In 1929 the firm moved into a much larger building. The structure is still a landmark on Main Street. Courtesy, Harris County Heritage Society; Litterst-Dixon Collection

By the late 1920s, even small independent Houston grocers had changed their marketing practices. With the coming of national brands and standardized packaging and advertising, every store began to appear more and more like every other. The grocers used every device offered by the distributors to make their stores look modern. Courtesy, Harris County Heritage Society; Litterst-Dixon Collection

Houston and Galveston were the center of the oceangoing export trade in cotton during the 1920s and 1930s. Thanks to good land and excellent ports, the region came to dominate the cotton markets of the world. Courtesy, Rosenberg Library

Cotton, sold through brokers in the Houston Cotton Exchange, was an important part of the economic life of the city in the 1920s. With the ship channel allowing vessels to come up to the port, more cotton than ever came through the city. The first cotton from each season was always marked with a special ceremony, denoting the continuing importance of cotton to the Houston economy. Courtesy, Harris County Heritage Society; Litterst-Dixon Collection

FIRST BALE
OF NEW COTTON CROP
1927-1928
RAISED BY
Mr. M. Chapa Montalvo
San Manuel, Hidalgo County, Texas
Ginned By
Cotton Belt Gin Co. Edinburg, Tex.
SHIPPED BY
Mr. J. J. Cavazos Mission, Tex.
CONSIGNED TO
WM. D. CLEVELAND & SONS
HOUSTON, TEX.

Far Left:
Cotton shipped into Houston was stored in large warehouses to await sale and shipment to the factories that would turn it into fabric. At various times of the year, these warehouses would be bulging with cotton bales. Courtesy, Harris County Heritage Society; Litterst-Dixon Collection

Left:
Before cotton could be marketed through the Cotton Exchange, it needed to be graded. Samples were taken and graded for quality and length of fiber by experts employed by the Cotton Exchange and by various merchants and factors. Courtesy, Harris County Heritage Society; Litterst-Dixon Collection

Mechanization came slowly to the farmlands around Houston, as it did throughout the country. Although railroads had penetrated the countryside and trucks were available to take cotton to the markets, most farmers still relied on mules and wagons to carry their cotton to the gins or the markets. Courtesy, Harris County Heritage Society; Litterst-Dixon Collection

Mayor Oscar Holcombe often met with local civic leaders and visitors in his efforts to shape the destiny of the city. Here he is seen meeting with a leader of a local civic club as a part of his program. Courtesy, Harris County Heritage Society; Litterst-Dixon Collection

Service stations were the last stage in the marketing operations of the major oil companies such as the Texas Company. Founded by Joseph Cullinan in 1901, the firm grew rapidly in the years after World War I. Motorists such as the driver of this Hupmobile found the company's service stations a necessity for survival. Courtesy, Harris County Heritage Society; Litterst-Dixon Collection

Later that year bank deposits reached an all-time high in Houston and the city appeared fully recovered from the Depression. In February 1939 Harris County taxpayers approved a $500,000 bond issue for a flood-control and drainage program, which upon completion was estimated to cost $23 million. Yet in the midst of these indications of progress, Houstonians cast an anxious eye toward European developments. When on September 1, 1939, Hitler's legions invaded Poland, most felt it was only a matter of time until the United States became involved. As the tempo of national defense increased, improvements were made at Ellington Field and Camp Wallace, both situated just outside the city limits. A number of industrial plants, including Humble Oil and Refining, Sheffield Steel, and Cameron Iron Works, were awarded contracts to furnish war materials, and in September 1940, marking the first peacetime draft in American history, 77,177 young men registered in Harris County.

The year 1941 dawned with its completion of Mayor Oscar Holcombe's seventh term; he was succeeded by C.A. (Neal) Pickett. Reflecting the increasingly ominous military situation, it was announced in Washington on April 1, 1941, that an ordnance depot would be built on a 4,700-acre tract opposite the San Jacinto battlefield.

Slips and docks along a lengthy frontage of the ship channel would be constructed so the depot could serve as a storage and distribution point for all Gulf Coast military bases. Also in 1941 the federal government awarded the Hughes Tool Company a contract to manufacture bomber parts for the army and navy, and Ellington Field's first contingent of airmen arrived for training that spring.

The summer passed uneventfully, and in November Houstonians learned that two Japanese envoys had arrived in San Francisco on a diplomatic mission to Washington. Commenting to reporters that they hoped to, "score a touchdown for peace," Saburo Kurusu and Kichisaburo Nomura flew to the nation's capital for protracted talks with Secretary of State Cordell Hull. The diplomats and Hull were still engaged in discussion when on December 7, 1941, Japan launched a devastating sneak attack on the United States naval base at Pearl Harbor. Responding to President Roosevelt's "day of infamy" address the next day, Congress declared war against Japan with but one dissenting vote. In addition to all of its other consequences, World War II would have a profound effect upon the history of the city of Houston.

MAGNOLIA PARK
SUBDIVISION OF
HOUSTON, TEXAS

PARTIAL VIEW HOUSTON HARBOR (U. S. S. "WINDOM" AT ANCHOR)

SCENE
MAGNOLIA PARK

MAIN STREET
HOUSTON

PRESENTED BY
MAGNOLIA PARK LAND CO.
916 TEXAS AVE.   OLD PHONE 2800
HOUSTON, TEXAS

As Houston began to grow after 1900, many areas were developed as residential subdivisions serving different markets around the city. Magnolia Park was located near the ship channel and attracted workers in the plants and on the docks of the port. It became popular with the Mexican community, but still served a large Anglo population as well. Courtesy, Houston Metropolitan Research Center; Houston Public Library

153

Once the rail network into Houston was completed, cotton was shipped to the city for delivery to oceangoing ships that were anchored off Galveston. The barges of cotton that departed from the Houston waterfront were great attractions for visitors and symbolized the city's role in the shipment of agricultural products in the late 19th and early 20th centuries. Courtesy, Barker Texas History Center; University of Texas

As the Mexican-Americans began to flock to Houston, they often found work in the port area as longshoremen, unloading the banana boats and other vessels that brought the produce of the world to Houston for distribution to Texas and the middle United States. Courtesy, Houston Metropolitan Research Center; Houston Public Library

Facing page:
At the heart of the intellectual life of the Mexican-American community were periodicals such as the Mexican-American literary magazine, Gaceta Mexicana, which was the outlet for a number of local writers in the 1920s and was developed by local entrepreneurs for the community. Courtesy, Houston Metropolitan Research Center; Houston Public Library

Gaceta Mexicana

REVISTA QUINCENAL

ORGANO-DE-LA-LIBRERIA-HISPANO-AMERICANA

| Vol. 1 Núm 7 | JOSE SARABIA, Administrador | Mayo 15 de 1928 |

Una Esperanza para el Arte.

Félix de la Isla

Jóven mexicano, que en la festividad patriótica del día
5 de Mayo en esta ciudad, obtuvo gran éxito cantan-
do en traje de caräcter la hermosa composición argen-
tina "Queja Pampera."

Facing page:
Captured in a portrait made of terra-cotta tiles and on display at San Jacinto Monument, Jesse Jones was the central figure in the development of Houston in the first half of the 20th century. He controlled most of the downtown properties and, with his architect Alfred Finn, built many of the office buildings of the era. He also played a major role in San Jacinto's development as an historic site. Courtesy, San Jacinto Monument

Daughter of the first native-born governor of Texas, Miss Ima Hogg devoted her life to the development of charitable and cultural institutions in Houston. In addition to assembling a distinguished collection of Early American decorative arts in her family's estate, Bayou Bend, Miss Hogg played an important role in the development of the symphony and also in the development of mental health activities. Courtesy, Bayou Bend Collection, Gift of Miss Ima Hogg; Houston Museum of Fine Arts

Designed by Houston's prominent residential architect, John Staub, in 1927, Bayou Bend was the center of development in the River Oaks area. It is now open to the public and symbolizes the charitable activities of many Houstonians. Courtesy, Bayou Bend Collection, Gift of Miss Ima Hogg; Houston Museum of Fine Arts

Facing page:
In Houston's Mexican-American community, Cinco de Mayo has been an event that has united the people. A celebration of Mexican revolutionary tradition and nationalism, the day has been marked with public programs such as a 1944 celebration at Jefferson Davis High School, a musical event in honor of the Mexican Revolution. Courtesy Houston Metropolitan Research Center; Houston Public Library

Completed in 1939, Houston's modern city hall is a statement of the WPA-style of architecture that was popular throughout the country. Thera Case's painting captures the park-like surroundings of the building, which was on property given to the city by George Hermann. Photo by Story J. Sloane III, Harris County Heritage Society

The visit of the heavy cruiser Houston *to the city in 1930 marked the official celebration of 10 years of amazing growth stimulated by the ship channel. The cruiser was a symbol of the city, for she had been named after an intense campaign on the part of the citizens, including a mass mailing by schoolchildren. When she was sunk in 1942, the* Houston *became the symbol of World War II for the city. Courtesy, Barker Texas History Center; University of Texas*

5 DE MAYO DE 1944.

LA FEDERACION DE SOCIEDADES MEXICANAS
Y
LATINO-AMERICANAS

PRESENTA

Una

Velada Literario Musical

In the first half of the
20th century, the Houston
Negro Chamber of Commerce
was an important part of the
black establishment in the city. It
provided a network for the black
business community to establish
ties and networks. Courtesy,
Texas Room; Houston Public
Library

CHAPTER VII

THE STRUGGLE FOR CIVIL RIGHTS

T housands of Texas blacks, many of them from Houston, enlisted in the armed services after Pearl Harbor. High black enlistment had begun during the Great Depression, when the principal motivation had been economic. Segregation prevailed in the military all during the conflict, overseas as well as at home. Although Houston was spared the type of terrible riot that it had endured in 1917, white demonstrations resulted in the removal of the black 54th Coast Artillery from Camp Wallace on the outskirts of Galveston. In Houston itself, in order to minimize the possibilities of friction, an interracial committee of civilians and military officers was founded in 1943 to monitor the situation. Black pilots training at nearby Ellington Field found most recreational facilities in the city closed to them and were dependent upon the black community for amusement. A Reserve Officer Training Corps was located at nearby Prairie View, one of the few situated on a black college campus in the United States. The irony of risking one's life in the struggle against tyranny abroad while failing to enjoy the blessings of democracy at home was not lost upon Texas blacks. One of them, a poet, summed up his feelings in this fashion:

On a train in Texas German prisoners eat
With white American soldiers, seat by seat
While black American soldiers sit apart
The white men eating meat, the black men heart

The campaign for equal treatment for blacks and Mexican-Americans in Houston was intensified by the nation's entry into World War II. Blacks adopted the slogan, "Win a Double Victory," which referred to both the war for the enjoyment of civil rights at home and the war being fought abroad. In fact, the struggle for civil rights began before the war and, in the case of blacks, was closely tied to the rise of the National Association for the Advancement of Colored People (NAACP) in Texas. Suits were planned and initiated combatting racial discrimination in the areas of voting rights, employment, jury service, and education.

At the first Texas state conference of the NAACP, held in Dallas on June 18 and 19, 1937, delegates from Houston, among them Sidney Hasgett and Clifton F. Richardson, joined those from Dallas, Waco, San Antonio, and Marshall, and Richard D. Evans, a Waco attorney, was elected president. The next year the state convention met in Houston, but soon the local chapter was wracked with turmoil. An audit ordered by the national office revealed grave financial irregularities and also the fact that the chapter had become a virtual spokesman for the programs of the Houston Negro Chamber of Commerce. Walter White, national president of the NAACP, considered revoking the charter of the Houston branch, but when the Reverend Albert A. Lucas consented to serve as the new local president, a semblance of order was restored.

Part of the difficulty that beset the Houston office was based on a personality conflict. Clifton F. Richardson, a longtime worker for civil rights and one of the first local leaders of the NAACP, ran Houston's principal black newspaper, The Informer, first published on May 24, 1919. Two attor-

Mack H. Hannah, Jr., had backed Lulu B. White for the presidency of the Houston NAACP chapter. Hannah, who had operated a rubber plant in Beaumont during World War II, used his profits to start an insurance and building and loan business. He was the wealthiest black businessman in Texas in the 1960s. Courtesy, University of Texas, Institute of Texan Cultures, San Antonio

neys, Carter W. Wesley and James M. Nabrit, Jr., wrested control of the paper from Richardson in 1930 and then actively criticized his past leadership. Angry at what had transpired and lamenting the sale of his newspaper, Richardson then started a rival publication, *The Defender.* In 1939 Richardson lost the presidency of the Houston NAACP chapter to Lulu B. White, who enjoyed the backing of such prominent and wealthy Houston blacks as Mack H. Hannah, Jr., Hobart S. Taylor, Sr., and Carter W. Wesley. Within a year Richardson passed away. He had been the true founding spirit of the Houston NAACP, and at the time of his death, the local chapter could boast of almost 1,500 members.

For almost 20 years from the time of its founding in Texas the major ambition of the NAACP was to gain the right to vote in Democratic primary elections. Since the Republican party was almost nonexistent in Texas at the time, the Democratic primary contest was the only significant race. In March 1940 black leaders from all over the state met at Olivet Baptist Church in Houston and determined to raise funds to pursue a primary case through the courts.

The task that confronted Thurgood Marshall, then the leading attorney for the NAACP in civil-rights cases, was to override the Supreme Court's ruling in *Grovey* v. *Townsend* (1935). In that case the Houston

In the years before World War I, Houston's black community developed its own leaders. Affiliated with the church and working in small business, men such as those in this singing group played an important role in shaping life among the blacks in Houston. Courtesy, Texas Room; Houston Public Library

black law firm of Atkins, Nabrit, and Wesley had filed suit on behalf of R.R. Grovey, a Houston barber and political activist, against Harris County Clerk Albert Townsend for the denial of an absentee ballot in the 1934 Democratic primary. Both the state courts and the United States Supreme Court had found against Grovey. The judges found the Democratic party to be a "private organization," which could set its own rules for membership and participation in the primary: no rights of federal citizenship guaranteed to blacks under the 14th or 15th amendments had been breached.

Another Texas white primary case that eventually reached the Supreme Court began in January 1941 when NAACP lawyers filed suit in behalf of Sidney Hasgett, a black Houston laborer, against Harris County election judge Theodore Werner. Hasgett sought $5,000 in damages for being refused a vote in the Democratic runoff primary held on August 24, 1940, in Houston. The case was heard in United States District Court on May 3, 1941, and, relying on the ruling in *Grovey* v. *Townsend*, Justice Thomas M. Kennerly of Houston found against Hasgett.

Race was not a factor in the *United States* v. *Classic* (1941) case, which dealt with falsification of ballots in a Louisiana election for the U.S. House of Representatives. Speaking for the majority in a five-to-three opinion, Chief Justice Harlan P. Stone held that, "the authority of Congress . . . includes the authority to regulate primary elections . . . when they are a step in the exercise by the people of their choice of representatives in Congress." After reviewing this decision, Thurgood Marshall persuaded the Houston NAACP chapter to drop their planned appeal of *Hasgett* and find a case more in line with *Classic.*

Dr. Lonnie E. Smith, a black Houston dentist, had been denied a vote in the 1940 Democratic primary for elections to the United States Congress. Smith was a willing plaintiff and suit was filed against S.E. Allwright, the precinct election judge who refused the ballot. After both the District Court, Justice Kennerly again presiding, and the Fifth Circuit Court of Appeals found against Smith, Marshall and W.J. Durham, Dallas attorney and chairman of the Legal Committee of the NAACP in Texas, took the case to the United States Supreme Court.

James Nabrit, Jr., seen at right, was a partner in the Houston law firm that had filed suit on behalf of a Houston barber and political activist who had been denied an absentee ballot in the 1934 Democratic primary. The lawsuit proved to be unsuccessful. Pictured here with Nabrit are NAACP attorneys George E.C. Hayes (left) and Thurgood Marshall (center). From the Ebony *Collection*

The precedent setting constitutional case of *Smith* v. *Allwright* was argued before the United States Supreme Court on January 12, 1944. The attorneys for Smith, Thurgood Marshall and William Hastie, argued that the Texas "white primary" violated the 14th, 15th, and 17th amendments to the United States Constitution. On April 3, 1944, the United States Supreme Court handed down its ruling in *Smith* v. *Allwright*. By a vote of eight to one (Justice Owen Roberts dissenting), the jurists stated that the Democratic primary in Texas was by law a part of the machinery for choosing state and national officials. The primary was an integral part of the electoral process in Texas and therefore the white primary was in violation of the 15th amendment. It was a historic victory for black civil rights. Lulu B. White of the Houston NAACP chapter spoke of the decision as the "second emancipation of the Negro." As for Smith, his comment in *The Informer* summed up the situation aptly: "I guess I feel about like all the other Negroes in Texas and the South. I am happy to be able to vote and see Negroes free in the real sense of the word."

The practical benefits of the decision in *Smith* v. *Allwright* were not long in coming. After the April decision there was time enough for blacks who held poll tax receipts or exemptions to vote in the July primary race. In Houston the Harris County executive committee of the Democratic party instructed all precinct judges to permit blacks to vote without interference. On election day no racial trouble of any kind was reported and of an estimated 5,000 registered black voters in the city, 2,618, or about half, voted. Some 158,000 whites were registered in Harris County, and 55,645, or about a third, cast ballots. While the above figure was encouraging for those involved in the struggle to gain black suffrage, the fact remained that only three percent of the black population in Harris County was registered to vote.

White response to the legality of black voting was tentative. In 1945 Mayor Otis Massey created an "Advisory Committee of Affairs of Colored People" principally to

Marian Anderson, seen here performing in Washington, D.C., performed in Houston four times. Her last concert in the city was given at the City Auditorium to a capacity crowd. The audience was integrated. From the Ebony *Collection*

ease the apprehensions of the white community. Other such committees were also established, but Professor Chandler Davidson, in his seminal work *Negro Politics and the Rise of the Civil Rights Movement in Houston, Texas,* states that most local black leaders saw such gestures as essentially token and lacking in substance. However, some basic progress was made at the county level. Increasingly aware of their importance in local contests, Houston blacks organized the Harris County Council of Organizations (HCCO), an informal coalition of civic clubs designed to protect black rights. Among its leading members were Mack Hannah and the Reverend L.H. Simpson. In 1946 a number of black delegates were elected to attend the Harris County Democratic convention, 18 blacks were appointed by the county tax assessor's office, and five were elected precinct chairmen. For the first time since 1923, a black candidate from Harris County, Erma LeRoy, ran in 1948 for a seat in the state legislature. Campaigning as an independent, she was defeated, but it was a start.

The long campaign to gain the ballot on an equal basis tended to overshadow the advances made by Houston blacks in the fight against segregated facilities. Although on the statute books mixed seating was illegal until the early 1950s, as early as March 1931 the celebrated tenor Roland

Hayes performed in concert before an integrated audience in Houston at the City Auditorium. Hayes returned to the city four years later, again singing to an integrated audience. An artist who enjoyed even greater success in Houston was Marian Anderson. Anderson first sang in Houston for a benefit concert for the Bethlehem Settlement House for underprivileged black children. She appeared in the city again in 1939, 1940, and just prior to Pearl Harbor in November 1941. On the last occasion the City Auditorium was filled to capacity and the audience was integrated in accordance with Marion Anderson's wishes. She performed works by Scarlatti, Handel, and Brahms, as well as an old spiritual, "Sometimes I Feel Like a Motherless Child."

The above, however, were exceptions to the general rule of the "color line." At a 1933 Houston Civic Opera presentation of *Aida,* in which a number of black Houstonians played roles as Ethiopian slaves, segregated seating prevailed. When a local performance of *Tosca* was produced in 1944, the white demand for tickets was so great that the "colored balcony" seats of the City Auditorium were sold to whites; the only opportunity that black opera enthusiasts had to view the production was at two dress rehearsals. During most of the 1930s, the only tickets available to the Houston Symphony concerts for black patrons were for "special reserved seats." In 1944, after many years of performing afternoon concerts for white schoolchildren, a Sunday afternoon concert was staged for black children for the first time. Although conductor Ernst Hoffman pronounced the event a great success, it still served to perpetuate the practice of segregation.

Unfortunately, the "color line" was not limited to musical performances. It was also observed during the first great showing of the work of black artists in the United States in September 1930 in Houston. The exhibit, presented by the Houston Museum of Fine Arts, consisted of 73 examples of painting and sculpture on the theme of black development. Blacks could only view the exhibit on one day each month that the museum set aside for "colored patrons" or by special appointment. This was all the more ironic since black children had contributed pennies to the expense of bringing the exhibit to Houston in the first place. Of course, the end result of such restrictive practices was the lack of any meaningful black patronage of the museum. By 1945 the museum trustees extended black visiting hours to include Friday afternoons in addition to the one day a month. Even at a showing of 100 drawings and paintings by black children in 1946 the limitations on attendance were still maintained.

Despite the exclusionary policies of the Houston Museum of Fine Arts, the work of black artists did receive some exposure elsewhere in the city. In 1933 the dedication of the Fifth Ward Branch Library in the black section of town was accompanied by an exhibit of the paintings of eight black artists. The next year the show was repeated in the Negro Carnegie Branch Library, and in 1937, the works of Frank F. Sheinall, a black artist from Galveston, were displayed there. In May 1949 the First Annual Festival of Fine Arts was held at Texas Southern University in Houston. The show featured the work of John T. Biggers, an art instructor at TSU and one of the most creative black artists ever to work in Houston. In 1950 one of his drawings, "The Cradle," won the $200 Purchase Prize awarded by the Museum of Fine Arts, and in 1954 an entire show at the museum was devoted to his paintings and sculpture.

Black cultural endeavors in Houston extended to the columns of *The Informer.* The weekly paper published the works of short-story writers and poets until the outbreak of World War II. Wartime limitations on newsprint curtailed this program, but during the postwar period the newspaper again tried to encourage such publication. In 1949 the paper sponsored a short-story contest, won by David Abner, an undergraduate student at Texas Southern University. Houston's black community was also active in the theater. In March 1931 the Houston Negro Little Theatre was organized as an amateur company. During the Great Depresssion adequate financing was difficult to acquire, but the company made its debut in 1935 with a one-act mystery drama, *No Sabe.* The performance was well-received by a predominantly black audience of almost 300. That year the group also performed Oscar Wilde's *Lady Windermere's Fan,* and in November 1941 the troupe put on Thorton Wilder's *Our Town.* However, the Houston Negro Little Theatre did not perform again until 1953, when it staged a highly acclaimed performance of Tennessee Williams' *The Glass Menagerie.*

In 1949 the work of Houston artist John T. Biggers was featured in the First Annual Festival of Fine Arts at Texas Southern University. Then in 1954 and 1968 the Houston Museum of Fine Arts held special exhibitions of his artwork. Courtesy, University of Texas, Institute of Texan Cultures, San Antonio

Access of blacks to libraries in the city was another issue of great significance during this period. In Houston the Colored Library Association, led by Ernest O. Smith, was founded in 1907 to provide library service and to raise money to purchase books. In 1911 the Carnegie Corporation authorized a grant of $15,000 to be used to build a separate library for blacks in Houston. The Negro Carnegie Branch Library, as it was officially called, was completed in 1913 and in 1924 was placed under the jurisdiction of the Library Board of the City of Houston. In 1934 three more libraries were funded within the black community as subdivisions of the main Negro Carnegie Branch Library.

Houston blacks, among them civil-rights lawyer James Nabrit, deplored the failure of the city to provide equal library facilities. In the columns of *The Informer*, Nabrit emphasized that of the approximately 300,000 volumes in the Houston public library system, less then 6,000 could be found in the four black libraries. Employees of the black libraries received lower salaries and operated in cramped quarters with inade-

quate lighting and restroom facilities. The situation improved somewhat when in 1933 James A. Hulbert became the first professionally trained librarian to accept a position in Houston. Hulbert envisioned the Negro Carnegie Branch Library as the center of black cultural and artistic life in the city. Although he did not meet this goal, Hulbert was responsible for a substantial increase in book usage and circulation at the black libraries. However, after his departure in 1936 and during the war years, the programs offered by the libraries fell off and interest seemed to decline.

In 1950, reflecting the postwar demand for a semblance of equal rights, efforts were made to gain access for blacks to the Main Branch of the Houston Public Library. The Houston NAACP chapter made this a priority and in an attempt to avoid a lawsuit, the Library Board doubled the budget of the Negro Carnegie Branch Library. However, this tactic failed to appease the black community. Upon the strong recommendation of Mayor Roy Hofheinz, the board, pressured by the threat of legal action

In the years immediately after the Civil War, formal educational institutions funded by public money were created to serve the black community. In the late 1870s the system was regularized and formal public schooling was established for both black and white. The Fourth Ward High School served black students in the late 19th century. Courtesy, Texas Room; Houston Public Library

Developed in the early 20th century, the Conroe Normal and Industrial College was the first black higher educational institution established in the area. Classes such as this 1927 one studied vocational as well as academic subjects. Courtesy, Texas Room; Houston Public Library

and the fact that a suit had recently been won desegregating the municipal golf courses, opened all its branches to the use of "all persons." Although these advances were laudable, it was not until the 1960s that black librarians were hired or that there was black membership on the Houston Library Board.

Segregation in education continued in Houston. The amount of money appropriated by the school board per student was much higher at white schools than black. Physical plants and facilities were initially superior and maintained better at white schools as well, and the standards demanded of teachers when hired for the first time were more rigid and exacting at the white schools.

Until the mid-1920s there had been one state-supported university for blacks in Texas. As originally conceived in 1878, Prairie View A & M was envisioned as an agricultural school. In 1901 the state legislature provided funds to establish a program there in "classical and scientific" studies, but professional and pre-professional classes languished for lack of adequate funding. Some of the slack was taken up by the 20 or

so private black colleges in the state, but, without exception, adequate financial resources proved a constant problem.

In 1937 the Texas legislature increased the appropriation for the black school at Prairie View, enabling it to offer graduate study. However, although a few master's degrees were awarded and two faculty members with doctoral degrees were hired in the physical sciences, the program at Prairie View was in no way comparable to the University of Texas. In 1939 the general appropriation for Prairie View was slightly increased again, but it was still foolish to pretend that its facilities were equal to those of the University of Texas at Austin. A decision in the legislature to establish a separate law school at Prairie View was blunted by the approach of World War II.

Spurred by the sacrifices made by blacks in the war, the issue came to the fore again upon the conclusion of the fighting. At a meeting of all Texas branches of the NAACP in Houston, it was agreed that having abolished the white primary, the next attack would be against discriminatory policies in public education, starting with graduate and professional education. Anti-

Houston's educational system always included opportunities for at least some physical education classes even in the 1870s. The students at Houston College, such as these women, took part in physical activities. Courtesy, Texas Room; Houston Public Library

cipating what was in the offing, the legislature upgraded Prairie View to a "State University" and authorized graduate training in law, medicine, pharmacy, engineering, and "any other course taught at the University of Texas." In theory, equal training at separate institutions now existed, but the facts were much different.

As Houston had been the focal point of the cases challenging the white primary, so would it be in education. In 1946 Heman M. Sweatt, an honor graduate of Wiley College and a World War II veteran, applied to the law school of the University of Texas at Austin. Sweatt, a native Houstonian employed as a mailman at the time, was denied admission solely on the grounds of his color. Once again Thurgood Marshall, on behalf of the NAACP, headed the legal team assisted by James Nabrit. A state judge ruled that since no black law school existed in Texas, Sweatt must be permitted to enroll at Austin unless equal facilities were guaranteed elsewhere within six months.

In the 1946 election every candidate for governor pledged to continue segregation at all state universities. Meanwhile the legislature sought to create a separate law school for blacks by hiring two black attorneys in Houston to offer courses in a rented building adjoining their offices. When no stu-

dents applied for admission and the subterfuge was roundly condemned by black leaders, a new tack was tried. Now space was rented in Austin in a basement near the state capitol. Classes would be taught by University of Texas faculty and black students would have access to both state and University libraries. Only three students, one of them from Houston, enrolled. A difference of opinion resulted among the leadership of the Houston black community; some were inclined to accept the situation in Austin as a step forward, while others agreed with the NAACP decision to take the Sweatt case to the Supreme Court if necessary.

The Sweatt matter indirectly led to the establishment of Texas Southern University, the principal state university for blacks located in Houston. Texas Southern University traces its origins back to 1926. In that year, a group of Houston black leaders, despairing of any other solution, arranged for Wiley College at Marshall to offer extension courses at the Jack Yates High School in Houston. In 1927 this program was assimilated into the curriculum of the Houston Colored Junior College, which was set up to provide further education for the graduates of Houston's three black high schools. The junior college was municipally controlled and functioned until 1934 when an upper division was added. In 1935 the upper division became the Houston College for Negroes, a branch of the University of Houston, and the lower division remained Houston Colored Junior College. In quick order the degree programs of the Houston College for Negroes were approved by the Texas State Department of Education and the Southern Association of College and Secondary Schools.

After World War II the Houston College for Negroes launched a fund-raising campaign that proved eminently successful. Encouraged by a gift of $100,000 from Hugh Roy Cullen, the major benefactor of the University of Houston, $283,000 was ultimately raised through the contributions of white and black Houstonians. In 1947 the legislature earmarked a special appropriation to locate a black university in Houston. A 53-acre campus was located near the University of Houston and by the fall of 1947, Texas State University for Negroes (later called Texas Southern University) opened its doors to some 2,000 students. The temporary law school was then moved from Austin to Houston, but

Sweatt reiterated his determination not to attend a segregated institution.

Meanwhile the Sweatt case worked its way through the labyrinth of state and federal courts. Before the Texas Court of Civil Appeals and the Supreme Court of Texas, Attorney General Price Daniel successfully argued that the Texas State University for Negroes provided a "separate but equal" legal education. But applications for admission to medical school and for professional degrees in other fields were also before the Board of Regents of the University of Texas and it was apparent that some decision must soon be reached. In April 1950 Thurgood Marshall of the NAACP and Price Daniel, representing the state of Texas, appeared to argue before the United States Supreme Court. In June the Supreme Court handed down its opinion that the law school in Houston was not equal in any way to the established University of Texas Law School; the faculty, library holdings, moot court and law review facilities were decidedly inferior. Sweatt was thus confirmed in his constitutional right to enter the University of Texas. He was 40 years old when finally admitted and had not attended a college

Located on the west side of the the city near Buffalo Bayou, Houston College served the needs of the black community for a number of years. The 1914 football team played games with a number of other black schools in the region. Courtesy, Texas Room; Houston Public Library

class since 1937. Thus it came as no surprise that he was dismissed within a year because of failing grades. In a sense, he had willingly martyred himself in the cause of black education. Finally, within five years after the historic court fight the Texas Southern University Law School in Houston was accredited by the American Bar Association and the American Association of Law Schools.

Segregated facilities remained in place in Houston's public schools all during the 1940s. Funding for schools in black neighborhoods continued to be inferior and discrepancies persisted in teacher compensation, physical plants, and the like. Yet the Sweatt case was a harbinger of the future and pointed the way to the decision in *Brown* v. *Board of Education* (1954) that "separate but equal" policies are unconstitutional.

The sting of segregation was felt not only by blacks, but also by Mexican-Americans, who numbered about 55,000 in Houston in 1945. They were, for example, refused service at restaurants, and burial in predominantly Anglo cemeteries. They were condemned to residential segregation, and they, too, determined to fight back. As it was for blacks, World War II was also a decisive era for many Mexican-Americans. Experiencing relative equality of treatment during their

military service, they anticipated the same treatment upon their return to civilian life. Between 6,500 and 7,500 Mexican-Americans had enlisted, and many had been decorated for bravery in action. In the immediate postwar period, a chapter of the American GI Forum, founded in 1948 by Dr. Hector Garcia, was quickly organized in Houston. A voter registration plan was implemented and a policy of opposing educational segregation was also proclaimed. In addition, a drive to aid needy families and provide scholarships for deserving students was also announced. However, while the GI Forum attracted the backing of many Houston Mexican-Americans, it was neither the first nor the most successful of the Latin protest groups.

Houston's Mexican-American community dates back to the period of the Republic and early statehood. In the first half of the 20th century, most Houstonians of Mexican-American ancestry lived in the Magnolia Park and Houston Ship Channel sections of town. In more recent years, a substantial community has developed on the north side and to a lesser degree in the southwest sections of the city. Our Lady of Guadalupe Church on Navigation Boulevard, in the heart of the older Mexican community, attracts the greatest number of parishioners to Roman Catholic church ser-

Neighborhood restaurants served as the centers for much of community life in Houston's different ethnic neighborhoods. The La Consentida Cafe at 1700 Washington was one of the social centers for the Mexican-American community in the 1930s. Courtesy, Houston Metropolitan Research Center; Houston Public Library

vices, while St. Hyacinth (San Jacinto) on Center Street and Annunciation Cathedral on Texas Avenue also have their adherents. Two Protestant churches, Iglesia Bautista West-End and Iglesia De Dios-Israelita, conduct services entirely in Spanish.

There are two Spanish-English community newspapers available to Mexican-Americans residing in Houston, *El Sol* and *Compass*. Of the publications, the latter is generally less content with the political status quo. Occupational groups, both professional and non-professional, abound, and

there is a local Mexican Chamber of Commerce subsidized by the business community. The most effective social service group is *Familias Unidas*, which employs as its motto, "Por el Progresso y Cultura de Nuestra Juventud" ("For the Progress and Culture of Our Youth"), and other clubs exist to commemorate Mexican holidays with a parade or fiesta. Finally, the League of Latin American Citizens (LULAC) and the Political Association of Spanish Speaking Organizations (PASO) together boast a membership of about 40 percent of the Houston Mexican-American community. PASO claims to be the strongest Mexican political organization in Harris County, but there is no doubt that the LULAC organization is the most effective on a state and national level.

LULAC was the very first organization of Mexican-Americans to wage a struggle for equal rights. The movement incorporated two splinter groups already functioning as protest organizations—the League of Latin-American Citizens and the Order of Sons of America. South Texas, where the concentration of Mexican-Americans was greatest, inspired this activity, and on April 17, 1929, at Corpus Christi, the League of United Latin-American Citizens was founded. A Houston chapter was formed in 1934. In the LULAC constitution, loyalty to the United States was put beyond ques-

Houston has become the site of a group of great medical institutions. Centered in the area around Hermann Park, close to both downtown and Rice University, these medical institutions have served the community, the nation, and the world, caring for rich and poor alike. Courtesy, Texas Room; Houston Public Library

As Houston's Mexican community continued to grow, Our Lady of Guadalupe provided more different services and religious activities for it. This religious procession took place in the 1940s. Courtesy, Houston Metropolitan Research Center; Houston Public Library

Right:
The Club Cultural Recreativeo Mexico Bello was organized within the Mexican community to serve the social needs of the leaders within that community. Active for many years, the club sponsored a number of social events and also served to bring the leaders of the Mexican community together for many different functions. Courtesy, Houston Metropolitan Research Center; Houston Public Library

Far right:
The Depression hit all parts of the Houston community. For some the prices of stores such as La Casa Verde were beyond reach. Courtesy, Houston Metropolitan Research Center; Houston Public Library

Right:
Although Houston had always had a small Mexican-American population, the turmoil in Mexico during the early 20th century caused many, such as this family, to migrate north to find stability and escape from the dangers of revolution. Courtesy, Houston Metropolitan Center; Houston Public Library

Right:
Orchestras tipicas, accompanied by Mexican dancers, provided popular entertainment for the Mexican-American community in Houston during the 1920s and 1930s. This orchestra tipica was being filmed by RCA for a short subject on Mexican music and dance to be distributed by Pathe. With their costumes and music, the entertainers were an important part of the Mexican tradition in Houston. Courtesy, Houston Metropolitan Research Center; Houston Public Library

–CLUB CULTURAL RECREATIVO MEXICO BELLO.– –1932–

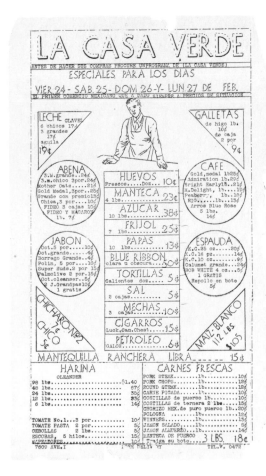

In the 1920s Houstonians were beginning to take advantage of the new medium of radio. The big clear channel stations brought the outside world to the city and then KTRH, KPRC, and KXYZ gradually came on the air, bringing local broadcasts to the city. Furniture stores, such as the Alamo Furniture Company (pictured here), sold radios to all ranks of the community. This store served the Mexican-American community, providing it with the latest in electronics as well as furniture. Courtesy, Houston Metropolitan Research Center; Houston Public Library

Below left:
Small grocery stores such as the Reyes Food Store in Magnolia Park served most neighborhoods in Houston well into the 1930s and 1940s. Owned by members of the community, these convenient stores were an important part in the group of social institutions that made up Houston in the years preceding World War II. Courtesy, Houston Metropolitan Research Center; Houston Public Library

Below:
Jose Sarabia's bookstore at 1800 Congress was the center of Mexican intellectual life in Houston during the 1920s. Courtesy, Houston Metropolitan Research Center; Houston Public Library

El Puerto, *an English-language paper for the Mexican-American community, was one of the agents of change designed to bridge the gap between Mexican-American and Anglo residents. Courtesy, Houston Metropolitan Research Center; Houston Public Library*

Over the years, the Mexican-American community began to develop its own institutions. Among the most important were the sports associations. Courtesy, Houston Metropolitan Research Center; Houston Public Library

tion and the obligations of American citizenship were also duly noted. On the other hand members pledged to employ every legal strategem available to end discrimination against Mexican-Americans. Specifically, the delegates vowed to oppose any prohibitions against voting, integrated schools, or their right to serve on juries.

Another declared purpose of the League was to "promulgate the English language among Mexican-Americans." At the same time Latins must be made conscious of their history in Texas and the Southwest in order to stir pride in their heritage. To achieve these aims a monetary fund was established ensuring frequent access to the courts for the protection of civil rights. Cautious in their aims and anxious to work within existing political and economic alignments, the Houston LULAC chapter reflected the dominant middle class origins of the group.

Following the example of the NAACP, the LULACS turned to the courts to assure equal rights for Mexican-Americans. On June 15, 1948, the Texas Supreme Court issued an injunction against segregated education for Mexican-Americans beyond the first grade, in which classes could be segregated for the purpose of special instruction. However, conditions in Houston schools did not change overnight, and segregation continued.

Another class action lawsuit on behalf of Houston's Mexican-American community challenged de facto residential segregation. Until about 1950 most Mexican-Americans in Houston lived on the east side of the city in the area between Canal and Navigation streets. As the community became better educated and tended more toward a middle-class orientation, attempts were made to move into some of the city's more desirable residential areas. It was here that restrictive covenants, barring Mexicans from living in specific neighborhoods, were frequently encountered. While a Houston case was pending in the state courts, the Supreme Court of the United States outlawed restrictive covenants as in violation of the 14th amendment to the constitution. Still, the case had little practical effect on residential segregation of Mexicans; their inability to afford better housing continued to be the decisive factor.

Traditionally, in Texas, Mexican-Americans had been slow to exercise their political rights. Often the pawns of Anglo bosses, particularly in South Texas, Mexican-Americans tended to vote for Democratic candidates in both state and national elections. Never particularly militant, they watched with interest as blacks began to insist upon the right to enter into the mainstream of Houston's political life. Eventually, businessman Lauro Cruz, a conservative

176

KLVL, established in 1956, was the first radio station to offer Spanish programming for the Mexican-American community. Although its owner, Felix Morales, had planned to broadcast in English, he realized that the need for Spanish-language programming was sufficient to merit a Spanish station. Courtesy, Houston Metropolitan Research Center; Houston Public Library

member of LULAC, became the first Mexican-American from Houston elected to the Texas legislature.

No national political figure has had a greater appeal to Mexican-Americans in Houston or throughout Texas than the late John F. Kennedy. A "Viva Kennedy" club was organized by Albert Fuentes in Houston in 1960. While national Democratic candidates had done well with Mexican-Americans in Texas from the 1930s on, John F. Kennedy surpassed them all. Of the 17 counties in Texas (not including Harris) where more than 50 percent of the population had Spanish surnames, Kennedy failed to carry only one. Perhaps even more impressive was the fact that of the 24 counties (including Harris) in the state with a Spanish surname population of 30 to 49.9 percent, Kennedy triumphed in 19.

The "Viva Kennedy" clubs had been so successful in turning out the vote that leaders of the party decided to create a permanent organization. In February 1961 delegates from Houston attended a statewide meeting in Victoria, Texas, at which the Political Association of Spanish-Speaking Organizations (PASO) was established. While the aims of PASO were similar to other Mexican-American organizations, the group was distinct in its emphasis on political action to achieve equal rights. No racial

or ethnic barriers to membership in PASO were stipulated, and the participation of all minority groups was welcomed. Since its establishment, the Houston chapter of PASO has been among the most vigorous in Texas.

In conclusion, Houston's minorities of color made substantial gains in civil rights during and immediately after World War II. Both groups began by emphasizing access to state and federal courts in pursuit of their rights. In this connection the city of Houston played a disproportionate role in the civil liberties arena since *Grovey v. Townsend, Smith* v. *Allwright,* and *Sweatt* v. *Painter* all involved Houstonians as plaintiffs. After winning legal victories on several fronts, both blacks and Mexican-Americans then turned to the franchise as a method of making their demands felt. Not since 1881 had a black sat in the state senate at Austin, but that was now realized with the election of Barbara Jordan in 1966 as senator from Harris County. In the same election, Curtis Graves was elected to the state house of representatives. In 1961 the first Mexican-American to serve in the United States Congress House of Representatives, Henry Gonzales of San Antonio, was elected. Leaders of both groups were cognizant of the fact that their people had begun to enter the mainstream of politics, but that much still remained to be achieved.

"Glamburger" Girls were the glamour girls of Houston during the war years. Employed by restaurants such as Prince's, a chain of drive-ins, the girls entered contests on Galveston Island and elsewhere, showing off their skills as waitresses and their daring costumes designed by their employers. The 1943 winner is on the right. Courtesy, Rosenberg Library

CHAPTER VIII

BUSINESS, POLITICS, AND THE ARTS: HOUSTON'S HEADY MIX

O n the eve of World War II, Houston could claim 385,000 inhabitants, 340,000 more than in 1900. After this rapid growth, the city's tremendous urban expansion continued unabated. Attracted by a favorable business climate, the population reached 690,000 in 1954, and by 1960 the city and county together were home to virtually one million people.

Among those who participated in Houston's expansion was entrepreneur Glen H. McCarthy, whose flamboyant life-style and rags-to-riches career masked a shrewd record as a successful oilman and land speculator. In 1944 McCarthy purchased 15 acres of land at the intersection of South Main Street and Bellaire Boulevard for $175,000. Until that time all of the city's major hotels were located downtown and only a handful of apartment hotels were situated in outlying residential areas. When in 1946 McCarthy began development of the Shamrock Hotel more than five miles from downtown Houston, a new stage in the city's growth commenced. Preliminary plans for the McCarthy Center also included seven apartment hotels, an ice-skating rink, a swimming pool, and a department store; most of these never progressed further than the architect's drawing board.

On St. Patrick's Day, 1949, the Shamrock Hotel was opened to the public. What followed has become a part of the folklore of the city of Houston. Almost 50,000 people turned out to see about 100 Hollywood stars brought in to witness the Dorothy Lamour radio broadcast from the hotel. Gene Autry, Lana Turner, Pat O'Brien, and other household names of that era were present and were nearly crushed by the surging crowd. It took Mayor Oscar Holcombe some two hours to gain entrance to the hotel, and other local political figures gave up trying. When the crowd became particularly unruly, NBC cancelled the radio show. Edna Ferber's memorable novel, *Giant,* and the movie starring James Dean that followed have immortalized opening night at the Shamrock.

By 1950, however, the hotel's builder was reported to be in serious financial difficulties. Because of increased state regulation, oil production in Texas was down, and McCarthy had incurred large debts in order to construct the Shamrock. While the hotel's operations were self-sustaining, other McCarthy holdings were not, and the hotel was acquired in a foreclosure proceeding by the Equitable Life Assurance Society. They, in turn, sold the hotel to the Hilton chain, and in 1955 the structure was renamed the Shamrock Hilton. Symbolically, the portrait of Glen McCarthy that had hung in the lobby since opening day was now replaced with that of Conrad Hilton. Although McCarthy lost his prized property, his foresight in building far from the downtown area was remarkable. Shortly after the Shamrock was built, Prudential Insurance Company announced the location of a Southwestern office near the site of the Shamrock, and this was followed by the construction of the Fannin National Bank in the same locale.

As had giants like Glen McCarthy in the oil business, leaders in other enterprises contributed more than just industry to the city. For example, Monroe D. Anderson of Anderson, Clayton & Company brought to Houston the beginnings of what has become a worldwide reputation for excellent medical facilities.

The origins of Anderson, Clayton & Company, the world's largest cotton concern, were modest. Founded in Oklahoma City in 1904, the company moved to Houston in 1916 to be at the center of the cotton business. The original partners were Frank E. Anderson, his brother Monroe D.

Anderson, and William L. Clayton, all of whom had prior experience in the cotton trade in Tennessee and Mississippi. They expanded the company's markets and began to diversify. Thus when the cotton market suffered a decline in the 1960s, the company was able to fall back on its interests in insurance and manufacturing.

In 1940 Will Clayton left Anderson, Clayton & Company to serve the federal government in Washington, eventually influencing the formation of the Marshall Plan. But the greater importance of the company to Houston lay principally in the charitable contributions of Monroe D. Anderson.

In 1936 Monroe Anderson, who had never married, established the M.D. Anderson Foundation, which at Anderson's death in 1939 received the major share of his estate, amounting to some $20 million. The trustees made a grant to Rice Institute for a classroom building and to the University of Houston for a library, but their principal accomplishment was the creation of the Texas Medical Center. University of Texas President Homer T. Rainey, Mayor Oscar Holcombe, Harris County Judge Roy Hofheinz, and Foundation trustees began negotiations to purchase land from the city next to Hermann Hospital for the erection of a cancer research hospital to be supervised by the University of Texas. The land was

purchased in 1942, and the first building was completed the next year. Today the M.D. Anderson Hospital and Tumor Institute is among the leading such facilities in the world. With President Rainey's enthusiastic approval, the University of Texas Dental School then relocated to the Medical Center, followed in 1943 by the Baylor Medical School.

Over the years the Texas Medical Center has expanded to include the Methodist Hospital, St. Luke's Episcopal Hospital, Texas Children's Hospital, Ben Taub Charity Hospital (Harris County), the University of Houston College of Nursing, and the University of Texas Medical School at Houston. The center has become a mecca for patients throughout the world seeking the latest developments in diagnostic methods and medical treatment. Dr. Michael DeBakey and Dr. Denton Cooley have brought fame to the Texas Medical Center through their pioneering work in cardiac surgery and organ transplantation. Presently much interest and hope is focused on the cancer research being done at the M.D. Anderson Hospital and Tumor Institute testing the use of interferon. Although it has never been widely publicized, the Anderson Foundation has also contributed liberally to the support of city and county charity hospitals.

In medicine and in other areas, the climate of growth in Houston encouraged improvements in the quality of life. As the

The ABC network radio show "Saturday at the Shamrock" attracted all the major stars during its heyday. When new movies such as African Queen were released, the stars, like Humphrey Bogart, appeared with Shamrock owner Glenn McCarthy and host Fred Nahas to gag, perform, and promote their pictures. Courtesy, Harris County Heritage Society

Houston's rise as an economic and population center was symbolized by the increasing number of visits from national celebrities and leaders. General Douglas MacArthur came to Houston in the early 1950s as a part of his effort to build a national constituency. Courtesy, Harris County Heritage Society

The Museum of Fine Arts houses a collection ranging from ancient Greek and Egyptian art to contemporary masterpieces. It is the city's major museum.

Bayou City grew into a thoroughly 20th-century metropolis, it gained many of the features that make urban life attractive and stimulating, including up-to-date facilities for and offerings in the arts. In the postwar period, Houston made great strides in the area of visual arts. The holdings and facilities of the Houston Museum of Fine Arts were expanded, and the Contemporary Arts Museum and the Rothko Chapel, both initiated after World War II, enhanced the city's position as a Southwestern art center.

A number of paintings by Frederick Remington, which depict life in the West and the story of the American cowboy, were donated to the Houston Museum of Fine Arts by Ima Hogg in 1942 and remain an important part of the museum's holdings. In 1953 the museum's facilities were increased with the addition of the Robert Lee Blaffer Memorial Wing, which now holds an impressionist collection; in 1958 Cullinan Hall, featuring a more modern type of architecture, was dedicated; and in recent years a sculpture garden has been added.

Located across from the Museum of Fine Arts is the Contemporary Arts Museum, founded in 1949. In 1955 Dr. Jermayne MacAgy of San Francisco was employed as its professional director. A devotee of modern art anxious to bring the best of such works to the attention of Houstonians,

MacAgy provided skillful leadership. However, in 1959 she resigned in order to accept a position at St. Thomas University in Houston and was replaced by Sebastian J. Adler. The Contemporary Arts Museum has enjoyed the patronage of John and Dominique de Menil, who have devoted much time and wealth to its success.

The de Menil family has made further contributions to the advancement of fine art in Houston. In 1964 they commissioned the Rothko Chapel, in which 14 of Mark Rothko's abstract expressionist paintings create a meditative atmosphere lit through a single skylight. The chapel was dedicated in 1971, one year after the artist's death. The de Menils also commissioned the Barnett Newman sculpture, the *Broken Obelisk,* which stands in a pond outside the chapel as

The Alley Theatre is home to the nation's oldest resident professional Equity group. Founded in 1947, the theater company has gone on to international renown.

a memorial to Dr. Martin Luther King, Jr.

As in visual arts, Houston has made great strides in the performing arts since World War II. In 1947 a small group of theater enthusiasts accepted the gift of a studio, partially situated in the alley at 3617 Main Street. The Alley Theatre was so successful that less than two years later it moved to new headquarters at 709 Berry Street. There for 19 years it staged more than 150 productions and built its reputation. From its inception the guiding genius of the troupe was Nina Vance, who acted as director, fund raiser, and liaison to the general theater-going public. Alley productions were often built around one recognized Broadway or Hollywood star, while featuring a local supporting cast. Such performers as Ray Walston, Jimmy Jeter, and Jeanette Clift all gained their first acting experience with the Alley, which is one of the oldest of the nation's resident professional Equity groups.

In 1959 the Ford Foundation made a grant to the Alley to further its work, and in 1962 it awarded $2.1 million in matching funds for the construction of a new theater across from the future site of Jones Hall. The Alley is now housed in a $3.5-million theater with two playhouses that seat 800 upstairs. The Arena Theatre downstairs has a capacity of 300 seats. Although Nina Vance has passed away, the Alley, under new leadership, continues to present a full and varied season each year. Also, semi-professional groups such as the Channing Players housed in Fellowship Hall, are flourishing. The Stages Theatre on Franklin Avenue and Chocolate Bayou Theatre on Lamar Avenue feature local casts and avant-garde productions. Also, the Houston Shakespeare Society performs with a cast of non-professionals.

In addition to the talent these groups bring to the stage, the Houston Ballet, originally founded in 1955, has developed as a major force in the cultural life of the city under the leadership of Ben Stevenson. A recent trip to China spotlighted the company's achievements and led to an important cultural exchange when a Chinese troupe later came to Houston. Generous funding for the Houston Ballet has been provided by local businessmen and corporations eager to further the success of the young group.

The Society for the Performing Arts also plays an important part in Houston's cultural offerings. A non-profit agency, the SPA was the creation of John H. Jones, Jr., editor of the Houston *Chronicle* and a nephew of Jesse Jones. When the Jesse H. Jones Hall for the Performing Arts was completed in October 1966 with funding from the Houston Endowment, it was anticipated that the Houston Symphony and the Houston Grand Opera would be its principal tenants. However, since this would account for only two or three nights a week at best, the SPA was chartered and charged with bringing the "finest international touring attractions" to Houston. Since its inception in 1966, the Society has presented such diverse attractions as the Mexican Ballet Folklorico, the American Folk Ballet, *Hello Dolly, Fiddler on the Roof,* and the Obernkirchen Children's Choir, as well as world-renowned individual performers.

While the increasingly metropolitan Bayou City was acquiring modern facilities in the arts and sciences, its growth continued to be fueled by the oil and gas boom.

A successful company in the energy area has been the Houston Pipe Line Company,

Baylor University College of Medicine, in the Texas Medical Center, became world famous with the cardiovascular surgery and organ transplantation work of Dr. Michael DeBakey and Dr. Denton Cooley.

William "Hopalong Cassidy" Boyd visited Houston for charitable events in the early 1950s, bringing his own special style to Houston children, who copied his dress. Courtesy, Harris County Heritage Society

which became the major supplier of the Houston Natural Gas Company organized in the same year. Located originally in the Scanlan Building in downtown Houston, both Houston Pipe Line and Houston Natural Gas moved their offices to the newly completed Petroleum Building in 1927. A 22-story edifice, the Petroleum Building was the headquarters for a number of Houston-based oil companies and was on the way to becoming the landmark that it is today.

Until 1927 the Houston Gas and Fuel Company had been contracted by the City Council to provide the city with gas, but in that year Houston Natural offered the city a 10-year contract at a lower rate than Houston Gas and Fuel was offering, and from then on the Bayou City market belonged to Houston Natural Gas. In 1933 Frank C. Smith, a local banker, became president of Houston Natural Gas. He accurately foresaw the unmatched postwar growth of the city and by 1947 the company had installed more than 100,000 meters in Houston. By 1953 two hundred thousand meters had been installed and in that same year Houston Natural Gas Production Company was formed to obtain drilling properties and to participate in the search for oil and gas. The acquisition in 1957 of the McCarthy Oil and Gas Corporation, founded by Glen McCarthy, facilitated this aspect of the company's business.

Houston Natural entered the present phase of its growth in 1967 when, after 40 years in the Petroleum Building, it moved to its present quarters in the 26-story Houston Natural Gas Building. It has since acquired several subsidiaries, including Liquid Carbonic Corporation, one of the nation's largest producers of carbon dioxide, and Intratax Gas Company, created to operate a West Texas transmission system. Houston Natural celebrated 50 years of operation in 1975, and its growth has matched that of the city over the same span.

Chartered on March 16, 1925, the most successful Houston firm in the natural gas field was the Tennessee Gas Transmission Company, founded by H. Gardner Symonds. The company was organized in 1944 and just 12 years later had assets of more than a billion dollars. Renamed Tenneco, Inc., in 1946, the company became involved in the manufacture of automotive components and tractors as well as chemical and natural gas pipelines.

An energy company projected to bring downtown Houston many new facilities is the Texas Eastern Transmission Corporation. Texas Eastern began by purchasing the "Big Inch" and "Little Inch" pipelines, which were built during World War II and effectively linked Texas to Eastern markets. From the production and transportation of natural gas supplies, the company moved into the manufacture of petrochemicals. However, it is as the primary developer of the Houston Center that Texas Eastern has become best known. The project encompasses a 33-block central business district, which upon completion will double the size of the city's downtown business area. Slated to be completed in 1990, the Houston Center's plans include a convention center, hotels, people-mover vehicles, and enclosed parking for some 40,000 cars.

The oil business had always been the benchmark of Houston's growth since Spindletop, so the tidelands controversy of the 1950s era generated a great deal of emotion in Houston. The dispute had its origins back in 1933 when Secretary of Interior Harold Ickes stated that the federal government had no right to issue drilling permits in leases for submerged coastal lands and that such authority belonged to the states. However, by 1937 Ickes had experienced a change of heart after the discovery of the Wilmington-Long Beach oil field off California. The United States government now brought suit to prevent the exploitation of that field by a California company, and in 1946 the Supreme Court ruled that California's tidelands were the property of the federal government.

Texas challenged the California case in 1950, and the Supreme Court's ruling was eagerly anticipated by the Houston oil fraternity, but again the decision was in favor of the federal government. The dispute then moved to offshore lands. In the 1952 Presidential election, Adlai Stevenson, the Democratic nominee, endorsed federal ownership of the tidelands, while Dwight Eisenhower, his Republican opponent, announced his backing for state control. Houston oilmen led an ultimately unsuccessful attempt to place Eisenhower's name as the Democratic nominee on the ballot in Texas, though he was the Republican candidate everywhere else.

As he had pledged to do, Eisenhower soon signed legislation returning to Texas title to the submerged lands 10.5 miles out to sea. The bill actually restored state titles to their "historic limits," which meant three

miles for all states except Texas and Florida. The latter were covered by Spanish law, which had granted title for "three leagues," about 10.5 miles.

Benign political viewpoints in Washington, D.C., and Austin combined with constantly increasing demand to make Houston the oil, gas, and petrochemical capital of the world. This status ensured the growth of banking, insurance, and investments tied to the search for oil and gas. Thoughtful economists, however, wondered whether this span of unrivaled growth since Spindletop in 1901 was destined to continue. By the early 1980s the world surplus of oil, OPEC's pricing policy, increasing conservation, and concern over the dangers of pollution had drastically changed the oil industry. The day of the colorful, independent oilman seems to be a thing of the past, and the future of the industry is uncertain.

While legislation and politics on the national level affected Houston business interests, local politics in the postwar period impacted public services, notably education. There were more than 80,000 students attending 126 public schools in Houston in 1949 when contention first arose over a school board resolution to accept federal aid for lunches. The proposal was attacked by the Committee for Sound American Education (CSAE), an ultra-conservative group, on the grounds that it would result in eventual federal control and supervision. However, compromise was reached when the board agreed to collect private funds for lunches. Opposition to the federal lunch program remained vocal until 1968, when the board finally agreed to accept funds from Washington.

The next controversy arose in October 1949 when the local board banned Professor Frank Magruder's *American Government*, a textbook that had been in use for many years, because of an alleged favorable reference to communism. Charges against the use of particular textbooks in history and government courses continued. Issues such as these were raised in the decidedly conservative political climate of Houston in the 1950s. In this period the Houston

Although Houston's career as a cattle town has been sporadic, the stock show that grew up in the city has attracted the interest of the cattle culture long before the modern revival of Saturday night cowboys. Western entertainers such as Roy Rogers made the stock show and the Shamrock stops on their tours in the early 1950s. Courtesy, Harris County Heritage Society

Chronicle and much of the city's business elite strongly supported the tactics of Senator Joe McCarthy.

One organization in Houston that flourished in this atmosphere of anti-liberalism was the "Minute Women of the U.S.A." This ultra-conservative political group was founded in Connecticut in 1949 by Suzanne S. Stevenson for the purpose of opposing "communism" in government and in the public schools. In 1951 a chapter of the Minute Women was organized in Houston and it rapidly became the most powerful of the local anti-communist groups. In its wake came organizations committed to many of the same beliefs, such as the Harris County Republican Women's Club, the American Legion, and the Doctors for Freedom. At meetings of the Houston School Board the Minute Women voiced their opposition to desegregation, federal assistance to education, and American membership in the United Nations. Board members complained that the routine business of educational matters was often left undone because of the ideological debates, and political divisions among classroom teachers and administrative personnel interfered with the daily business of educating children.

In the November 1952 school board election, candidates running under the banner of the "Committee for Sound American Education," which represented the interests of the Minute Women, won two of the four contested seats. With the election concluded, the Minute Women sought the removal of George Ebey.

Earlier in the year Ebey, an educator with a history of involvement with liberal causes and a reputation as an able administrator, was hired as deputy superintendent by William E. Moreland, superintendent of public schools in Houston. Moreland later said that he had selected Ebey on the basis of his high recommendations from Columbia University and his vast administrative experience. Moreland had not concerned himself with Ebey's political beliefs, which were admittedly liberal, but hardly radical.

At a board meeting a local attorney, John P. Rogge, accused Ebey of communist sympathies. The educator defended himself vigorously, and was completely exonerated of the charges by an FBI report; nevertheless, the board by a 4-3 vote refused to renew his contract. Chairman James Delmar insisted that Ebey had been dismissed because of a poor job rating, but both the Houston Teacher's Association and the National Education Association condemned Ebey's firing. The entire episode reflected the strong conservative emphasis in Houston politics at that time.

If communism was the issue during the Cold War, desegregation became the problem at a later date. In 1954 the United States Supreme Court handed down its decision in the landmark case of *Brown* v. *Board of Education of Topeka, Kansas,* in which it called the "separate but equal" doctrine discriminatory and gave the United States District Courts responsibility for the integration of educational facilities. In 1956 the Houston School Board ordered integration of the administrative wing of the public schools but postponed desegregation of the pupils until a construction program aimed at providing equal and adequate facilities everywhere for all students could be completed. Impatient with these dilatory tactics, the local NAACP chapter filed suit to compel desegregation.

By November 1956 the conservatives again controlled the school board, and Mrs. Dallas Dyer, a member of the Minute Women, was its chairman. The board issued a statement in May 1957 pledging no desegregation of the Houston schools until 1960, when the ongoing building program would be finished. In the interim, Federal District Judge Ben C. Connally had ordered desegregation with "all deliberate speed" but had carefully refrained from setting an exact date. Mrs. Dyer and school board attorney Joe Reynolds said there would be no appeal as the school trustees felt the order to be a wise decision. Judge Connally's decision was moderate, but the board took advantage of the absence of a starting date by postponing any attempt to begin desegregation. Judge Connally believed that a local plan of desegregation should be instituted because court-ordered plans in the past had led to resentment and violence.

Then in 1958, for the first time in the history of the board, an Afro-American, Hattie Mae White, was elected to a seat, which she held until defeated for reelection in 1967. Pressed by Judge Connally to submit a workable plan of desegregation by June 1, 1960, the board submitted a proposal to integrate one elementary, one junior high, and one high school. Now, clearly out of patience, Connally stated that desegregation must commence in all first grades in September 1960 and continue at one grade a year after that. But, through the enforcement of rigid requirements, only 12 black children out of a student population of more than 175,000 were able to attend an integrated school in September 1960.

Subsequent attempts to remedy the problem of segregation included a federal court order to abandon grade-by-grade integration in favor of immediate desegregation of all grades; federal court-ordered pairing and rezoning of predominantly segregated schools; and the Magnet School Program. The Houston School Board has complied with all federal orders and regulations in regard to integration, and the city fortunately has been spared the violence and disorder which has scarred some other areas.

While in the area of education intense political and social struggles were being waged, the power struggle that had characterized relations between the mayor and the City Council during the Great Depression and New Deal era was resolved. In 1942 Houston adopted a city-manager form of government, with eight councilmen and a part-time mayor, who was paid the paltry sum of $2,000 per year. John North Edy, who had been city manager of Dallas, was brought to Houston as city manager. But in 1946 the "Old Gray Fox" won reelection on a platform advocating a strong mayor. Oscar Holcombe's salary was set at $20,000 and the mayor's job was defined as full-time. Also, in the 1946 election the city charter was amended to combine the responsibilities of the mayor and the former city manager. In practice this meant that the mayor functioned as the executive branch of government and also prepared the agenda for the legislative branch (City Council). Also, the mayor appointed all city department heads

In the years after World War II, oil exploration moved offshore into the Texas Gulf waters. The early rigs were small affairs, serviced by converted LST's and similar craft. This well was at a depth of 11,017 feet when this photograph was shot in 1949. Courtesy, Rosenberg Library

with the sole exception of the city controller, who was elected.

Buttressed by this authority, the office of mayor has attracted strong personalities in the Oscar Holcombe tradition. Perhaps the most dynamic was Roy Hofheinz, whose full and colorful life has become part of the Houston legend. He served as mayor in 1953-1955, between Holcombe's last two terms. Born on April 10, 1912, in Beaumont, young Roy moved to Houston in 1928 after the death of his father, Fritz, who had driven a laundry truck for a living. Roy worked his way through Rice Institute and the Houston Law School, graduating at the age of 19. Hofheinz was a successful attorney, but the political life attracted him. He was elected to the state legislature at the age of 22, and at 24 he was elected to the post of Harris County judge, the youngest man ever to hold such an office in the United States.

Referred to thereafter as the "Judge," Hofheinz remembered his term as county judge as the most rewarding of his life. He presided over the work of three courts and four county boards, including the county hospital board. He was responsible for the inclusion of the county hospital (Ben Taub) in the Texas Medical Center as well as the formation of the Harris County Probate Court. From his law practice, investments in land, and ownership of radio and television stations, he became a millionaire.

In 1953, at the age of 40, the "Boy Millionaire" was elected mayor of Houston. Although he became embroiled in a 1955 struggle over proposed charter changes that almost resulted in his impeachment, Hofheinz can be credited as a successful mayor. He was responsible for revamping the city purchasing department, which resulted in substantial savings to taxpayers. He also carried through a public-works and street-building program that greatly facilitated the city's growth and progress. Probably his most significant achievement as mayor was the construction of the Houston International Airport. Completed in 1954, the facility was renamed the William P. Hobby Airport in 1976. While it has since been superseded in the amount of both passenger and freight traffic it handles by Houston Intercontinental Airport, "Hobby" marked Houston's debut as a major Southern air terminal.

Despite his political involvements, Hofheinz will best be remembered as the builder of the Harris County Domed Stadium, better known as the Houston Astrodome. Completed and opened to the public in 1965, the "Dome" has since

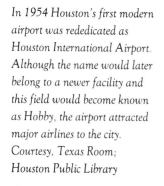

In 1954 Houston's first modern airport was rededicated as Houston International Airport. Although the name would later belong to a newer facility and this field would become known as Hobby, the airport attracted major airlines to the city. Courtesy, Texas Room; Houston Public Library

become the prototype for many stadiums built in the United States and abroad. Hofheinz maintained that he got the idea for the Astrodome while viewing the Roman Colosseum, which had a "velarium" or awning pulled by slaves and pulleys when weather conditions were inclement.

The Astrodome, which is today the most commonly recognized site in Houston, was for a while a subject of controversy. In 1958 Harris County voters approved a $20 million bond issue for a combined football and baseball stadium. The Houston Sports Association then offered to lease the stadium when completed at a rental sufficient to redeem the bonds; the Sports Association would control and supervise the facility, and the county would build according to the plans of the HSA. However, the 1958 issue did not sell well and was cancelled, and a new and larger bond issue was proposed. The risk was obvious: if the Houston Sports Association failed—and there was a good chance it might—the county taxpayers would be saddled with the debt. Opponents of the Astrodome protested that it was unwise to assume a public debt on behalf of a private corporation. However, the project was endorsed by powerful factions within the city and promoted brilliantly by Hofheinz. The bond issue and yet another one were overwhelmingly approved.

The Astrodome was completed at a cost of almost $50 million and opened in April

1965, with an exhibition baseball game between the Astros and the New York Yankees. The Houston Sports Association, with Roy Hofheinz and R.E. "Bob" Smith as the principal partners, had been awarded a major-league franchise in 1960, and the Colt 45s began major-league play in 1962; by 1964 they had become the Houston Astros. On opening night for the Astrodome, Governor John Connally threw out the first ball, President Lyndon B. Johnson sat in the "skybox" with Hofheinz, and the Astros triumphed in 12 innings, 2-1. In 1968 the Houston Oilers, owned since the team was chartered in 1959 by K.S. Bud Adams, president of the Ada Oil Company, began to play their games in the Astrodome, and fan interest has been at a high pitch ever since.

The postwar era was one of continued growth and development for the city of Houston. Business expansion and virtually full employment were made possible by the post World War II economic boom. In Bayou City fashion much of this new wealth went into significant and lasting charitable endeavors, such as the famed Texas Medical Center. Vigorous support was also given to the arts and the cultural life of the city attained new heights. Finally, although it required persistent legal action and was characterized by the tactics of delay, a beginning was made toward equal educational opportunities for all.

On January 3, 1962, leaders from Houston and the nation joined Houston political leader and entrepreneur Roy Hofheinz to dedicate the Harris County Domed Stadium, also called the "Eighth Wonder of the World." The first of the indoor stadiums, the structure was a record setting architectural achievement. Courtesy, Texas Room; Houston Public Library

Houston's Fat Stock Show, symbolized by western equipment and photographs of men performing in rodeos, has become one of the major rodeo and stock display events in the country. Since 1965 it has been held in the Astrodome. For many years before it was held in various open-air arenas around the city. It brings together great rodeo performers, fine stock, and a variety of animals raised for the event. Courtesy, Harris County Heritage Society

CHAPTER IX

REACH FOR THE STARS: HOUSTON, CITY OF THE FUTURE

The Lyndon B. Johnson Space Center in Houston controls the flights of spaceships that lift off from Cape Canaveral. Here we see the Columbia *taking off on its third flight. Courtesy, National Aeronautics and Space Administration*

Houston in 1960 was a city on the verge of enormous change. The village founded amidst so much travail by the Allen brothers could now claim a metropolitan population of 1,251,700. A $3-billion oil and petrochemical industry, along with a ship channel whose business reached $68 million in that same year, defined the economic character of the city.

On September 19, 1961, the most significant event in Houston's postwar development took place when James E. Webb of the National Aeronautics and Space Administration announced that the city had been designated as the site of a new space center that would serve as the hub of the nation's space exploration program. Houston had prevailed over the candidacy of some 20 other cities. The facility would be constructed on a tract of land at Clear Lake, 22 miles southeast of downtown Houston.

The fine art of politics "Texas style" could be seen in Houston's designation as the space center. Congressman Albert Thomas, longtime spokesman for the city, was chairman of the House Appropriations subcommittee, which controlled the funds of the National Aeronautics and Space Administration, and Lyndon Johnson was chairman of the National Space Committee. However, there were yet other reasons to explain why Houston was selected rather than Boston, Los Angeles, New Orleans, Dallas, and Jacksonville, Florida, all of which made presentations. The ship channel and port facilities could readily transport space hardware to the other main NASA location at Cape Canaveral, Florida, and Houston's tremendous industrial complex, which was responsible for roughly 38.6 percent of the country's oil tool production, 32 percent of its petroleum resources, and close to 75 percent of petrochemical manufacturing, was capable of supporting an aerospace center. The city, which has a temperate climate, also has several major research centers at Rice, the University of Houston, and the Texas Medical Center.

By the spring of 1962 work had begun at Clear Lake on the construction of the Spacecraft Center. Brown and Root, Incorpo-

Lyndon Johnson served as chairman of the National Space Committee when Clear Lake, located about 22 miles southeast of downtown Houston, was chosen as the site for a space center. From Cirker, Dictionary of American Portraits, *Dover, 1967*

rated, a leading Houston firm, was awarded the contract to build the main complex. Since the center would not be completed until 1964, NASA leased temporary facilities in Houston, which now acquired the appellation, "Space City, U.S.A." On July 4, 1962, the Chamber of Commerce staged a truly Texan welcome for the astronauts and their families as well as Robert R. Gilruth, director of the Manned Spacecraft Center, and Colonel John "Shorty" Powers, the "Voice of Mercury Control." Astronaut John Glenn, the first American to circle the earth, and Congressman Albert Thomas, without whom none of the festivities that day would have been possible, were also enthusiastically cheered. Thousands of Houstonians witnessed the Independence Day parade and were especially captivated by a Mercury spacecraft mounted on a long trailer.

On the evening of September 11, 1962, President John F. Kennedy arrived in Houston to personally inspect the facilities at the Manned Spacecraft Center. Obviously inspired by what he saw, he then proceeded to Rice Stadium for a planned address. There, before some 50,000 Houstonians, the young President sketched a bright future for the city and the nation. The city would reap benefits as scientists and engineers would be attracted to its environs. More than $200 million would be invested in plant equipment, and salaries amounting to more than $60 million annually would be paid out, and presumably spent, in Houston. Less than a month after Kennedy's speech, Astronaut Walter M. Shirra, Jr., flew an Atlas rocket on a six-orbit ride into space.

From the beginning NASA officials were anxious to establish cordial relations with the people of Houston. Upon request, speakers were quickly provided for school and college audiences, and a NASA spacemobile featuring displays of rockets and other space hardware was made available as an exhibit to any school that requested it. Gilruth understood the worth of favorable publicity and friendly local relations when seeking additional congressional appropriations for the Spacecraft Center.

Work continued on the Mercury, Gemini, and Apollo projects. Nine new astronauts were chosen to work with the original seven Mercury pilots, who would serve as senior officers on all prospective voyages. By the summer of 1964, the permanent center at Clear Lake had been completed on land originally donated by Rice Institute. Of the structures in the permanent complex, the Integrated Mission Control Center was the most important. From that site all prior preparations and flight operations would be controlled. Although "lift-offs" would continue from Cape Kennedy (formerly Cape Canaveral) in Florida, the missions, once airborne, would be directed from Houston.

After the successful Mercury and Gemini projects, the Manned Spacecraft Center prepared for the Apollo moon landing. One

On the southeast side of Houston the National Aeronautics and Space Administration has built a great complex of buildings, the Lyndon B. Johnson Space Center. From this complex the United States' space program is directed and control is maintained for the space missions. Courtesy, National Aeronautics and Space Administration

With the report, "Houston,
Eagle has landed," the U.S.
space crew of Armstrong and
Aldrin descended to the moon,
becoming the first to set foot on
another planetary body.
Controlled from Houston's
Johnson Space Center, the event
marked the beginning of a new
era for man. Courtesy, National
Aeronautics and Space
Administration

technician said of the air of excitement, "We work in a place where 13,000 men can feel like Columbus." On July 16, 1969, commander Neil Armstrong, pilot Michael Collins, and Edwin E. Aldrin, Jr., embarked on their historic adventure. The attention of the world was riveted on Cape Kennedy and the Manned Spacecraft Center at Houston when the flight began.

The long-anticipated departure to the moon went flawlessly. Apollo II, the command ship, completed 2.5 orbits around the earth and then started off toward the moon, more than 200,000 miles in the distance. Once in the moon's orbit, Armstrong and Aldrin transferred into a small lunar module attached to the nose of Apollo II, which separated from the mother ship. Then, after orbiting the moon to a predetermined position, they landed on the moon at 4:17 p.m. Eastern Daylight Time on July 20, 1969. After receiving permission from Mission Control Center in Houston, they buckled on their cumbersome space suits, opened the hatch, and prepared to step out on the surface of the moon.

More than any single factor since Spindletop in 1901, the presence of NASA in the greater Houston-Harris County area has been responsible for the city's continued growth. The University of Houston Bureau of Business Research forecast that the Spacecraft Center would attract 200,000 new residents within 20 years, and a Texas National Bank survey hazarded a guess that the population of Greater Houston would reach eight million in less than 50 years. In 1963 the Houston Chamber of Commerce published a study which concluded that the location of the Manned Spacecraft Center in Houston would commence an economic boom similar to the opening of the ship channel in 1916. Also, the city would escape an unhealthy dependence on the volatile oil-petrochemical industry while new capital was diverted to aerospace and electronic endeavors. In addition to studies and projections for the future, there were immediate results. More than one hundred aerospace firms with space-related contracts leased offices in Houston. Such well-known companies as McDonnell Aircraft, Grumman Aircraft, Lockheed, and Boeing all located in Houston as did General Electric and International Business Machines. Research grants, lavishly funded by the federal government, were awarded in 1962 to Rice Institute and the University of Houston for aerospace research, and by 1967 some $30 million was being spent annually in the city by NASA employees.

In the past several decades, Houston has truly become a 20th-century supercity, a space-age metropolis. Along with its tremendous success has come the challenge of accommodating this growth with up-to-date facilities and public services. The mayors of Houston have had to deal with problems in areas such as transportation and water supply while also handling continuing tasks, such as ameliorating ethnic and racial discrimination.

During the postwar boom Houston had only four mayors. After Oscar Holcombe and Roy Hofheinz came Lewis Cutrer (1958-1964) and Louie Welch (1964-1974). Cutrer, a native of Mississippi,

Fred Hofheinz, who was elected mayor of Houston in 1974, served until 1978, at which time he declined to run for reelection. He was a liberal mayor who was widely supported by the city's minorities.

As events associated with the national civil rights movement brought new attention to the problems of minorities, the Mexican-American community saw the development of its own political voice, the Raza Unida. This organization played an important role in the development of a political consciousness in Houston's Mexican-American community. Courtesy, Houston Metropolitan Research Center; Houston Public Library

prospered in Houston as a lawyer and businessman. Believed to be the spokesman of the conservative Houston business community, he confounded his critics by ending racial discrimination in all public building facilities in 1962. On behalf of the city, he also arranged for the purchase of land upon which the first jet field, Houston Intercontinental Airport, was ultimately built. He also blocked attempts on the part of some neighboring communities to annex lands in the path of the airport's expansion. His successor in office, Louie Welch, a successful automotive-parts dealer and real-estate speculator, had the common touch and seemed to genuinely enjoy the rough and tumble of a Houston political campaign. Certainly his most important accomplishment in office was guaranteeing Houston's water supply for the future. In 1964, over the concerted opposition of Dallas and Fort Worth, Welch signed an agreement with the Trinity River Authority that was later approved by Houston voters. This and the $200-million Lake Livingston project in 1973 assured Houston's industrial and residential expansion at a time when other cities were desperately seeking new supplies of water.

Houston politics took on a familiar appearance in the mid-1970s when Fred Hofheinz, son of the former mayor, was

elected to the city's highest office in 1974. Hofheinz, an intelligent man with an advanced degree in economics, professed decidedly liberal views and enjoyed the almost complete support of the black and Latin communities in Houston. In an attempt to inspire confidence in apprehensive business circles, Hofheinz was active in promoting Houston's business climate before Chamber of Commerce groups throughout the country.

Because he was receptive to the minority constituencies, Hofheinz was particularly sensitive to charges of police brutality. Although no civilian review board was created as urged by blacks and Mexican-Americans, there was a drive to recruit more police officers from among those groups. It was obvious that substantial additions to the police force were necessary because the crime rate had begun to escalate rapidly in the mid-1970s. With dubious distinction, Houston eased past both New York and Detroit as the "murder capital" of the United States. Short of supervisory manpower, the city was also woefully lacking in the facilities to adequately house prisoners.

During his term in office Mayor Fred Hofheinz continued to be opposed by some political factions in the city. He became the target of a smear campaign, and, having had his fill of local politics, declined to stand for

reelection. On November 22, 1978, Jim McConn, a local builder and former city councilman, defeated Frank Briscoe, who had served earlier as Harris County district attorney, in the contest for mayor.

The new urban executive faced myriad problems for which there were no easy solutions. According to the United States Census Bureau, Houston was the fastest-growing major city in the nation. Including surrounding metropolitan areas, its population was 2.5 million in 1979, making it the fifth-largest city in the country. The city itself expanded to more than 521 square miles, seven times its size after World War II. Such rapid growth placed a strain on municipal services and local government. In addition to the ever-upward homicide rate, Houston now ranked third in the nation in automobile fatalities. The streets were poorly main-

tained, and traffic jams assumed legendary proportions.

Responsibility for solving many of these problems lay with the City Council, which took on even greater importance. Black and Hispanic groups had long insisted that they enjoyed little if any voice in public policy-making. In response to pressure to make local government more representative, a new voting arrangement was instituted whereby 9 of the 14 Council members would be elected from designated geographical areas; previously all members had been elected at large. The new system made possible the election of four black or Mexican-American candidates, and Judson Robinson emerged on the Council as a leader of the black constituency and Ben Reyes as a spokesman for the Mexican-American group.

As the sense of identity of the Mexican-American community grew in the 1960s and 1970s, celebrations such as Cinco de Mayo assumed greater importance for the community. It drew individuals to centers such as Allen's Landing for celebrations of their Mexican heritage. Courtesy, Houston Metropolitan Research Center; Houston Public Library

The affable and easy-going Mayor Jim McConn faced a difficult campaign for reelection in 1979. It was alleged that he had pressured city contractors to provide funds for his campaign and that he had used such funds to satisfy his Las Vegas gambling debts. During the campaign it was revealed that the mayor's construction company was near bankruptcy, and confidence in McConn was further eroded. McConn was also faulted for his frequent trips outside the city and for inattention to the daily business of governing. Councilman Louis Macey, a persistent critic of the mayor, ran a strong campaign and on election day forced McConn into a runoff, but in the end McConn prevailed.

By 1980 Houston was attracting 1,000 new families a month to its environs. While a sign of vigorous expansion and a vital economy, traffic problems along the city's freeways became almost unmanageable. Accordingly, after an intense campaign backed by Mayor McConn and downtown business interests, city voters approved creation of the Metropolitan Transit Authority. It has since examined several proposals, including one for a subway system modelled on the ultra-modern Mexico City line.

Houstonians had a particular interest in the 1980 Presidential campaign. Vice-Presidential candidate George Bush, a native of Connecticut and graduate of Yale, had been a successful oilman in Houston before his interest turned to public service.

On November 17, 1981, Kathryn ("Kathy") Jean Whitmire was elected mayor of Houston. The first woman to hold that office, she had a background in accounting and had previously served as city controller, an elective position. From that vantage point she had been a consistent critic of Mayor McConn's financial practices and failure to live within the city budget. Mounting a disciplined campaign, Whitmire cut substantially into McConn's base of minority support. Surprisingly, Whitmire was also backed by many among the city's business elite who had grown disenchanted by the incumbent's financial difficulties. To dramatize her commitment to minority participation in city government, Whitmire named a black, Lee Brown, to head the city's police department.

In the decade of the 1980s, Houstonians seem to be increasingly concerned not so much with size, but with the quality of urban life. Concern for the rights of

Ben Reyes has been one of the leaders in the political development of the Mexican-American community in Houston since the 1960s. Courtesy, Houston Metropolitan Research Center; Houston Public Library

minorities has been increasingly manifested, and Houston's newest ethnic minority, the Vietnamese, have already begun to enter the mainstream of Houston's economic and educational life. Citizen interest in combatting the problems of pollution, snarled traffic, and an ever-increasing crime rate is at an all-time peak. Specific performance is expected of elected officials and the voters are quick to demand change if they do not see the promised results. Yet there has been no slack in the willingness of private and corporate interests to work to improve the tone of daily life.

The concern of Houstonians about their city is reflected in their efforts to retain its colorful past. The city and county have both been involved in the area of historic preservation. Founded in 1954, the Harris County Heritage Society is a "private, non-profit membership organization dedicated to preserving a segment of Houston's past." The society's major accomplishment has been the creation of Houston Park, an accredited outdoor museum. Within the park area can be found the Kellum-Noble House, built in 1847 and probably the oldest brick house in Houston, and St. John Church, constructed in 1891 by German farmers for their Evangelical Lutheran congregation. First located in northwest Harris County, the church, still containing its origi-

nal pulpit, was later moved to its present site. The "Long Row," a replica of Houston's first commercial building, constructed for the Allen Brothers in 1837, and the "Old Place," a cedar log cabin built on the west bank of Clear Creek and thought to be the oldest structure in Harris County, are also located in this unique outdoor museum. Thus, in the shadow of vibrant downtown Houston, are some gracious reminders of the city's more leisurely past.

While the Harris County Heritage Society has been the principal organization dedicated to the preservation of the area's past, other bodies have also been at work. In 1971 the Greater Houston Preservation Alliance was created to maintain or restore to their original form some of Houston's oldest and most interesting buildings. Aided by federal grants, the work of this agency is proceeding apace. Still another group, the Houston Oldtown Association, is interested in converting Market Square into a New Orleans French Quarter type of development. Located near Buffalo Bayou at the base of the original city, the restaurants and shops that constitute the Market Square locale make an interesting place for tourists to visit. Finally, the projected Houston Museum of History, when completely funded and constructed, will coordinate all of the above activities and add greatly to the retention of Houston's past.

Professional historians are also at work trying to document and explain the Bayou City's record. In 1974 the National Endowment for the Humanities awarded a $116,000 grant to be shared by the University of Houston, Texas Southern University, Rice University, and the Houston Public Library. This project, known as the Houston Metropolitan Archives and Research Center (HMARC), has as its mission the "organization of a program that would locate and preserve historical records relating to the development of the Houston area." Originally housed at Rice University, in the summer of 1976 the project was transferred to the Houston Public Library and came under the supervision of Director David Henington. A new division within the li-

Elected in 1981 as Houston's first woman mayor, Kathy Whitmire was faced with a city whose population growth was slowing down due to the national recession. The temporary ebb in Houston's growth has created new types of problems. Courtesy, Texas Room; Houston Public Library

With the move of the San Diego Rockets to Houston in 1972, the city had acquired major league athletic franchises in the three major sports. Almost always in contention, the Rockets, playing in the Summit, stand on the brink of another period of greatness led by the young Ralph Samson. Terry Teagle, former Baylor star, is one of the young players counted on to help rebuild the Rockets. Courtesy, Houston Rockets

brary was then organized, known as the Houston Metropolitan Research Center (HMRC). Based in the Julia Ideson Building, the Research Center seeks to collect the data of Houston's past. In this connection, private papers, manuscripts, and oral interviews with Houstonians from all walks of life are being assembled. A particular effort is being made to emphasize the historical contributions of Houston's black and Hispanic communities.

Almost 150 years ago, on April 21, 1836, the battle of San Jacinto was fought and Texas won its independence. The victorious commander, General Sam Houston, could have little inkling that his name would later grace one of the most dynamic cities of the 20th century. The 1980 census figures revealed that the state of Texas had 6.3 percent of the nation's population and accounted for 13 percent of its growth in the 1970s. During that decade, Texas expanded at a rate more than double the national average, second only to Florida among the 50 states. Within the boundaries of the Lone Star State, Houston outpaced Dallas and San Antonio to become the fifth-largest city in the nation. If current trends persist and the migration from the Northeast and Midwest to the "Sunbelt" states continues, Houston will become even larger. Houston's role in the exploration of space is symbolic of its orientation toward the future—a future made possible by the willingness of its citizens to give of their time and resources. Although perhaps unknown today, the counterparts of William Marsh Rice, Jesse Jones, George Hermann, and Monroe Anderson stand ready to help in the future.

Jeff McKissack's "The Orange Show" is a unique museum assembled as a tribute to the orange by its originator over many years of individual work. In many respects, it is a perfect example of modern Houston Folk Art, combining mechanical and still exhibits in a unique celebration of the orange. Courtesy, Texas Room; Houston Public Library

THE ORANGE SHOW

Modern Houston's downtown is a contrast of skyscrapers in the International style and 19th-century historic buildings preserved in Sam Houston Park by the Harris County Heritage Society. The 1908 statue, Spirit of the Confederacy, is in the foreground. Photo by Story Sloane III, Harris County Heritage Society

Far right:
At the entrance to Hermann Park, the statue of Sam Houston serves as a symbol of the city and of its ties to the founder of the Republic. The park, established in 1925 as the result of a gift to the city from George Hermann shortly before his death, is one of Houston's major parks and an example of the tradition of private giving typical in the city. Photo by Story Sloane III, Harris County Heritage Society

Right:
Made in Troy, New York, the Scanlan Fountain was shipped to Houston and placed in front of the home of Timothy Scanlan, Reconstruction mayor of the city. Gracing the front of this mansion on South Main for many years, the fountain was finally moved to Sam Houston Park after the Scanlan home was torn down. Courtesy, Harris County Heritage Society

Built in an area annexed to Houston in the 20th century, St. John Church is typical of the small rural churches that dotted the Texas countryside in the second half of the 19th century and early 20th century. Home of a German-speaking Evangelical Lutheran congregation drawn from neighboring farms, the church reminds modern Houstonians that Harris County has been a rural area for much of its history, despite the presence of a major urban center as early as 1836. Courtesy, Harris County Heritage Society

Shadowing the 1868 San Felipe Cottage, a modest urban residence preserved in downtown Houston, are the modern skyscrapers of 1983 Houston. Springing up from behind the cottage are two Philip Johnson buildings, the Republic Bank Center still under construction, and, almost hidden behind it, the angular Pennzoil Place, which marked the beginning of the end of the International style in Houston and the beginning of the collaboration between Johnson and Gerald Hines. Behind both is I.M. Pei's 75-story Texas Commerce Bank Building. Courtesy, Harris County Heritage Society

Nationally famous Rice University, first known as Rice Institute, began operations in 1912 with a substantial endowment left by William Marsh Rice. Rice had wanted Houston to have a university "dedicated to the advancement of art, literature and science."

Above:
The mounted police patrol may be seen in Houston's parks and the downtown area and at parades and festivals. The unit is a part of the modern traditions of Houston. Photo by Story J. Sloane III, Harris County Heritage Society

Right:
In 1908 the local chapter of the Daughters of the Confederacy unveiled L. Amateis' monument, The Spirit of the Confederacy, in Sam Houston Park. Produced in the fashionable art nouveau manner, it is one of the earlier pieces of public sculpture in Houston. Courtesy, Harris County Heritage Society

For Houstonians summer is often a dash between one air-conditioned space and another. Yet, on occasion, residents picnic in the parks, celebrating national and state holidays in spite of the heat and humidity of the Houston summer. Photo by Story J. Sloane III, Harris County Heritage Society

In the 1970s, Houston football came of age in the NFL with the arrival of Earl Campbell. The great running back gave the Houston Oilers a new offense that took them to the NFL playoffs. More important, Campbell became a symbol of the best in professional athletics, playing a role in providing leadership for the community. Courtesy, Houston Oilers

The Houston Ship Channel accommodates vessels the size of the one in the foreground and large tankers that come to the city's refineries and petroleum storage terminals.

The Port of Houston is the busiest port in the Southwest.

Many of Houston's residents enjoy participating in outdoor recreational activities such as horseback riding.

Bluebonnets lining one of Houston's roads add a splash of color to the landscape.

A full moon hangs over the Houston skyline of 1971, a skyline that has undergone many changes as the city has developed. In the 1980s Houston stands as one of America's fastest growing cities.

CHAPTER X
PARTNERS IN PROGRESS

History—by its nature—is a look back, whereby past events are arranged—sometimes emphasized—in due order. Often these events hold a clue to the future. Such is the case in Houston's business world.

The community was established for land speculation by Augustus C. Allen and his brother, John K. Allen, after they paid $1,000 down and notes totaling $4,000 to Elizabeth E. Parrott (widow of John Austin and wife of T.F.L. Parrott) for the lower league granted to her by her late husband. The tract was situated on a waterway—now known around the world as the Houston Ship Channel—that would play a vital role in the development of Houston into one of the world's most vibrant business communities.

The Allen brothers, in an advertisement in the *Telegraph and Texas Register* on August 30, 1836, noted that their new town was located on the west bank of Buffalo Bayou at "a point which must ever command the trade of the largest and richest portion of Texas. As the country shall improve, railroads will become in use, and will be extended from this point to the Brazos [River], and up the same, also from this up to the head waters of the San Jacinto River, embracing that rich country, and in a few years the whole trade of the upper Brazos will make its way into Galveston Bay through this channel.

"The town of Houston must be the place where arms, ammunition, and provisions for the government will be stored, because, situated in the very heart of the country, it combines security and the means of easy distribution, and a natural armory will no doubt very soon be established at this point."

Today the Port of Houston is the third largest port in the United States. And the city has become the energy capital of the world; thanks to rich resources and the port, tremendous volumes of crude oil flow into and out of the area.

In the early 1970s another tag was placed on Houston: "International City." Due to the energy crisis, the big petrochemical complex on the ship channel, and low real estate prices, the city became a favorite of world investors—especially those from England, Canada, West Germany, Mexico, and several South American and Middle Eastern countries.

From the first years of Houston's founding, those involved in "trade," our current-day merchants, have held a major influence in the city's commercial devlopment. Until 1875 the general pattern of trade was much the same—merchants exchanged a variety of goods for the products of the countryside. However, by the early 1900s an improved transportation network allowed trade to be conducted at greater distances.

Houston's development has been unique. Perhaps because it is a relatively young city, and an affluent one, it is receptive to new ideas and new undertakings. For example, Houston is a showcase for the best modern architecture of the 1970s. In 1979 the city became the first in the United States to issue more than one billion dollars in building permits.

Much of this growth has been led by Houston's real estate industry, an industry deeply involved in helping to develop such landmarks as the Harris County Domed Stadium, the Manned Spacecraft Center, the Houston Medical Center, and the Houston Ship Channel.

The organizations you will meet on the following pages have chosen to support this important civic event. They are representative of the businesses that have helped make Houston the "International City" with the talent, skills, and determination that are the lifeblood of a thriving community.

HARRIS COUNTY HISTORICAL SOCIETY

"San Jacinto, fought 21 years after Waterloo, was the 16th decisive battle of the world. It wrought the independence of Texas and opened the way to the Pacific."

—Clarence R. Wharton, in "The Isle of Mal Hado"

The Harris County Historical Society was founded October 2, 1923, on the 88th anniversary of the Battle of Gonzales, where Anglo-Texan colonists leveled on Mexican dragoons and fired the first shot of the Texas war for independence.

A son of Sam Houston, Colonel Andrew Jackson Houston, was elected first president of the Society. Other officers were Mrs. Adele Briscoe Looscan, an outstanding historian, honorary president; Clarence R. Wharton, Sam Houston Dixon, Mrs. I.B. McFarland, and Mrs. Florence Hoover, vice-presidents; A.G. Mallison, secretary/treasurer; and Miss Julia Ideson, custodian of records.

Mrs. Adele Briscoe Looscan (1848-1935) was an honorary life president of the Harris County Historical Society.

Among the founders were sons, daughters, and grandchildren of signers of the Texas Declaration of Independence or veterans of San Jacinto, who had detailed knowledge of historic events. They organized to share their knowledge and impart their belief in a destiny of greatness for Houston.

Officially, the Society's purpose is stated in the charter issued it by the state of Texas in 1939: "historical, literary, and educational, namely the discovery, collection, preservation, and publication of historical records and data relating to Harris County, Texas."

Sixty years after its founding, the Society remains on the course established by its charter. It offers a rallying ground to the history-minded and those who have written, or aspire to write, on local or sectional history. The meeting place becomes a clearinghouse of ideas. Members are encouraged to report discoveries of endangered historic records so that possibilities of preservation may be explored.

One member's report led to an agreement with a church more than 100 years old, permitting the Society to copy the earliest birth, marriage, and death records of the church on microfilm and place the film in the public library.

The Society has sponsored the publication of books and pamphlets, joined in recording oral history and popular Texas music of the past, funded portrait restoration, encouraged teaching of Texas history, and intervened in public proposals to alter the names and uses of historic roads and sites.

At monthly meetings from October to June, it presents qualified speakers on subjects of interest or concern to the membership. The Society maintains close contact with the Houston Public Library and Houston Metropolitan Archives and cooperates with other historical organizations. It has acted as co-host of several state historical groups and is supported by the dues of its members.

—Edgar E. Lackner, member, board of directors, Harris County Historical Society.

Colonel Andrew Jackson Houston, a son of Sam Houston, was the first president of the Harris County Historical Society. (Courtesy of the Houston Public Library.)

FISK ELECTRIC COMPANY

J.R. Fisk, founder of the Fisk Electric Company.

Twenty-one-year-old John R. Fisk, fascinated with electrical lighting, knew there were many unknowns in the then-infant industry in 1913. But like many successful businessmen before him, Fisk was not afraid to venture into untried areas when an opportunity held promise.

Although only 19 percent of electrical equipment was being manufactured in the United States in 1913, there were indications of big changes ahead. A researcher, William D. Coolidge, had just received a patent for his method of using high temperatures to draw tungsten into fine filaments. These long-burning filaments replaced the Swan-Edison carbon units used previously.

It also was the year that Fisk decided to start an electrical service company in his

father's backyard, a move that was to make the young man, already tall in stature at six foot, five inches, a major factor in the business world. Today many of Houston's skyscrapers are lighted due to the efforts of the organization Fisk founded.

In the early 1920s Fisk Electric, with a staff of 20 persons, moved to new facilities across from the Southern Pacific Railroad station. Fisk was especially proud of his part during the next decade of helping modernize the old Humble Building downtown, and the wiring of many of the mansions in the River Oaks section of Houston. However, his most treasured and memorable electrical project was the wiring of the San Jacinto Monument, which was dedicated in 1936 in observance of the Texas Centennial.

From the Southern Pacific site, Fisk Electric next moved in 1933 into a two-story structure in the 3100 block of Milam Street, next door to a live-poultry establishment. Fisk gradually acquired all of the property in the block.

The company incorporated under Texas laws in 1931, and continued to expand its scope of operations along with the growth of Houston. Many wartime contracts were filled in the 1940s, and the building boom that began soon after World War II is still going on.

Fisk died in December 1954 but his philosophies have been carried out by management since. The firm has

experienced fantastic growth since that time, success many in the business credit to his wife, Ila Morgan Fisk, board chairman until her death in 1971. Their nephew, Lloyd Davis, is current president and board chairman. Fisk Electric now employs more than 1,500 people in operations in Houston, Dallas, New Orleans, Baton Rouge, San Antonio, Saudi Arabia, and Egypt.

Among the organization's projects are the Harris County Domed Stadium, Bank of the Southwest Tower, Pennzoil Building, One Shell Plaza, Texas Commerce Tower, First International Plaza, First City Tower, Marathon Oil Building, and Houston Centers I-II-III.

Since the firm was founded some 70 years ago, executives at Fisk have not been afraid to try new ventures. In 1971, for example, the company formed Fisk Telephone Systems to take advantage of a Federal Communications Commission ruling that customer-owned telephone equipment could be connected to major telephone networks. After establishing itself in the interconnect business, Fisk then sold the operation to Centel Business Systems. In August 1982 Fisk Electric was acquired by William Press Group of London, England. These are other examples of the right moves at the right time.

Headquarters of Fisk Electric Company—111 T.C. Jester at the corner of Washington Avenue.

SAKOWITZ

At the turn of the century Galveston was the main fashion and cultural center of Texas. But disaster struck in 1900, when the island was hit by a hurricane that killed thousands of people and destroyed most businesses. One such business was owned by Louis Sakowitz, a Russian immigrant.

After the storm two of his sons, Tobias and Simon, went to work for other Galveston merchants and by 1902 they had saved some $2,000. Although their father reopened his ship's chandlery, which catered to the needs of merchant seamen, the two brothers decided to open their own gentlemen's haberdashery on Market Street.

Before long, Tobias and Simon were casting an eye toward expansion, and a second store was opened in Houston—a city many folks were beginning to say could someday be larger than Galveston. Simon headed for Houston to run the store, Sakowitz Brothers, at 308 Main Street.

In 1917 the Houston store was expanded to include the corner at Preston Avenue, the store in Galveston was

---

The interior of the first Sakowitz store in Houston, 308 Main Street. Tobias Sakowitz is on the left behind the counter and Simon Sakowitz is at far right. The photo was taken in 1910.

---

closed, and Tobias moved his family to Houston in an old Reo to help his brother. During the 1920s Sakowitz became a prominent name in retailing, and in 1929 another major expansion took place when the company moved into six levels of a new 35-story structure built by Jesse Jones, a leading citizen, at the corner of Main and Rusk.

Expansion has not stopped since. The firm now operates major Texas stores, shops, and boutiques in Houston, Dallas, Midland, Amarillo, and in Scottsdale, Arizona, and is scheduled to open new stores in San Antonio and Tulsa, Oklahoma, in February 1984.

And, during all of this growth, management at Sakowitz has remained a family business. Simon died in 1966 at the age of 82, active in the firm's operation until the last week of his life. Tobias died at the age of 88 in 1970. Management reins had long since been assumed by Bernard Sakowitz, son of Tobias, who had entered the business in 1929, expanded the merchandise lines, and diversified the fashion specialties, and was active as president until 1975 and as chairman of the board until his death in 1981.

Today the company is headed by Robert T. Sakowitz, son of Bernard, making it the last privately held fashion specialty merchandiser of any appreciable size in the United States that is still totally

owned and operated by the founding family.

Mr. Sakowitz notes that while the company has grown from a single unit to a multi-store operation, "we have still maintained a small-store philosophy as reflected not only in the larger stores but in our small shops and boutiques."

Sakowitz launched the first French couturier (Courreges) boutique in America, was the first to market the Yves St. Laurent Rive Gauche line in free-standing boutiques in Houston and Dallas, and innovated other concepts such as Fiorucci, Sakowitz' Wine Auctions in-store, annual theme festivals, and the world-renowned *Sakowitz' Christmas Catalog* highlighting Ultimate Gifts.

The Gulf Building, at 720 Main Street, was the home of Sakowitz from 1929 to 1951.

Three generations involved with Sakowitz are Tobias Sakowitz (seated), his son Bernard (standing at left), and grandson, Robert T. (standing at right).

SPAW-GLASS INC.

Spaw-Glass Inc. has completed numerous contracts involving restoration of existing structures, the largest being the Hogg Building (shown here).

Alabama-born T.F. Glass, Jr., new to Houston in 1937, was faced with a decision of where to sit as he walked into calculus class at Rice University. Little did he know at the time that it would be one of the most important decisions of his life.

Officially, Houston's Spaw-Glass Inc. was formed on February 3, 1953, in a one-room office on Times Boulevard in the Village. Unofficially, association of the two principals began as Glass settled down into his seat in class with Louis D. Spaw, Jr., and Frances Chapman.

Glass married Miss Chapman and Spaw also met and married Wanda Hoencke while at Rice. Some years later they became business partners when they formed the construction company with assets of two mortgaged cars, two mortgaged houses, $27,000 in borrowed cash, six stockholders, and no contracts. Presently, Glass is chairman of the board

and Spaw serves as the president of the Top 400 construction firm.

On March 23, 1953, the new firm landed its first job—$1,100 to remodel a residence in Bellaire. That contract is still on display in the firm's corporate offices. By the end of that first year the business had completed a volume of $512,013 and was able to show a small profit.

The company's first money loser came the second year on a $447.50 contract to build a Little League grandstand. The job lost $3.75. Also in the early years some residential work was performed, including 62 FHA-insured residences and 10 private homes.

Since that time Spaw-Glass Inc. has served as general contractor on hundreds of structures, including office buildings, schools, hospitals, clinics, high-rise apartment buildings, wharves, parking garages, and other types of projects such as the one-million-square-foot Albert Thomas Convention and Exhibit Center, the firm's largest undertaking to date. In 1968 Spaw-Glass received a contract to

build Miller Outdoor Theatre, a "Cor-Ten" steel job, a difficult one both to estimate and to build.

In 1982 total contracts under way by all Spaw-Glass Inc. divisions, subsidiaries, and joint ventures exceeded $360 million. Diversified construction contracts included four million square feet of office space, three hotels, three condominiums, several schools and hospitals, and retail stores within large area malls.

The corporation also has completed numerous contracts involving the rehabilitation and restoration of existing structures. The largest of these is the Hogg Building, actually three adjoining facilities, erected by William Clifford Hogg in 1921. Two other such projects are the Kiam Building and the 1907 Republic Building, a classic example of early 20th-century Chicago School architecture. The five-story Kiam Building was one of Houston's first skyscrapers when constructed in 1893 and contained the first electric elevator west of the Mississippi River. The Kiam, Hogg, and Republic structures are listed on the National Register of Historic Places.

Concorde Tower, a 22-story downtown office building with 502,000 square feet of office space, was built by Spaw-Glass Inc. for owner/developer Realand U.S.A.

WILLIAMS BROTHERS CONSTRUCTION COMPANY

It's only right that Williams Brothers Construction Company should be headquartered almost under a freeway overpass bridge on the outskirts of Houston's downtown core. For Williams Brothers and freeway bridges seem to go together.

Even its headquarters building, a two-story Federal-style structure, reflects Williams Brothers' business philosophy that all employees—from top officers to part-time workers—are part of the same corporate family. The building, which has oil paintings by board chairman Claude Kress Williams, could easily be taken for someone's residence in another location.

Low employee turnover has been and will continue to be a key factor at Williams Brothers, says James D. Pitcock, Jr., president, who tries to visit job sites as much as possible. Pitcock, in a style of management somewhat unique for a firm with 700 employees, has job superintendents report directly to him. Absence of a general superintendent is unusual in the construction industry.

The construction of this bridge over the Ship Channel is a Williams Brothers' project.

The company was started as a new venture in 1955 by Claude Kress Williams and John Kress Williams, members of the well-known Kress Stores family. The brothers moved to Houston from Long Island, New York. Pitcock, then employed by the Houston construction firm of Farnsworth & Chambers for the previous five years, with a degree in civil engineering from Texas A&M University, was enlisted to assist the brothers in establishing the firm.

A Houston freeway under construction—another Williams Brothers undertaking during the 1960s.

Originally, each brother retained 45 percent of the corporation and Pitcock held 10 percent. However, in the late 1950s, ownership was restructured so that each of the principals held one-third of the company. Subsequently, in 1964, John Kress Williams' interest was bought out; thus the remaining two men now each own 50 percent of the corporation.

Other officers include Ray Haley, vice-president, and Astrid Matfield, secretary/treasurer.

The headquarters facility and much of the equipment used by the firm is owned by a partnership consisting of Pitcock and Williams and is leased to the corporation. Pitcock is the chief operating officer.

Until 1977, Williams Brothers was involved principally in bridge building and earth moving on public-sector construction work in and near the Houston area. In that year, however, the Texas legislature significantly increased its already inadequate highway budget in response to the extraordinary growth that had been taking place throughout the region.

Many contractors, such as Williams Brothers, could not keep up with the volume of jobs being let with the equipment on hand. Pitcock, with the help of a $5-million loan from Citibank of New York, purchased $15 million worth of new equipment over the following few years, which permitted the firm to broaden its operations into the paving, concrete, sand, and gravel business.

On May 1, 1978, Williams Brothers acquired all of the outstanding stock of Jack Cogbill Inc., a trucking company.

That subsidiary now derives about 80 percent of its total revenue from trucking operations for Williams Brothers and about 20 percent from such operations for others.

As the company has grown in capabilities, it has been less involved in joint venturing projects and currently handles most of its projects by itself.

While the Williams Brothers headquarters in the 3800 block of Milam also has served as the job office in the past (mainly because some 90 percent of its business was in the Houston area), the firm in recent years has established a significant presence in Louisiana, opening offices in Baton Rouge and Rayne. Today approximately 25 percent of Williams Brothers business is in Louisiana.

Top management has taken several steps to retain the close relationship among key personnel that has prevailed through the years, including weekly meetings with all supervisors, two-way radio systems in all offices and about 200 vehicles (three systems, four frequencies), and Pitcock's normal practice of visiting each site within the area and keeping close communication with all elements of the business.

Among other properties used by the company are a sand production plant in Humble, two paint shops, six concrete plants scattered around Houston, and a hot-mix plant at the edge of Houston's

A Williams Brothers' bridge project on State Highway 87 between Sabine Pass and Port Arthur.

central district.

Williams Brothers, the country's fifth largest federal aid highway contractor, is a major bridge builder. Its primary customers are the Department of Highways and Public Transportation for the state of Texas in the two counties of Harris and Brazoria.

James D. Pitcock, Jr., is nationally recognized as an authority on highway construction and funding problems and has been involved at both the state and national levels of the Associated General Contractors of America (AGC) and is scheduled to become national president in 1984. His other industry-community activities include active participation in the Texas Good Roads/Transportation Association, the American Road Builders' Association, and on the Houston Chamber of Commerce's Transportation Committee. In 1970 he was appointed by Governor Preston Smith to a six-year term as a member of the State Board of Registration for Professional Engineers; in 1976 he was appointed by President Gerald Ford as a public member of the National Transportation Study Committee; in 1978 he was appointed as a member of the Texas Deepwater Port Authority by Governor Dolph Briscoe; and in 1980 he was appointed as a member of the Texas 2000 Commission by Governor Bill Clements.

The Williams Brothers Construction Company was the contractor for this bridge spanning the Mississippi River at Luling, Louisiana.

COOPER INDUSTRIES

Charles Cooper, sitting on a hill overlooking Zanesville, Ohio, had reached an emotional nadir. His father had died some months before and along with his brother, Elias, he had to leave the family farm at Mt. Vernon, Ohio, to eke out a living digging and hauling coal.

It was the summer of 1833 as Cooper looked down from his hilltop resting spot at the smoke drifting from the Old David Foundry chimney. Suddenly he jumped to his feet. "Foundry"—the word was never far from Cooper's thoughts during the remainder of his life. What happened next would dizzy any of today's money dealers.

As Cooper recalled many years later, "I sold one of my three horses for $50 and took one of Brown's notes payable in coal for that amount delivered in Zanesville. I sold that note to Cose & Co. paper mill men, and their note for the same payable in paper at wholesale. This note I took to Granville, Licking County, and traded to P.A. Taylor & Co., blast furnace men, for the bottom and staves for our first cupola to melt iron in."

Financing out of the way, the two brothers moved back to Mt. Vernon to set up their foundry in the northwest corner of town. Charles and Elias, along with a horse, constituted the entire work force.

The horse, harnessed to a system of wooden shafts and gears, walked a circle to generate enough power to blow air into the cupola. The Cooper brothers carried iron, cleaned ladles, and charged the furnace by hand, producing from 500 to 700 pounds of metal in an afternoon. Their products included maple syrup kettles, plows, stoves, sorghum grinders, mill irons, and wagon boxes. From such beginnings developed Cooper Industries, today a diversified manufacturing firm with revenues of some $3 billion.

By 1842 the Cooper brothers were producing and selling carding machines and special power machinery as well as plows and other items. They soon expanded to a two-story machine shop. Then the railroad came.

Like many towns, Mt. Vernon benefited from the arrival of the railroad. In Cooper's case, the immediate boost came from transportation links to the steel

In 1833 Charles Cooper (shown here) founded the C. & G. Cooper Co., forerunner of today's Cooper Industries, together with his brother Elias.

industry. Many of the firm's "blowing engines" were shipped to Ohio's Hanging Rock District, where 60-foot-high furnaces were chiseled out of solid rock or constructed of heavy stone masonry. Some of the engines continued to operate for over a half-century.

The company built a wood-burning locomotive, the first manufactured west of the Allegheny Mountains, in 1853. It built and sold its first Corliss engines, with patented oscillating valves that permitted full bursts of pressure and steady speeds, in 1869. The engines were huge. Some had

pistons measuring seven feet in diameter.

The Cooper traction engine appeared in 1875. It applied power from the steam engine to the vehicle's own wheels. Although most people would call it a traction engine for years afterwards, it was America's first farm tractor.

The corporation moved into the 20th century, reeling from the blows of a general business downturn, not the first such economic downcycle faced by Cooper. This time the surge of vitality came from below the surface. Natural gas was being discovered in new fields around the country and shipped through pipelines; an entire new industry was developing. Cooper officials decided to become involved.

In 1909 the company's first natural gas engine-compressor combination was installed on a short pipeline in West Virginia. A complicated horizontal two-cylinder machine, it had such slow action that one Cooper salesman said the piston "goes out today and comes back tomorrow." However, the machine provided long service, and just as important, initiated an even longer relationship between Cooper and the new energy industry.

One of Cooper Industries' early portable engines, manufactured in 1870, was purchased from a Missouri farmer in 1954 and returned to Mt. Vernon, Ohio, where it is maintained by Cooper.

Cooper joined forces with the Bessemer Gas Engine Company in the late 1920s. Cooper needed additional production units to meet the demand for large natural gas engine-compressor engines. Bessemer, having stretched its fiscal capabilities in extensive diesel development, was in need of new capital. By 1929 Cooper had 33 buildings and 765 employees. Bessemer had 29 buildings, including one of the world's largest industrial plant foundries, and 1,180 employees. The merger made Cooper-Bessemer the largest builder of gas engines and compressors in America.

During the following years Cooper continued to expand both internally and by acquisition. Cooper diversified into the manufacture of hand tools with the acquisition of Lufkin Rule Company in 1967. Since then, Lufkin® has been joined by seven other well-known hand tool brand names.

To reflect the decision to broaden the company's product offerings, Cooper-Bessemer changed its name to Cooper Industries in 1965. Two years later and some 130 years after the Cooper brothers founded the firm in Mt. Vernon, it was decided to move the corporate headquarters to Houston.

Major changes in the recent past have been the acquisition of Gardner-Denver (1979) and Kirsch and Crouse-Hinds (1981). Five months before Cooper acquired Crouse-Hinds, that firm had acquired the Belden Corporation.

The acquisition of Gardner-Denver expanded Cooper's presence in the energy

This blowing engine, produced in Mt. Vernon, Ohio, had to be taken to a plant in Columbus for assembly because of its height. This crew of more than 200 Cooper employees did the job in 1907. Later, a building extension in Mt. Vernon made it possible to assemble the giant engines there.

industry. The firm, in addition to manufacturing compression equipment, became a producer of drilling equipment such as mud pumps, swivels, rotary tables, draw works, mud-handling equipment, instrumentation, and more.

The acquisition of Kirsch, a manufacturer of drapery hardware,

The first Corliss steam engine produced by Cooper began a new manufacturing era for the company.

expanded Cooper's position in the tools and hardware markets. The acquisition of Crouse-Hinds and Belden put Cooper into the market of electrical and electronic products, an entirely new area for the business.

Robert Cizik, president, chief executive officer, and chairman of the board, notes that the firm's size and scope have changed dramatically. In a single decade, Cooper Industries has grown from essentially a one-product company to a diversified corporation in three lines of business: compression and drilling equipment, tools and hardware, and electrical and electronic products.

STEWART & STEVENSON SERVICES, INC.

Stewart & Stevenson Services, Inc., from its first moments, was geared toward horsepower. And, from the beginning, it was a class operation.

In 1903 two young Texas craftsmen decided to pool their talents and resources to form a blacksmith and carriage-making business to be known as C. Jim Stewart & Stevenson. C. Jim Stewart would handle the blacksmithing and J.R. Stevenson would perform the carriage and wood-work. Each would invest $300 to get the partnership started.

They began their venture near the banks of the muddy Buffalo Bayou in Houston, and when they opened their doors they offered customers the first "horse-shoeing parlor" in the community, where "horseshoeing is carefully executed."

The basic philosophy of the two men was simple: hard work, integrity, and a dogged determination to get the job done right, even when others said it could not be done. Such principles were clearly defined in the original partnership agreement, which noted that "C.J. Stewart shall do the general blacksmith work connected with said business and said Joe R. Stevenson shall do woodwork, but both shall do such things in and about said business which shall be necessary."

During the first two years, the horse-and-buggy business went well for the partners (J.R. Stevenson always referred to the two men as "pardners") and their cooperative craftsmanship earned them a

By 1916 the Stewart & Stevenson carriage and blacksmith shop had added automobile repair to its services.

rapidly growing business. Soon they became dealers and manufacturers of fine wagons and were adding other craftsmen to help with the ever-increasing work load.

By 1905 the firm enjoyed an enviable reputation in Houston, and it was this reputation that earned the partners their first job on a horseless carriage—a badly burned Dixie Flyer. Damage to the vehicle was so extensive that a new handcrafted, wooden, four-door body was created and installed. It was the beginning of the transition from horseshoes to horsepower for the company.

The horse-and-buggy days began to fade rapidly as a steady stream of motorized vehicles—autos, trucks, and buses—

The interior of the Stewart & Stevenson carriage and blacksmith shop in 1903.

appeared on the scene. Stewart & Stevenson often was called upon to modify and service various types of vehicles for a variety of applications.

As the business grew, so did the need for additional craftsmen. The two partners always made sure that the people they hired were not only experts in their fields, but also were willing to pitch in and help wherever needed. While Stewart died in 1938 and Stevenson died in 1953, that simple hiring guideline still serves the company today, some three-quarters of a century later.

The firm decided to venture further into the power business in 1938. It was a move that kicked off a tremendous growth

Employees of Stewart & Stevenson about to embark for their annual picnic back in the 1920s.

sold a few marine propulsion engines for shrimp boats and small tugs along the Texas coast.

With the coming of World War II a few years later, Stewart & Stevenson found itself in the position of having to switch from selling engines commercially to doing business with the federal government. The firm was restricted to selling its diesel products to aid the war effort. It was at this time that Stewart & Stevenson initiated its policy of searching for innovative ideas and finding better ways to apply diesel engines to various needs.

The company's first contract with the government was for 35 mobile diesel generator sets, which had to be capable of running on Russian M-4 heavy fuel. The consistency of this fuel appeared to be similar to SAE 90 transmission oil, except that when it was cold it took on a waxy appearance and feel.

To obtain the contract, Stewart & Stevenson had to guarantee the capability of the diesel generator set (which it would assemble, utilizing a basic GM Detroit Diesel engine), a generator purchased from another firm, a base fabricated by Stewart & Stevenson, and other hardware manufactured by the company to put the generator set together and mount it in an insulated trailer. Detroit Diesel told Stewart & Stevenson that the model M-7 engines it planned to use on the project would not burn the heavy Russian fuel

surge for Stewart & Stevenson.

General Motors was introducing a new, untried diesel engine that defied virtually every "accepted" principle of the time, and GM was looking for companies with solid service backgrounds that could help market the engine. Stewart & Stevenson applied for and was granted a franchise to distribute this new "Series 71" GM diesel.

The business philosophy for this new diesel engine distributorship would be to analyze the customer's needs and to provide a complete engine-driven job on a "turnkey" basis, with one single responsibility.

The move by Stewart & Stevenson came at a time when farmers were seeking to expand agricultural operations in the

In the early 1920s the firm sold and modified trucks, one of which is shown on its way through downtown Houston.

Houston-Galveston areas. The firm's Engine Division, as the diesel distributorship was called, sold a large number of the engines to rice farmers, cotton growers, lumber mills, and other small power users.

The company started out selling the engines in about the same configuration in which it purchased them from Detroit Diesel: to rice farmers for powering irrigation pumps; to cotton ginners for powering cotton gins; to canning plants in the Rio Grande Valley; and to cafes, movie houses, and tourist courts for prime power generation. In addition, the firm

219

and that there was no way to process the fuel to make it suitable for such an operation.

Stewart & Stevenson, in turn, held the position that the engine would burn any fuel it could get into the cylinder. The firm recognized that operation at extremely cold temperatures would make it difficult to handle heavy fuel. However, the company modified the engines, utilizing an edge-type duplex fuel filter and a simple heater and boiler to circulate hot water through the engines during a pre-start period in extremely low temperatures, and installed a fuel tank in the base of the unit, with provisions for exhaust from the engine to be bypassed through exhaust heaters in the tank to heat the heavy fuel.

The arrangement was extremely successful, resulting in an additional order for 50 similar units, a later order for 350 large GM Detroit Diesel-powered units, and then an order for 500 more.

Later, during World War II, when Detroit Diesel had been given responsibility by the government to remanufacture approximately 4,000 General Sherman tanks, Stewart & Stevenson was asked by Detroit Diesel to take on the manufacture of these 4,000 engines as a subcontractor to the Detroit firm.

Stewart & Stevenson, already overloaded with war work and with no facilities at the time to undertake the project, declined the offer. Detroit Diesel was persistent, refusing to take "no" for an answer. Finally, the Houston firm said it would give the project a try.

During the Berlin airlift in 1948-49 these Stewart & Stevenson/General Motors-powered 250-kilowatt generator sets were loaded on a C-131 aircraft for transport to Ramsden Air Force Base in Germany.

The plan was to have a facility thrown together at the firm's Harrisburg property within 90 days. The price tag would be some $1,900 per pair of 6-71 engines. Detroit Diesel argued that the figure was too low, and that the Houston firm should increase the price to the government.

Stewart & Stevenson rejected the suggested price increase and began to remanufacture the engines at a rate of 40 per day, virtually unheard of at that time. After the contract was completed, Stewart & Stevenson returned some one million dollars to the federal government which it felt was excess profit on the project.

In the mid-1940s this Stewart & Stevenson engine was in use at an East Texas sawmill.

During the war thousands of engines were remanufactured for use in tanks and jeeps, and thousands of generator sets were built to provide electric power in military camps, radar installations, and other locations where regular electric power was not available or had been bombed out. Those engines and generator sets came from Houston.

At the end of the war the Engine Division of C. Jim Stewart & Stevenson had grown to such proportions that it was decided to split the division from the parent corporation. It became a separate company called Stewart & Stevenson Services, Inc.

To develop sufficient peacetime business and also to maintain the size of the wartime organization was no small chore for Stewart & Stevenson. The firm did what it always had done when needed—it developed many "firsts" in the field of diesel power.

During the early 1950s Stewart & Stevenson developed a 45-kilowatt precise-power diesel generator set, using a Detroit Diesel basic engine for operation at its rated load, under conditions of

10,000-foot elevation with a very critical weight requirement.

To do this required modification of the model 3-71 GM Detroit Diesel engine, inasmuch as the standard engine would not produce the 45-kilowatt rating under the requirements of the specifications. The firm innovated with a modified version of the 3-71 engine, which later was referred to by the Army Corps of Engineers as a "Stewart & Stevenson Model 3-71 (Mod E) Engine." It was the only engine on the qualified products list for the U.S. military for this particular requirement. Thousands of the units were manufactured and sold.

Also during the 1950s Stewart & Stevenson was the first and only company to produce a quad (four single engines driving through a common gear box, into a single shaft) 110 unit. These units primarily were sold in the oil field drilling market.

At about this time, two Stewart & Stevenson employees, Bill Collette and Fred Mitchell, came up with the idea of directly connecting a Detroit Diesel engine to a vertical deep-well turbine pump. The conventional way of driving a vertical deep-well turbine pump with a diesel engine was to install a right-angle gear drive on the discharge head of the pump, and then connect the conventional engine to the horizontal shaft of the right-angle drive through a spicer shaft and universal joint couplings.

The Stewart & Stevenson method would eliminate the right-angle gear drive and simply set the engine on its flywheel end, put the crankshaft in a vertical position, and direct-connect to the pump. This would simplify the installation, increase the efficiency by eliminating the right-angle gear drive, and reduce space requirements by two-thirds.

Of course, to stand the engine up on its end would interfere with the lubrication system, and to direct-connect the pump shaft to the engine flywheel would create a thrust problem on the engine crankshaft. Stewart & Stevenson modified the engine to change the lubrication system, so that it would operate successfully in the vertical crankshaft position, and also devised a thrust adapter to take the thrust off the engine crankshaft.

When Detroit Diesel heard that Stewart & Stevenson was planning to run the engine in a vertical crankshaft mode, it notified the Houston company that there were 46 reasons why it could not be done. Stewart & Stevenson pursued the project nonetheless, completed it successfully, and has marketed hundreds of the vertical crankshaft engines throughout the world—not only on irrigation pumps, but on fire pumps, stand-by generator sets, and other applications where space is critical.

Today the Engine Division builds, fabricates, or assembles just about anything that utilizes a diesel or gas turbine engine as the prime mover. The firm's International Switchboard Corporation subsidiary offers a complete line of switchgear and control products.

Other subsidiaries include the International Electric Corporation, formed in 1979 to manufacture commercial generators under license from Delco Products Division of General Motors; Stewart & Stevenson Power, Inc., based in Denver and operating primarily in Colorado, Wyoming, and Nebraska (a separate General Motors Detroit Diesel Allison Division distributor); Stewart & Stevenson de Venezuela, South America, organized in 1975 to operate in Venezuela as the sole distributor for the GM diesel division engines and transmissions in that country; Saudi Diesel, formed in 1978 as the Detroit Diesel Allison product distributor in Saudi Arabia, with headquarters in Alkhobar and plans for branches in Riyadh and Jeddah; Material Handling, founded in 1959 with a franchise granted by the Hyster Corporation for the sale of that firm's lift trucks and associated equipment in Southeast Texas, with headquarters in Houston and branches in Beaumont, San Antonio, Galveston, and Harlingen; Machinery Acceptance Corporation, begun in 1957 to finance the sales of highly diversified products for Stewart & Stevenson customers; Stewart & Stevenson Realty, Inc., organized to consolidate all Stewart & Stevenson real estate; and Thermo-King, formed to sell and service Thermo-King refrigeration

This marine engine, just one of many diverse products marketed by Stewart & Stevenson Services, Inc., is a far cry from the firm's horse-and-buggy beginnings.

These are the Stewart & Stevenson facilities in 1982, with downtown Houston in the background.

equipment to the transportation industry.

Stewart & Stevenson went public in 1976. It is traded on the national over-the-counter market, but it continues to be a closely held corporation with approximately 50 percent of the stock owned by the Stewart and Stevenson families.

Today the company has operations around the world and employs more than 2,500 people. It utilizes 876,500 square feet of floor space throughout the Houston area—considerably more than the less than 3,000 square feet that the business began with in 1903. In fiscal 1982 Stewart & Stevenson's sales increased 31 percent to a record $463 million. The Engine Operations accounted for 87 percent of the firm's sales for the year. Net earnings increased to a new high of $15.2 million, up 87 percent from the $8.2 million for the previous year.

Horsepower definitely has taken this Houston enterprise a long way from that original blacksmith and carriage shop at 1712 Congress Avenue.

WESTHEIMER COMPANIES

For many years Westheimer Transfer and Storage and Westheimer Rigging and Heavy Hauling Company operated under the slogan, "We move anything," and, in response to Houston's phenomenal growth, the firm literally has done so.

Corporate records show that in its history Westheimer has moved multimillion-dollar art exhibits, oil companies, banks, and once even a town—when Houston annexed a smaller city and all official records were transferred. When the Houston branch of the Federal Reserve Bank moved to a new location, Westheimer was called upon to haul more than $30 million in cash.

Founded in 1883 by a German immigrant, Sigmund Joseph Westheimer, the business specialized in moving household furniture by means of horse-drawn wagons and, instead of a mechanic, had a resident veterinarian to care for the horses. Today the veterinarian has been replaced by specialists to maintain a fleet of modern moving equipment.

When Sigmund Westheimer retired in 1923, he sold the business to Ben S. Hurwitz, who had begun working for the company as a teenager. Under his guidance the firm expanded in many areas and in 1929 became an agent for Allied Van Lines, of which Hurwitz was a member of the board of directors.

Westheimer Transfer's corporate headquarters is located on Kirby Drive at the Southwest Freeway on a five-acre tract, including a 100,000-square-foot office/warehouse terminal, a full-service vehicle maintenance facility, and a department for international shipments. Westheimer has 25 acres on the Southwest Freeway at Stancliffe for a future office and warehouse terminal.

In addition to residential moving and storage, the company's expertise also extends to office relocations and international transfers.

Also, to keep up with Houston's industrial expansion, Westheimer Rigging and Heavy Hauling Company was established in response to a need to haul and erect heavy industrial equipment. Sigmund Westheimer would have enjoyed seeing the firm that bears his name one day provide services to an entity

involved in space travel and exploration, the National Aeronautics and Space Administration. Westheimer Rigging Company has grown to be an international leader and has been the recipient of many distinguished national awards.

Westheimer Rigging Company's corporate headquarters, warehouse facilities, and equipment yard are located

The Westheimer Transfer Company was founded in 1883 along with its slogan: "We move anything."

at 117 Eastwood Street. Westheimer also owns a 15-acre parcel at 12301 Amelia Street, which serves as a terminal for many of the company's cranes, heavy hauling trucks, and other special equipment.

Westheimer is proud to have been a partner in the progress that Houston has enjoyed and is equally proud of the involvement in and contributions to the community of many of its associates, who serve on the boards and committees of many local schools and charitable and cultural organizations.

Although "horsepower" was the original mode of transportation for Westheimer's, today the firm operates equipment including mobile and crawler cranes, specialized hauling equipment, heavy gin poles and guy derricks, hoists, and other accessory equipment.

BAXTER AND SWINFORD INC., REALTORS

Sam T. Swinford (left) and Ray W. Baxter (right), their tenure based on a firm commitment to the realtor's code of professional service to the public and a dedicated company loyalty.

Ray W. Baxter and Sam T. Swinford were having lunch in different parts of a restaurant off the Katy Freeway some 22 years ago when a mutual friend decided to introduce the two men.

A little while later, with only a handshake, Baxter and Swinford joined their business operations. They were short on cash and long on the desire to achieve.

Baxter, who was constructing and selling houses, and Swinford, who just recently had entered the real estate field, established a one-room office at Wycliffe and Memorial in 1960. At first they shared the building with a fence company, and when it went out of business, they eventually took over that space for use as an office.

"We look back now and have to smile when we think about that first operation," says Swinford. "For a restroom, we had to go across the street to the service station."

Today the firm has 120 associates and 35 other staff members at its 10 locations. Baxter is 1983 president of the Houston Board of Realtors. Swinford was president of the board in 1974.

"When we formed the company we wanted to be sure that people felt we were the kind of firm that liked doing business the old-fashioned way," Swinford says. "That's why we made the name 'Baxter and Swinford.'"

In 1965, with six employees including their first salesperson, Mary Kent (who is still with the firm today), the two men moved their business operation— including the small building—to a tract near the intersection of Kirkwood and Memorial Drive.

In 1970 the company, now with 15 agents, opened its first branch office, a unit off Highway 1960. It was also the year that Baxter and Swinford incorporated.

Since then, the organization has

continued to expand along the western fringes of Houston. Much of the firm's growth has been boosted by corporate transfers into and out of Houston.

"A milepost for the firm," asserts Baxter, "was our joining RELO (an intercity relocation group) in 1965. We have been very active in relocation services, and have handled a large amount of transfer business. The real estate business has become a nationwide situation."

In recent months, both Baxter and Swinford have noted a change in homebuyers. "Up until the 1970s, homebuyers were interested in bigger houses, even if they did not need four or five bedrooms and a formal living room," Baxter says. "Now, however, if they do not need those extra rooms, they buy a smaller house. Homebuyers are buying what they need, and little more."

Both men feel that the success of their organization results from "the family feeling" of its associates.

223

McCORMICK OIL & GAS COMPANY

McCormick Oil & Gas Company is a direct outgrowth of 11 years of exploration activities conducted by McCormick Oil & Gas Corporation. The firm began as a privately owned venture which was chartered on June 19, 1969, for the purpose of assuming the operations previously conducted by Sanford E. McCormick, who had operated as an independent since 1965.

On May 1, 1980, McCormick Oil & Gas became a public company, following the completion of an exchange of stock for approximately 81 percent of the interests in the McCormick Oil & Gas Programs for the years 1970 through 1977 and all of the corporate general partner's interest in the programs formed after 1977. The firm's securities are now traded on the over-the-counter market.

McCormick historically has concentrated its activities solely on exploration and production, with major emphasis being in the south-central states. In 1982 the company established a new exploration area in the mid-continent and the Rockies and in addition entered into its first foreign venture by acquiring all of the stock of Chapman Oil of Australia, Inc., which owns a 50-percent working interest in an exploration permit covering 3.84 million acres in the western part of Australia.

In 1969 the original staff consisted of approximately 30 people, and by 1982 that number had grown to approximately 160. The firm is headed by Sandy McCormick, president and board chairman, who began his career in the oil business in 1956 after receiving degrees from Yale University in 1953 and L'Ecole des Sciences Politiques in Paris, France, in 1954.

McCormick's home office always has been in Houston—originally on the 12th floor of the Tenneco Building, relocating

McCormick drills approximately 30 new exploration prospects a year. Shown here are two oil field workers on the floor of a drilling rig at a McCormick site. © 1982 Bob Gomel

Sanford E. McCormick, president and board chairman of McCormick Oil & Gas Company. © 1982 Bob Gomel

in 1979 to the 35th and 36th floors of Two Allen Center. In addition, the firm maintains an office in Lafayette, Louisiana, and employs consultants in Midland, Texas; Oklahoma City, Oklahoma; and Denver, Colorado.

The primary structure of the company consists of the president and two executive vice-presidents, one who oversees the areas of exploration and production, and one who is responsible for the financial activities.

McCormick drills approximately 30 new exploration prospects a year, and for 1982 had some $40 million of exploration funds available. By the end of 1982 McCormick had drilled a total of approximately 375 exploratory wells and 270 development wells since the offering of its first public drilling program in 1970.

The corporation and its predecessors have financed the majority of their exploration activities through the sale of public drilling programs, raising from as little as $2 million in 1970 to as much as $30 million in 1982. In addition, since 1974 certain industry partners also have been participants in the annual exploration activity, and as a public company, McCormick has undertaken a significant direct investment itself.

BERING'S

August C. Bering III, chairman and chief executive officer of Bering's.

The death of a team of oxen in 1842 brought about the birth of a firm which became the forerunner of Bering's in the 6100 block of Westheimer.

Conrad and August Bering emigrated that year from Kassel, Germany, and were headed for a land grant at Fredricksburg. When their team of oxen died they abandoned the idea of homesteading in the hill country and went into business in Houston. Both brothers were cabinetmakers, so it was logical that they chose lumber and cabinetmaking for their Houston ventures.

Today August C. Bering III, a great-grandson of Conrad, and his sons, August IV and Norman J. Bering II, operate Bering's, founded as Bering Lumber Company in 1940 by August C. Bering, Jr., who died just three years later. After World War II, Bering Lumber Company entered into the retail lumber business with two employees. Previously, the firm had been a wholesale lumber operation.

In 1942 the lumber operation was relocated from its initial site at 7206 Capitol to the west side of Houston, where the construction of more expensive homes was burgeoning. August chose three business lots at the corner of Potomac and Westheimer Road, an area once owned by his great-uncle. At the time of the move the company had an inventory valued at some $10,000, primarily lumber, with some hardware and paint, a weekly payroll of around $600, and five employees.

When the building was enlarged in 1957, the hardware and paint departments were expanded and the electrical, plumbing, and lawn and garden departments were added. By 1962 annual sales exceeded one million dollars.

The firm added a second floor to house

offices and the accounting department, as well as adding additional warehouse space, in 1970. Just before the project was completed, a fire destroyed most of the facilities. Following the blaze, a new store was erected in three phases. A housewares department and gift shop were added, and the garden, paint, electrical, and plumbing departments were enlarged. The number of employees climbed to 85.

Bering's expanded again in 1978 with the opening of a new 17,000-square-foot facility to house the home improvement area, lumberyard, and the new containers and storage department.

August C. Bering III was voted chairman of the board and chief executive officer in 1981 by Bering's board of directors. August C. Bering IV, who had joined the firm in 1965, was named president and Norman J. Bering II, who had come aboard in 1971, became executive vice-president.

In April 1982 the company's name was changed from Bering Home Center, Inc., to Bering's, reflecting its change from strictly a lumber and hardware operation to a full-service hardlines department store.

The original Bering Lumber Company was located at 7206 Capitol, with the office in the house next door.

THE HORNE COMPANY, REALTORS

W.A. Horne,
founder of The Horne Company.

W.A. Horne was one of many people in the United States who was forced to change jobs when banks were instructed to get out of the real estate business during the time of the Great Depression. But for Horne and his sons, the move led to the development of a commercial real estate firm that has been involved in many of Houston's monumental transactions over the past five and one-half decades.

W.A. Horne relocated to Houston from Corpus Christi in the early 1920s to work as a real estate officer at the San Jacinto Bank & Trust. The bank was later merged into the Second National Bank, which became the Bank of the Southwest.

The San Jacinto Bank was financing and developing residential and commercial projects and employed 42 salesmen selling lots in 24 subdivisions. The bank would handle everything from platting the property, creating the lots and other development needs, to selling the lots to independent builders.

Horne left the bank in 1926. He specialized in brokerage work on commercial properties in the downtown area in the 1930s, when everything revolved around the Central Business District. Few, if any, shopping centers outside the central core existed at that time.

Today The Horne Company employs some 260 people and works throughout Houston's almost 7,000-square-mile area. The firm's founder died in 1979. However, his sons, Howard W. Horne, chairman of the board, and Robert A. Horne, senior vice-president, have remained active in The Horne Company. Other principals include Ronald J. Hoelscher, president and chief operating officer; Sidney V. Smith, senior vice-president; Stephen N. Montgomery, senior vice-president and president of The Office Network Inc. (an affiliation of major real estate firms in major U.S. markets); Drew Lewis, vice-president with the Office Building Division; and David L. Cook, vice-president and general manager of the Industrial Brokerage Division.

The Office Network was formed in 1977 by The Horne Company because, as Chairman Horne notes, "We wanted to identify other firms in major U.S. cities that had the same goals and objectives as we did and still do—specifically, giving good, informed service in the real estate field. Instead of opening branch operations in other cities, we formed The Office Network to fulfill the needs of our Houston clients in other cities." The Office Network consists of 21 real estate firms in 37 markets from New York to Los Angeles.

Although it began as a brokerage operation, The Horne Company today also has Office Building, General Brokerage, Industrial, Property Management, Equity Investment, Farm and Ranch, and Consulting divisions. These units are provided information by three extensive research departments.

As Houston has grown, so has The Horne Company. The corporation recently passed a milestone with the purchase and move to its own building located at Main and Jefferson in downtown Houston.

GULF RESOURCES & CHEMICAL CORPORATION

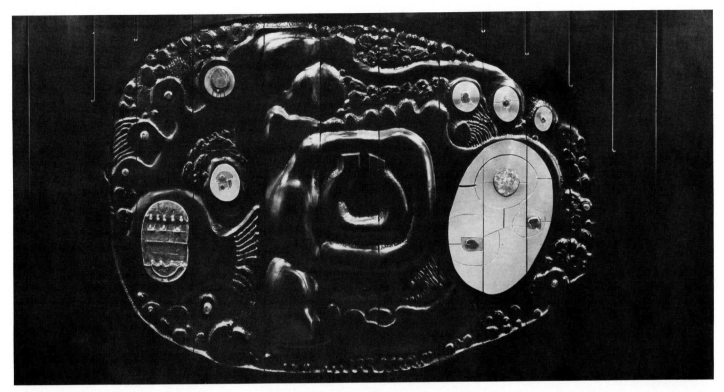

Gulf Resources, formed in 1951 as the Gulf Sulphur Corporation by three brothers, Lawrence, William, and Ashton Brady, in its early years directed efforts into exploration activities in the southeastern part of Mexico.

Such efforts proved the necessary commercial sulphur reserves to justify construction of a Frasch-processing sulphur plant in Salinas, Veracruz, Mexico. Construction of the plant began in 1954 and was completed in April 1956. Shortly thereafter, the Brady brothers sold 50 percent of the voting shares of the company to a group headed by Edward J. Hudson of Houston, and by Bear, Stearns & Co. of New York.

Production began in May 1956 and by the end of that year more than 180,000 tons of sulphur were produced and sold at a net loss to the firm of around $1.1 million. The following year also proved difficult as the company attempted to survive the period of transition from plant start-up to product manufacture. While sulphur production increased 40 percent in 1957 and all production was sold, operating losses climbed to $1.3 million due to depressed prices.

Losses continued until 1961, the year the firm was recapitalized by converting three outstanding classes of stock into one

single class of common stock, eliminating $300,000 in cumulative preferred dividends. Also, certain debts and accrued royalties totaling $6.4 million were exchanged for common stock, and an agreement was signed with the Mexican government to defer payment of all outstanding royalties over a three-year period. For the first time in its history, the company had a profit-net income of $300,000.

In 1962 sulphur production and sales increased, with net income climbing to $1.1 million in spite of continued oversupply and price cutting by producers. It also was the year Gulf built a modern grammar school for the village of Salinas.

Net income rose to $1.8 million in 1965. Exploration drilling resulted in the discovery of two new mineralized areas.

Diversification began in 1967, when Lithium Corporation of America was merged into Gulf Sulphur. Great Salt Lake Minerals & Chemicals Corporation was formed to take over the operations of Lithium Corporation at the Great Salt Lake. The firm's name was changed to Gulf Resources & Chemical Corporation.

The Bunker Hill Company was merged into Gulf Resources in 1968, providing further diversification in metals, minerals, and chemicals. Gulf Resources was listed

The refined metals and raw mineral ores incorporated in the wall sculpture of its corporate headquarters reception area suggest Gulf Resources' historical identification with a wide variety of natural resources.

on the New York Stock Exchange and began trading under the ticker symbol GRE. The following year marked the company's entry into oil and gas exploration, and C&K Coal Company was acquired in 1970.

Within three years revenues and earnings reached record levels of $145 million and $6.2 million, respectively. By 1980 revenues totaled $671 million, with net income of $25 million.

However, 1981 marked the beginning of a major recession, causing the company to reassess its investment goals. The board of directors decided to discontinue the company's lead, zinc, and silver mining and its smelting and refining operations.

Gulf Resources & Chemical Corporation remains a leading producer of a broad range of natural resources and energy-related products whose major products are oil and gas, coal, lithium chemicals and metal, fertilizers, salt, industrial explosives, specialty clays, and engineering services for the oil and gas industry.

227

NATIONAL CONVENIENCE STORES INCORPORATED

The story of National Convenience Stores is, in part, the story of Houston and the imagination and entrepreneurial spirit that fueled the successful business ventures that prevailed in the area in 1959—the year that a group of Houstonians chartered a company to operate five convenience stores as a franchise of U-Tote-M, Inc.

The business decision was an auspicious one. The five-store franchise grew during the next two decades into National Convenience Stores Incorporated, a New York Stock Exchange corporation of more than 1,000 stores which has annual sales of $750 million.

Organizers were F.J. Dyke, Jr.; Raymond W. Oeland, Jr.; William Key Wilde; F.J. Dyke, Sr.; and LeRoy Melcher, Sr. The founders elected F.J. "Jeff" Dyke, Jr., the first president and under his leadership the company immediately began its rapid sales growth and store expansion.

By the second year of its operation, when the firm entered the Southern California market, sales had climbed to one million dollars. In 1962, with 21 stores in operation, the company changed its name to National Drive-In Grocery Corporation. The following year it expanded into its third state, Nevada, and moved its national headquarters to Anaheim, California, to be nearer its concentration of West Coast stores.

Dyke dissolved the franchise agreement with U-Tote-M in 1964, creating an independent business which operated under the trade name of Stop N Go. The organization, now comprised of 70 stores, had $5 million in sales.

Eastward expansion began in 1965, when stores in Georgia were added, and was followed within the next two years by units in Tennessee and Mississippi. It was also in 1965 that the corporate headquarters was moved back to Houston, which was nearer the center of the firm's developing national network of stores.

At the end of its 1968 fiscal year, the company had 300 stores operating in six states with revenues of $39 million and a new name, National Convenience Stores Incorporated (NCS).

The company purchased the 57 Handee Food Stores in Houston in 1969.

One of the early Stop N Go Stores which, until 1965, were located in Texas, California, and Nevada.

To finance this acquisition, each of the directors personally guaranteed the note given by NCS with the expectation that the borrowed funds would be paid from the proceeds of a public offering planned for later that year. Circumstances prevented the offering and the directors remained liable for the debt for two years, during which period the future of NCS was in doubt.

NCS entered the self-serve gasoline business on a commission basis with the installation of non-owned equipment at a few of its stores in 1970. The firm also began the sale of fast foods in its stores and Dyke correctly predicted in the 1970 annual report that "prepared foods will play an increasingly important role in the convenience market industry."

These decisions were the first of many innovative actions NCS would take in succeeding years—actions that subsequently would distinguish the organization as the leader in the convenience store industry.

As a result of the company's first public offering of 291,000 shares of common stock in 1972, NCS made a strategic decision to own the gasoline installations at its stores, thereby significantly increasing its profits. It continued to make gasoline an integral part of its store program and in 1982 NCS ranked among the 50 largest gasoline retailers in the United States. The fast-food program continued to develop and the firm opened its first commissary in Houston in 1974.

In 1981 NCS opened a second

commissary in Southern California for the distribution of its products to Stop N Go stores in that state. The Houston commissary, by 1982, was providing 600 stores in Texas with appetizers and entrees as well as the freshly made sandwiches that were its initial products.

V.H. Van Horn succeeded Dyke as president and chief executive officer of NCS in 1975. Van Horn had joined NCS in 1966 as its first management trainee and moved through successive posts with the company.

At the time of his election to the NCS presidency, Van Horn faced a difficult situation. A national recession and the firm's aggressive new-store growth program had combined to adversely affect NCS's earnings. In a radical departure from conventional convenience store practice at the time, NCS decelerated its store expansion program and began to close marginally profitable or unprofitable stores.

The following year Van Horn, in a report to employees, stated his management philosophy: "NCS is in business to create customers and, by so doing, increase profitability. Our focus is on the quality of individual stores, market areas, earnings, and people rather than their quantity. We recognize our resources are limited and precious and must be deployed carefully to maximize returns.

National Convenience Stores Incorporated selects strategic locations for its Superstores, such as this one, which specialize in fast foods, gasoline, and nonfood items.

We are dedicated to creating an environment in which NCS people feel good about themselves, their relationships, their contributions, and their future growth."

It was tagged "responsive marketing." The results of the philosophy were immediately evident in the 1976 earnings increase of 111 percent and, for the first time, the board of directors declared a cash dividend.

In the annual report for fiscal 1977, NCS announced that it would double its $3.5 million in earnings during the next four years. The following year the predication was amended on the basis of the corporation's 1978 performance: The goal would be accomplished in three years instead of four.

NCS moved away from the drive-in grocery concept of a convenience store toward that of a specialty retailer, with emphasis on fast foods, nonfoods, and gasoline. A natural extension of the new specialty retailing was the Houston opening, in 1979, of the firm's first Superstore.

That Superstore contained 3,600 square feet of space, compared with the 2,400 square feet of the conventional convenience store. The company places its Superstores on prime, high-traffic corners and the additional space is devoted to the sale of fast foods, nonfoods, and gasoline.

It also was in 1979 that NCS made its second significant acquisition in Houston when it purchased the Texas Super Duper chain of 85 stores. The purchase, followed by the Mr. M acquisition which included 40 stores in Houston, brought to 271 the number of stores operated by NCS in the Houston area. It made NCS the largest operator of convenience stores in Houston.

The company's sales and earnings performance, coupled with its closely held stock, placed its status as an independent corporation in jeopardy in the 1970s.

Beginning in 1976, NCS expanded its shareholder base through the declaration of six stock dividends in seven years; through the listing of its stock for trading on the American Stock Exchange in 1979, followed by a move to the New York Stock Exchange in 1981; and through two common stock offerings in 1980 and 1982. The result of these efforts has been to transform a closely held regional firm to that of a corporation with a large national following and a diverse group of shareholders.

As NCS approaches its 25th anniversary, it can be said that the firm reflects the city of Houston—a city whose growth potential is limited only by the willingness of its leaders to be innovative and responsive to its opportunities.

FINGER FURNITURE COMPANY, INC.

Although Finger Furniture Company opened its first store in Houston in 1927, the history of the firm actually reaches back to 1901, to the small East Texas community of Shepherd where Sam Finger opened a general merchandise store to serve the farm families of San Jacinto County.

In 1903 he was joined by his bride, Annie, and together they operated S. Finger General Merchandise for the next 22 years, establishing a tradition of serving the public which continues to this day.

Sam Finger retired to Houston in 1925, leaving one of his four sons behind to run the Shepherd store. But his retirement was short-lived, for in 1927 he and his eldest son, Hyman, opened the Finger Radio and Furniture store in the 2900 block of South Main.

From the 1920s through succeeding years, Finger's continued to grow, opening new stores throughout Houston, selling radios, furniture, and appliances, and corporate growth kept pace with the dynamic growth of Houston.

In the 1950s the warehouse showroom concept was pioneered by Finger's, 20 years before the nationwide boom in this type of retailing in the late 1960s and the 1970s. The eight-acre Finger Furniture Center was opened on the Gulf Freeway in 1965, offering home furnishings displayed in hundreds of unique environmental room settings and vignettes.

Today Finger's includes the Finger Furniture Center, now covering 14 acres with the world's largest furniture store under one roof, and five branch locations: Finger's Sharpstown, Finger's Post Oak, Finger's North Central at Jensen Drive, Finger's Pasadena, and the largest branch store, Finger's Greenspoint, a 140,000-square-foot facility.

Warehouse, delivery, and service operations are completely streamlined, centralized, and computerized. Warehouse facilities provide more than $10 million in inventory for Finger's customers.

Leading the firm since the 1950s are S.P. Finger, president, and Aaron L. Finger, senior executive vice-president, two of founder Sam Finger's sons. The third generation of the Finger family is

The first Finger's store was founded in 1901 by Sam Finger in Shepherd, Texas.

represented by S.P. Finger's son, Robert, who is executive vice-president and general manager of the award-winning Finger Office Furniture, and Aaron Finger's son, Alan, who is executive vice-president and general manager of the rapidly growing Appliance Division. In 1981 Alan Finger's son, Steve, representing the fourth generation, joined the company.

Finger's board of directors includes S.P., Aaron L., Robert, and Alan Finger, Joseph P. Kost, company senior vice-president, and David W. Barg, company vice-president and treasurer.

The corporation has remained a Texas firm, family-owned and -operated, and has received many national awards, including Brand Names Retailer of the Year and Merchandiser of the Year.

Finger's magnificent Furniture Center on the Gulf Freeway occupies 14 acres and is the largest furniture store under one roof in the world. Built on the site of historic Buff Stadium, the store contains the Houston Sports Museum which features a commemorative marker of the old ballpark's homeplate and mementos of past and present sports greats.

CULLEN CENTER, INC.

In 1948 Hugh Roy Cullen purchased four acres of land west of Houston's downtown YMCA, marking the beginning of what was to become one of the city's major office developments.

He acquired the land that would become Cullen Center in piecemeal fashion. At one point during his acquisition of acreage, the outline of the continuous lots Cullen owned formed the shape of the state of Texas. This seemed appropriate for the oil operator, whose wealth has been used to finance educational and research facilities, and who formed the Cullen Foundation for charitable and educational purposes.

Planning for Cullen Center began in 1959 by members of the Cullen family and Welton Becket and Associates, Architects-Planners. The tract of land at that time was the largest singly owned, undeveloped area in downtown Houston.

The first phase of the project began in 1960, with the groundbreaking for the 500 Jefferson Building and an adjacent hotel. The 20-story office building was formally dedicated in the spring of 1963. The Whitehall, a 276-room hotel, was next. The Whitehall has hosted an array of such luminous guests as Prince Charles of Great Britain and Moshe Dayan, in addition to a variety of celebrities and entertainers, among them Johnny Carson, Ella Fitzgerald, and Elvis Presley.

The Marathon Manufacturing Building, the third facility of Cullen Center, was completed in 1971. Neuhaus and Taylor, Architects, were responsible for the design of the 20-story structure.

The fourth addition to Cullen Center was the Dresser Tower. Also designed by Neuhaus and Taylor, it was the third tallest building in the Houston skyline upon its completion in 1973. At 590 feet and 40 stories, it provided one million square feet of office space. Dresser Industries, as joint-venture partner with Cullen Center, located several of its major Houston operations in the facility. Dresser Tower was chosen as headquarters for the Houston American Revolution Bicentennial Commission. This commission was responsible for devising and coordinating appropriate observances in Houston of the U.S. Bicentennial.

All structures in Cullen Center are interconnected at the second level with elevated, enclosed pedestrian malls. Parking garages also are attached to each of the buildings in the Center. In addition to business offices and the hotel, the development houses various retail services and shops, a U.S. Post Office, and a medical clinic.

Most recently, Cullen Center, in a joint venture with PIC Realty, began construction of the 1600 Smith Street Building, designed by Morris * Aubry, Architects. This 55-story structure will be the first unit in a two-building office complex which is being developed as the latest addition to the Center.

Through the new complex, all of Cullen Center will be connected to the intricate downtown tunnel system. The landscaped plaza of the 1600 Smith Street Building will perpetuate Cullen Center's commitment to an aesthetic environment. The building is scheduled to be completed in the spring of 1984.

—Joan Marie Houck

The outline of Hugh Roy Cullen's land acquisition resembled the state of Texas in the early 1960s.

Cullen Center, two decades later.

HEITMANN, BERING-CORTES COMPANY

WHOLESALE HARDWARE AND INDUSTRIAL SUPPLIES

F.W. Heitmann & Co., as it was then known, had its start in 1865. Frederick William Heitmann, the original owner, came from Germany to Houston in 1855. At the corner of Main and Commerce, handy to Buffalo Bayou, he set up a cotton and forwarding business under the name of Allen and Heitmann.

The field was a prosperous one to be in during those early days. Wagon trains or prairie fleets almost a mile long trailed into Houston from all over Texas, bringing products from the interior.

F.W. Heitmann gave up the cotton and forwarding business to found a metal and hardware store in 1865. He kept the steamboats busy docking at the foot of Main Street with tools, iron, tin plates from England, and other merchandise from Germany and Sweden.

H.S. Fox, one of Houston's prominent bankers, came into the business in the early 1870s and the firm's name was changed to Fox and Heitmann. After that it became F.W. Heitmann & Co.

When the Civil War broke out Fox and Heitmann figured that they would make a fortune if they could run the Union ship blockade with a big load of cotton for England. They liquidated their business to raise capital to purchase the cotton. Heitmann went to Mexico to arrange the sailing from that country. Everything was in order and the ship set sail. Unfortunately, Union gun boats sank the ship *and* the Fox-Heitmann fortune two days out of port.

In 1881 the company moved to 113 Main, where it remained for 89 years. F.W. Heitmann's son, F.A. (Fritz) Heitmann, joined his father in the business after a few years studying and performing dentistry in Silver Cliff, Colorado.

Fritz's son, Fred W. Heitmann, joined the firm in 1941, and after serving in World War II became president in the early 1960s. He retained that position until his death in 1977.

Fred W. Heitmann loved to tell the story of the time his grandfather was hauling a 1,000-pound keg on a flat dray down to Franklin Avenue, when the keg rolled off the dray and immediately sank out of sight in Houston's notorious mud. He had to wait until dry weather before he could find it again.

The late G.E. Ploeger was the company's president for 50 years, both at its old location and at its new 10.5-acre headquarters which opened in 1957 with 150,000 square feet of floor space. The

The current Heitmann building contains more than 150,000 square feet of space and includes 15 loading docks and a railroad terminal.

warehouse is equal in size to eight football fields and stocks about 22,000 items, ranging from tiny nails to huge stock tanks.

This headquarters facility for the oldest forerunner of the Heitmann, Bering-Cortes Company was erected in 1865.

JAMES BUTE PAINT COMPANY

The history of an organization often is interesting in light of the personalities of its leaders. A strong character, surfacing again and again, in the Bute family has guided this firm throughout its history. The same strength, combined with 115 years' experience, has spawned the story of the James Bute Paint Company.

Its founder, a young Scot, visited Canada with his uncle, a sea captain, who unfortunately went down with his ship, depriving young James Bute of a mentor — as well as passage home.

After spending some time building bridges in Canada, James, a civil engineer by trade, was lured away from his profession by the unknown opportunities that often were hidden by the early-morning fog of the Texas Gulf Coast.

Upon arriving in Houston in 1867, he established a small paint store. He then would travel throughout South and Central Texas, taking orders for his fledgling enterprise — no easy task in those days just after the Civil War. When he would return home to Houston, the orders would be filled and again he would embark behind a team of oxen and deliver the goods. He continued to expand his business and in 1911 he erected the building that the firm occupies today.

Upon James' death in 1915, one of his sons, John Bute, assumed control of the business. With an office located on the top floor of the old Light Guard Armory and a penchant for shooting rabbits from a chauffeured convertible, John Bute was another character at the helm.

With John's death in 1929 and until 1960, the James Bute Paint Company was operated by a succession of non-family members. The second John Bute and James Bute III both worked for the firm during this time. However, their individual natures led to other ventures. John became a builder and James a rancher. In 1959, successful in their own right, the two men pooled their resources and purchased all of the outstanding stock, as James says, "if for no other reason than to give the firm a burial in the family name."

Undaunted and unprepared to let the venture fold, John Bute decided to try to instill it with new life. He built, as he had

James Bute, founder of the James Bute Company.

built before, in an unknown marketplace and prospered, eventually becoming the sole owner of the corporation.

The James Bute Paint Company now sells in a five-state area to independent hardware stores, lumberyards, and decorating centers. Today there are two additional Butes, John Burton and James IV, working within the

organization. If history repeats itself, which it surely will, the story of the James Bute Paint Company shall continue for another century.

From 1918 to 1928 the James Bute Company was located at Texas and Fannin streets.

ADAMS & PORTER ASSOCIATES, INC.

Early in the 1900s Henry Adams, after gaining valuable experience in the marine insurance business, came south from New York to Houston and worked a few years for Cravens & Kelly.

After further experience in the marine insurance field in Houston, Adams decided that it was time to establish his own business. In the meantime, he had met Henry Porter who was well acquainted in the thriving business community on the banks of Buffalo Bayou. In 1907, based on the handshake and mutual trust of Henry Adams and Henry Porter, the firm was founded. The place: Houston's Cotton Exchange Building, which in those days was the sight of many business deals made on a handshake.

A notice, which reads as follows, was sent to all their customers: "We take this means of informing you that on and after May 1, 1908, the General Agency of the United States Lloyds of New York and the Columbia Insurance Company of New Jersey, will be operated by Henry A. Adams and Henry L. Porter under the firm name of Adams & Porter. Hoping to be favored with a continuance of your valued business, we beg to remain very truly yours, Adams & Porter."

The fledgling enterprise's first office was established in the old Cotton Exchange Building on Franklin Avenue, which is now a historical landmark. The office later moved to the First National Bank Building at Main and Franklin, then to the new Cotton Exchange Building at Caroline and Prairie upon its completion in 1925.

On several occasions, Adams traveled to London in search of marine insurance markets. During one of his visits, he met Harry Hilliard, then with the London brokerage firm of Kennard, Arbon and Company, who subsequently came to America and joined Adams & Porter.

Soon afterward, World War I broke out and Hilliard, an English citizen, returned to fight with the Scottish Brigade. He was wounded in action, losing an eye, and spent several months in the hospital where he met the nurse who later became his bride. After the war he returned to Houston with his wife,

This 1908 photograph of the Adams & Porter staff includes the office boy (not identified), Henry Adams, and Henry Porter, left to right. The office was in the Cotton Exchange Building.

became an American citizen, and continued in the insurance business as a partner of Adams & Porter until his death.

Eight years after its founding, Adams & Porter/New York was established to realize closer contact with the important New York insurance market and to be near to war risk insurance underwriters during World War I, thereby serving its growing accounts more effectively.

Subsequently, William H. Young, with whom Adams had worked previously at another New York brokerage firm, joined Adams & Porter in New York. A close affiliation has existed since between the two autonomous offices operating in New York and Houston. Porter died in the early 1920s. Adams, Hilliard, and Young continued their active roles in the management of the two firms' offices until their deaths in later years.

During the intervening years, Adams' two sons joined the firm, Norman in Houston and John in New York. Norman died in 1971 and John is now retired. Two of Adams' grandsons are members of the firm today, Alexander in Houston and

David in New York. A great-grandson, DeGraaf, works in Houston, as does John, the grandson of Harry Hilliard.

During World War II, the U.S. government was involved in importing enormous amounts of strategic materials for the war effort, such as tin, chrome, rubber, lamb's wool, and industrial diamonds. In order to handle the insurance on these imports, the government set up the Defense Materials Insurance Committee and entrusted its operation to the five most prominent marine brokers in the United States, one of which was Adams & Porter.

In the early 1960s it was decided that both offices should change from partnerships to corporations; they operate as such today.

Adams & Porter grew up with the cotton business and indeed was privileged to have the appointment as broker for the largest cotton merchants. Cotton shipments were necessarily dependent on

Henry Adams, during the early 1900s, looking after a client's damaged cotton.

water transportaion during those early days. Consequently, cargo and hull covers were needed; hence the firm became extremely knowledgeable in the marine field. Historically, Adams & Porter has been known as a marine insurance house, but it has kept pace with the offshore petroleum industry as well. The firm has the distinction of insuring the first offshore drilling barge in the Gulf of Mexico. No such policy had ever existed and therefore it was a great challenge for Adams & Porter to draw up a policy to adequately handle the inherent problems associated with both drilling exposures and the usual perils of the sea.

Keeping pace also meant adjusting to its clients' increasing operations in all areas of the world, no matter how remote. The first actual expansion was the establishment of Adams & Porter offices in Brazil, 35 years ago, the first overseas office ever established by an American broker. Constant travel abroad and servicing clients' needs had become commonplace. Such servicing is most important where large claims have occurred overseas.

Adams & Porter Associates, Inc., has rapidly expanded and now employs 125 people. Most account executives responsible for clients' insurance are owners of the firm and all take an active part in the daily operations.

Today Adams & Porter occupies offices in its own building at 1819 St. James Place in San Felipe Green. The firm's growth has again made it necessary to move to larger quarters. A new facility will soon be constructed on Bering Drive, just north of Woodway.

The operation of the firm is the responsibility of its board of directors, composed of Richard R. McKay, chairman; Alexander Adams, vice-chairman; Hugh T. Wilson, president; John F. Marshall, Jr., executive vice-president; George P. Gardere, Jr., senior vice-president; and John V. Polk, Jr., senior vice-president.

The success of Adams & Porter is directly attributable to its employees and owners, who include Alexander Adams, Robert L. Barclay, Frank O. Colby, Marshall Crawford, John Currie, G.P. Gardere, Jr., James Glotfelty, John Hilliard, Stephen B. Holaday, Ralph Howard, Howard M. Marshall, John F. Marshall, Jr., Howard Mason, Richard McKay, Stephen G. McKinnon, James I. Montano, J. Carleton Parker, Joe H. Parker, W. Craig Plumhoff, John V. Polk, Jr., Benjamin Reynolds, Fred M. Schall, Dale Shivers, Dean Smith, Howard Sweeny, Gardner S. Thornton, Jerry Treadwell, Jeffry J. Wiley, and Hugh T. Wilson.

235

PAKHOED USA INC.

Pakhoed USA Inc., a wholly owned subsidiary of Pakhoed Holding N.V. of Rotterdam, The Netherlands, was organized in 1973 to develop a diversified services company for the energy industry. Its first development in the United States was a joint venture in Philadelphia with Ocean Terminals for the storage of two million barrels of oils and chemicals. The real breakthrough, however, came in 1975 when Pakhoed acquired Robertson Distribution Systems Inc. of Houston. Houston then became the corporate headquarters for Pakhoed USA Inc. operations.

Worldwide, the Pakhoed group of companies provides business and industry with services in the fields of dry and liquid bulk storage, environmental services, transport and distribution, and project development, as well as investment in and management of real estate. Headquartered in Rotterdam, Pakhoed has operations throughout the world. The firm as it exists today was established in 1967 out of a merger between two established Dutch companies. Blauwhoed, founded in 1616, developed real estate and provided stevedoring and warehousing for dry goods. Pakhuismeesteren, founded in 1818, accepted one of the first consignments of petroleum to arrive in the Port of Rotterdam in 1860. After the 1967 merger, a new corporate name, Pakhoed, was created from the first syllable of one company and the second syllable of the other. The firm's long history of materials handling and distribution is embodied by its logo, a red hat like those worn in 17th-century Holland by Dutch stevedores.

Since 1975 Pakhoed USA has continued to expand with the acquisition of additional tank storage facilities, the development of dry bulk operations, and the expansion of its environmental services subsidiary.

Today Pakhoed USA has four operating subsidiaries, three of which have facilities along the Houston Ship Channel. Paktank Corporation is an independent tank storage company specializing in the liquid storage of crude oil, petroleum products, chemicals, and refined products. Paktank owns or operates eight terminal facilities in

Paktank personnel are highly trained and able to handle the most difficult product storage and transfer situations.

the United States, two of which are located on the Houston Ship Channel at Deer Park and Galena Park.

Paktank completed a $20-million expansion project at its Deer Park terminal in May 1983. The expansion included the construction of an additional one million barrels of oil and chemical storage and a third ship/barge dock and common support facilities. Completion of the expansion increased Paktank's overall storage capacity in the U.S. to approximately 11 million barrels.

Pakhoed USA established Empak Inc. in 1975 to provide environmental services to its bulk liquid storage and transportation divisions. Today Empak offers commercial services to companies in the petrochemical, manufacturing, and distribution industries to meet the ever-increasing needs for effective and efficient

disposal and treatment of industrial wastes and product residues. Empak's modern facilities on the Houston Ship Channel are capable of processing a wide range of industrial wastes. These wastes are either treated prior to discharge to surface waters or disposed of by deepwell injection. In addition, Empak performs cleaning and purging operations on rail cars, tank trucks, and container units.

Paktank Florida Inc. provides storage and transshipment services for dry bulk cargo such as bulk chemicals, fertilizer ingredients, and salt. Located in the Port of Tampa, Paktank Florida maintains the largest and most modern bulk-handling terminal in the state of Florida. Paktank Florida also operates liquid sulphur terminals in the Tampa area.

Pakhoed USA's other subsidiary is Trafpak USA, an independent tank container operator which specializes in the transport of bulk liquid chemicals.

Pakhoed USA also is the parent company of Blauwhoed USA, its real estate investment division. A partnership was established in 1974 between Blauwhoed and Charles S. Ackerman of Atlanta to engage in real estate activities in the United States.

Ackerman & Company has developed national and international commercial and residential real estate brokerage operations in the United States, with offices in Atlanta, Baltimore, Chicago, Houston, Rotterdam, and London. In 1981 Ackerman acquired Shindler/Cummins Residential Inc., one of the largest brokerage firms in Houston, and has established Houston as its southwestern regional headquarters.

Pakhoed USA, presently a leader in the liquid terminaling industry, plans to continue to expand its operations through the growth of all existing subsidiaries in addition to the development of new activities compatible with its overall business.

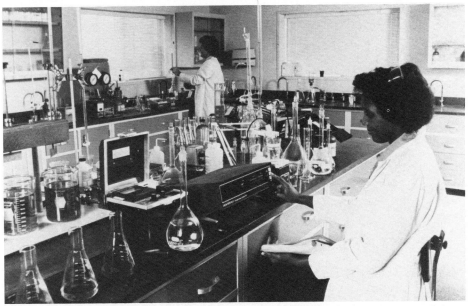

The site of Empak's liquid-waste deepwell injection facility.

A large, modern laboratory provides support for Empak waste treatment and disposal operations.

A view of one of Paktank's tank storage facilities, located on the Houston Ship Channel. Paktank operates two terminal facilities in the Houston area.

237

K.L. McGUIRT & COMPANY

As a boy growing up in Shreveport, Louisiana, K.L. "Mac" McGuirt dreamed of a future filled with promise for his native Southland. He knew he wanted to make a contribution toward that bountiful tomorrow.

In 1942 Mac and his young wife, Jean, took that first step and moved to Houston where he soon after began a real estate career as a salesman with Robert Newkirk in the then-rural Memorial Drive area.

He went on to found K.L. McGuirt & Company in 1948 with a small office on Memorial Drive in a locale that ultimately became one of the most prestigious areas of the city.

Much of the desirability of this location today is attributable to his efforts. Most of the Memorial area was not restricted to residential use. Mac, who could have profited greatly by marketing these unrestricted tracts for commercial use, opted to do everything he could to ensure that the land was sold for residential construction, working directly with home builders in the development of many of Memorial's finest subdivisions.

Another of Mac's goals was to upgrade the real estate profession. To achieve this end, he devoted many hours to serving the National Association of Realtors and other organizations to improve practices and ethics within the industry. For example, at the time of his unexpected death, he was vice-president-elect of the Texas Association of Realtors and was elected president of the Houston Board of Realtors just hours prior to his passing. He also had taught real estate classes at the University of Houston.

Mac's son, Don McGuirt, joined the firm in 1970 after graduation from Texas Christian University. Mac died in July of that year and responsibility for continuing the firm passed to Don.

By 1971 the northwest side of Houston was in the early stages of what was to be a tremendous growth period. This was the year Don opened an office in the FM 1960 area. Once again, K.L. McGuirt & Company was a major factor in pioneering a new and desirable place to live.

Early 1979 marked the opening of the firm's third office, this time on the far west side of the city to service neighborhoods near Highway 6. In 1980 the fourth office opened in the Galleria area, an office that houses residential, commercial, and corporate relocation departments, in addition to administrative offices.

K.L. McGuirt & Company now has more than 120 full-time agents, and the firm has participated in over one billion dollars in real estate sales.

Every morning thousands of Houston families begin the day in a home they purchased with the aid of McGuirt residential agents. Many work in offices, shops, and industrial facilities that were sold under the McGuirt commercial division.

Don McGuirt heads K.L. McGuirt & Company today.

K.L. McGuirt, founder of the firm that bears his name.

PORT OF HOUSTON AUTHORITY

Barbours Cut Terminal, located just 25 miles from the open Gulf of Mexico, is the Port of Houston Authority's ultramodern intermodal container facility.

Throughout its short history, the deepwater Port of Houston has devoted itself to spurring the economic development of Houston, serving as a key factor in the city's dynamic 20th-century growth.

Houston's population in 1980 was 35 times larger than it was in 1914, when the Houston Ship Channel was opened. During the same period, the populations of the Texas interior cities of Dallas and San Antonio had increased by factors of 20 and 15, respectively.

The port's 1981 contribution to the economies of the region, state, and nation was almost $3 billion, according to an economic impact study conducted during 1982 by Booz-Allen & Hamilton, Inc. The consulting firm found that 31,700 Texans were employed as a direct result of port activity in jobs that would vanish if the port were to close. Another 111,000 jobs were found to be indirectly related to port activity.

The port and Houston have grown in lockstep. The port is the nation's third largest, while Houston has become the nation's fourth largest city. More than 100 million tons of cargo were handled at docks along the Houston Ship Channel in each of the years 1979, 1980, and 1981. Houston exports more wheat and imports more steel than any other port in the United States. Foreign trade accounted for 50 million tons of cargo worth $26.4 billion in 1981.

While the Port of Houston includes many privately owned terminals, most of which serve the petrochemical complex located on the Houston Ship Channel, the facilities owned and operated by the Port of Houston Authority handle nearly 90 percent of the general cargo moving through the port. It is general cargo that has the greatest impact on the economy through job creation.

The Port Authority operates 36 general cargo docks in the historic Turning Basin area, including two which serve the six-million-bushel-capacity Houston Public Elevator. Other Port Authority facilities include the Manchester Wharves, the Bulk Materials Handling Plant on Greens Bayou for dry bulk shipments, and the newest and most modern intermodal container facility on the Gulf of Mexico, Barbours Cut Terminal.

Located just 25 miles or two and one-half hours from the open sea, Barbours Cut has three 1,000-foot wharves for container ships, a dock for barge-carrying ships, and a two-way platform for ships equipped with stern ramps for roll-on/roll-off cargo. Six large, 40-long-ton-capacity cranes are utilized at the terminal to load and unload ships with cargo containers.

Construction of the ultramodern terminal began in 1970. More than $100 million had been invested in the facility by 1983.

Building for the 21st century and beyond, the Port Authority awarded contracts for almost $20 million in new construction during 1982.

The projects include a 1,000-foot-long container wharf at Barbours Cut for $9.4 million, a project and general cargo dock adjacent to the Loop 610 bridge for $6 million, and a new ship loader for the Bulk Materials Handling Plant for $3.3 million.

As 1983 began the Port Authority was expecting authorization of a unique multisite Foreign Trade Zone. Through innovations such as these and through steady, paced growth, the Port of Houston will continue to spur the economic development of the city, state, and nation.

Unit 1 of Houston's municipal wharves in the 1870s.

SHIPPERS STEVEDORING COMPANY

Shippers Stevedoring Company, formed in 1969 by a group of investors headed by Jerry McManus of Houston, today provides a unique, total service from its base of operations at Clinton Drive on the Houston Ship Channel.

The firm has the only private, full-service dockside operation in Houston. It includes crating, storage, all cargo handling, and the largest marshaling area of its kind on the Gulf Coast.

In addition, McManus has said that plans call for expansion of the firm's marshaling area with the purchase of some 65 acres of land, a portion of the old San Jacinto Ordnance Depot. The depot was shut down by the government following World War II. The expansion, to include the depot tract, will more than double Shippers Stevedoring's marshaling and storage areas. The expansion tract is being purchased from the Bethlehem Steel Corporation.

Plans also call for the development of a rig-up yard and a new container-repair facility. An additional Ro/Ro ramp is also included in the expansion program.

"We formed Shippers Stevedoring," McManus says, "to fill a need. We wanted to offer services for all aspects of the shipping industry in this area. The time had come to give the younger generation a chance to innovate with some new ideas about cargo handling."

Shippers Stevedoring today boasts the port's largest-capacity roll-on, roll-off berth, deepest berths, and fastest cargo-handling speed at its two private terminals—AGRI Export and Jacinto Port. The expansion planned will be at the Jacinto Port operation.

Although the firm primarily handled grain and agricultural products in its early days, "We felt that as Houston and the Port of Houston grew and became more energy-oriented, facilities here should meet those needs," McManus says. "Thus, we developed the flexibility to meet any industry's needs."

In 1974 Shippers Stevedoring became the first company in the port to buy a 300-ton truck crane. Two years later it built the first Ro/Ro ramp. As many as seven vessels at a time can be accommodated 24 hours a day along the

3,500 feet of dock at berths that draft 38 feet.

Nine cranes aid the unloading and loading of cargo, which can be transferred directly from ship to truck or train, and vice versa. Fifteen rail tracks, switch engines, track scales, and grain hoppers constitute the greatest rail capacity in the port.

When cargo needs to be stored, it can be placed in a large, open area or in some

The Shippers Stevedoring Company built Houston's first Ro/Ro ramp at the AGRI Export facility and, combined with direct rail-to-vessel capabilities, the terminal's flexibility meets any of the shipping industry's needs.

Sophisticated Ro/Ro vessels, such as this one, work around the clock, a factor behind Shippers Stevedoring Company representing more total man-hours than any other operation in the Port of Houston.

272,000 square feet of warehouse space. Also, security is a special concern, with Shippers' premises completely fenced and guarded around the clock.

"Of course, nothing is too big for us to handle," McManus asserts. "We have the equipment to handle any commodity for loading and terminal operation in the port, and we have our own container-inspection facility."

Shippers Stevedoring formed the Shipside Crating Company to provide a total-control concept to shippers by offering custom-crating, -packing, and -bagging services at the AGRI Export and Jacinto Port terminals.

Versatility of the dockside crating company includes the availability of a variety of mobile lifting equipment ranging in capability from small forklifts to large truck cranes.

Although the average age of three executive managers and 10 divisional managers at Shippers Stevedoring is only 40 years, these individuals share approximately 286 years of experience in ship and cargo handling at ports on six continents.

The firm, which has been experiencing a revenue growth rate of some 15 percent the past two years, is the exclusive handler for at least six steamship lines.

"The management team is international in makeup with multilingual capabilities, which is a crucial factor in dealing with international shipping," McManus says. "This team directly oversees the work of operating vessels, controlling berthing space, and loading and unloading ships."

He continues that at present, competition for dockworkers is not too heavy due to the recession. However, in busier times, "the fact that Shippers Stevedoring puts in more total man-hours than any other operation in the port, including the public wharves, helps the firm in obtaining top employees," he says.

Vessels load at Shippers Stevedoring Company's deepwater Jacinto Port facility.

"We are guiding our own destiny," McManus adds. "We don't lock away our management behind layers of assistant clerks. Every shipment, every ship, is handled by an individual dockside supervisor. Should problems arise, our man is there to help solve them."

Grain and agricultural products were primarily handled at the AGRI Export terminal before the slip was completed in 1969.

GEOSOURCE INC.

Geosource Inc. is an international supplier of high-technology products and services primarily to the petroleum industry.

Founded in 1973 as a privately held company, Geosource has, like the city of Houston, grown rapidly since its beginnings. Sales have increased from $49 million in 1973 to over $799 million in 1982, when the company reached number 343 on the Fortune 500. Assets now exceed $629 million and it employs more than 10,000 people around the world.

Originally started to market satellite seismic surveying technology developed by Rockwell International, Geosource today is the most diverse oil services company in the industry. The firm offers over 200 products and services to its customers in more than 40 countries serving the three major segments of the petroleum industry: exploration, development, and processing and distribution.

The company's initial market entry was in the geophysical business with the acquisition of Ray Geophysical, which provided services and equipment in Europe, Africa, the Middle East, and North America. In June 1973 it acquired Petty Engineering, another firm engaged in geophysical services. Petty's primary market strength was in Latin America. These were combined to form the Petty-Ray Geophysical Division, the operating heart of what is today Geosource.

Today Geosource is the largest land geophysical company in the Free World, with over 100 land and 5 marine crews conducting geophysical services around the globe.

Geosource began diversifying its operations in 1975. It first entered the processing and distribution segment with the acquisition of Smith Meters from the A.O. Smith Corporation. Today Geosource participates in this market through Smith Meters and Systems, Wheatley Valves and Pumps, and Crosby safety relief valves.

The development market was also entered in 1975 with the acquisition of the Hunt Tool Company, which provided Geosource with a broad range of oil-

A typical wireline operation at a customer's site in West Texas.

242

A safety relief valve manufactured at the Crosby division in Wrentham, Massachusetts.

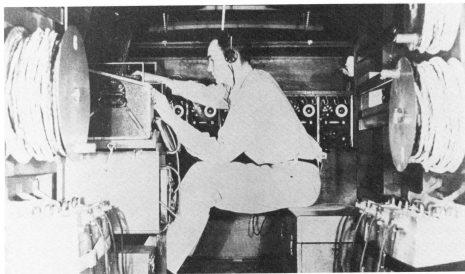

This 1931 photo shows the interior of an observing truck.

related services. Presence in the petroleum development market has expanded in recent years to include wireline, well stimulation, and drilling products and services.

Geosource had its beginnings in 1972, when Rockwell International developed a plan to set up a company to market technology related to seismic surveying by satellite. Besides this technology, Rockwell invested $5 million. Donaldson, Lufkin & Jenrette then provided one million dollars and the services of some of its corporate finance group. DLJ approached Aetna Life & Casualty as a source of additional working capital. Aetna put $10 million into the firm.

The Geosource story from then until now is a remarkable one. It became a public company in 1977, with Aetna holding approximately 30 percent of the stock. Aetna maintained that level of investment until July 1982 when the two companies agreed to merge. Geosource is now a wholly owned subsidiary of Aetna and continues to operate from its Houston-based executive offices.

Throughout its short history Geosource has been a leader in technological innovation. Some of its recent advancements include the Data Sentry and the MDS-14.

The Data Sentry is an example of converting a commodity-type product into an offering with design uniqueness. It is a

digital readout system which replaces the mechanical device traditionally used on a drilling rig. Geosource developed this product using microprocessor techniques originally developed for geophysical instrumentation.

The MDS-14 is a seismic data acquisition system which provides 240 full-resolution channels using an optical fiber data link. The MDS-14 will be expanded to over 1,000 channels which will represent the first major step toward full-resolution, three-dimensional seismic surveying.

Geosource is committed to providing its customers with the most technologically

advanced products and services available through its research and development activities. To meet this commitment, the company has established centers for technology in the areas of electronics and fluid flow technology. Separate from divisional engineering departments, these centers consolidate research activities and serve as focal points for state-of-the-art maintenance, design services, and intra-company communication.

At 10 years of age, Geosource already has made its mark in Texas. With its commitment to service and technological innovation it will continue growing as a partner in progress with its headquarters city, Houston.

The MDS-14 seismic data acquisition system.

TEXAS WESTERN MORTGAGE COMPANY

On May 1, 1978, the scene on the third floor of the Post Oak Bank Building at the offices of Texas Western Mortgage Company was a far cry from the plush carpets and large sofas usually associated with financial executives.

Other than its three partners, the staff of Texas Western on that spring day consisted of one part-time secretary. The four company personnel shared one card table, a telephone, and a few chairs on yet-to-be-carpeted concrete floors. Yet it was a start for the three young mortgage bankers—Dale Couch, president; Woody Taliaferro, executive vice-president; and Harvey Trammell, senior vice-president—all native Houstonians.

A week or so later, as furniture was in various stages of being uncrated and moved in, a potential customer looked in and inquired, "if we were moving in or moving out," recalls Trammell. And it has been that way for the company ever since—each day a new world, a new challenge. Texas Western began operations in one of the wildest interest rate markets in recent history.

Dale Couch and Woody Taliaferro discuss financing on a current project with Houston homebuilders J. Don and Linda Morris.

On May 1, 1978, Dale Couch (left) received the initial monthly payment from the first mortgagor of Texas Western Mortgage, Inc.

Within two months of its founding, the firm had increased its staff to seven employees. Carpet, telephones, and furniture were installed. And it began making FHA-insured loans. The secretary was a part-time employee for just three weeks.

"We started at a time when everyone else in the mortgage banking industry was retrenching," Couch states. "But we did not have a choice but to go after the business. We did not have the big loan portfolios that many of the larger mortgage companies enjoyed."

Texas Western, of course, did not have to conduct extensive market research to find out whether Houston was a suitable place to open a residential mortgage lending operation. Several study groups already had named the city as the top area for favorable development in investment in new plants and equipment for manufacturing operations.

And potential growth in the residential construction market was indicated by a number of sources, indications that later were to be proved by the Houston area leading the nation in new-home construction. Since 1980 the city of Houston has surpassed the $2-billion market for new commercial and residential construction.

"We knew the business was there; it was just a matter of how we went after it," Couch asserts. Texas Western concentrated in self-generated business, not by extensive merger programs or joint ventures. By its second year of business the firm was handling some $70 million in loans.

"We started when interest rates were climbing," explains Taliaferro. "And, as far as interest rates are concerned, we have been in uncharted waters ever since. At

Left to right are Texas Western Mortgage executive Harvey Trammell with Gemcraft Homes executives Russ Hutchins, Joe Ann Golden, Frank Romero, and Bob Hutchins.

office, and it would be a new world," Taliaferro recalls. "The best way to finance a house one day would have changed by the next day. Now, however, things have settled down and we usually suggest one of four types of loans for home buyers."

Much of the firm's business has been on the west side of Houston, a locale with great residential expansion in the past few years. Approximately seven million people currently live in the Houston area.

Today, some four years after it was founded, Texas Western has 50 employees at its 12,000-square-foot office facilities in the 4200 block of the Southwest Freeway. "We have put over $260 million in mortgage loans into the Houston economy," Couch states, "and by the end of 1983 that total should exceed $400 million. Our goal is to be the number one residential mortgage lender in Texas."

As to the future, the firm hopes to expand into the commercial loan market and possibly into other financial service areas, and there are plans to open offices in other Texas cities. Already, Texas Western has expanded into the property management and insurance fields.

"There really are no limits to our future growth," Couch asserts.

one time interest rates had climbed past the 19-percent mark, and almost no one was qualifying for a fixed-rate mortgage at that level."

One of the firm's challenges was to educate—builders, real estate brokers, and

The annual company barbecue—1983.

home buyers and sellers—about new types of available mortgages. It became a matter of matching the home buyer with the type of mortgage loan that was best suited for his needs. The loans have ranged from fixed-rate, 30-year mortgages to various adjustable-type mortgage loans.

"Each day we would walk into the

245

JAMES ORIGINAL CONEY ISLAND

A familiar sight in Houston.

Houston, 1923.

It was there and then that brothers James and Tom Papadakis started cooking up their own version of the American Dream—James Original Coney Island Hot Dog.

Immigrating from their native Greece in the early 1900s, the Papadakis brothers made their way to New York City where they first sampled a popular sandwich New Yorkers fondly referred to as a "Coney Island."

The brothers parted ways for a time. James worked in restaurants in Alaska, Washington, and Houston; Tom stayed in New York as a barber.

Attracted to the opportunities Houston offered, the two joined up in the Bayou City to found their own business. A flip of a coin decided which brother's name was to headline the family venture and in February 1923 the first James Original Coney Island opened its doors on Rusk Street.

Three years later the entrepreneurs moved into a new building in the 1000 block of Walker Street owned by "Silver Dollar" Jim West.

Tom's son, Jimmy Papadakis, remembers, "In all our years there was only one person, Jim West, who was allowed to make his own hot dog. He would come by and give every employee a silver dollar, then go behind the counter and make up his own hot dog."

The Walker Street store is still regarded as a favorite downtown eatery. The shop "was an equalizer, and still is," reflects Jimmy Papadakis. "The bootblack feels as much at home as the banker. The Walker shop has always been a melting pot, and that is the way Daddy and Uncle Jimmy wanted it."

But Houstonians weren't the only ones to try the James Original Coney Island's celebrated hot dogs and chili at the Walker shop. Jimmy recalls, "I looked up one day and saw a crowd of young women at the front door. Pretty soon John Wayne walked in and ordered a bowl of chili. After he tasted it he said, 'This is damn good chili.'"

One of the key reasons for James Original Coney Island's early success was the loyal core of employees at the downtown shop. Some are still with the company today.

"Daddy told me that not once during the Great Depression did they refuse to serve someone who could not pay," Jimmy recalls, "He said they would eventually get paid, one way or another. Daddy and Uncle Jimmy just loved people."

James Papadakis died in 1968; his brother Tom died in 1974.

Today Jimmy Papadakis and his

After sampling "Coney Island" sandwiches in New York, James (left) and Tom Papadakis introduced their own version in Houston in 1923.

brother-in-law, Louis Servos, run the 12 James Original Coney Island restaurants in the Houston area. They employ some 450 employees and serve Houstonians 30,000 hot dogs a day.

To this day not one single ingredient in any of the original recipes has ever changed.

Through the years many items have been added to the menu but the Coney Island sandwich is still the most popular. Houstonians consume 30,000 hot dogs each day at the 12 James Coney Island restaurants.

SUNILAND FURNITURE

Suniland has been a significant influence on elegant home interiors of Houston since the summer of 1927, a month before Lindbergh made his historic flight across the Atlantic. The first furniture order was delivered from Myers-Spalti Mfg., a Houston furniture maker, to a rambling two-story residence one mile from downtown.

The upstairs rooms at 3016 Main comprised the home of the owner, John C. Weston, and his family. On the bottom floor Suniland opened for business "out of the high-rent district." Weston, his wife, and two other employees took care of customers, in striking contrast to the 1983 staff of almost 500.

The first of several expansions occurred only a year after the opening of a new 17,000-square-foot building at 2817 Main, two blocks from the original site. Instead of a one-story-and-balcony structure, it developed into three floors, topped later by a fourth story.

Suniland's room displays drew applause from the furniture industry. "The showrooms make you believe the myths you hear about Texas," commented one furniture manufacturer. Interior design shows were a regular feature for many years.

An Office Furniture division was added in 1949, moving in two years to separate quarters at the corner of Milam and Francis. Later 2303 Main became its home, with 16,500 square feet to offer complete design facilities with experienced professional designers, architects, workroom facilities, and a comprehensive selection of office furnishings. Here Suniland Office Furniture remained until it rejoined the residential operation at 2800 Fondren.

Matching the pace of Office Furniture's progress, in 1955 home furnishings expanded to 100,000 square feet of showroom and other improvements. The 2817 Main structure with its contemporary gray aluminum and white marble, became a landmark on the Houston home fashion scene, providing fine furnishings and interior design assistance to a fourth generation of Houston homemakers.

In 1961 a new era began for Suniland.

A look at Suniland's original 3016 South Main home portrays an enduring dignity.

Even then Houston showed signs of being a 20th-century Pied Piper. People and corporations all over the world were listening to the crescendo rhythm of the city's growth. At that time, a pioneering furniture family moved from the West to South Texas. On June 26 the Kauffmans took over the ownership of Suniland and continued the firm's heritage of "family-owned" and "family-operated."

The years of planning began that day, culminating in the 1975 trek to the spacious housing of brick and glass at 2800 Fondren, between Richmond and

At its present 2800 Fondren location, modern architecture covers the inside story of Suniland's timeless quality.

Westheimer. The accelerated growth in Houston's southwest area coincided with the change in locations for more convenient customer access. About 200,000 square feet provide one-floor shopping and warehouse facilities with space for over 250 customer cars on its nine-acre tract.

A residential atmosphere was achieved in colorations, plantings, heavy beamed ceiling, and various roof elevations. All furniture, carpets and rugs, accessory, and custom departments are housed on the main floor with incandescent lighting to permit the customer to see colors and finishes as they will appear in his own home. On the second floor is an art gallery that doubles as an auditorium.

The entire Suniland operation now includes a modern mechanized warehouse with 90,000 square feet at 4001 Briarpark, the largest drapery workroom in the Southwest at 2818 Canal, and Suniland Clearance Center at 7301 Clarewood Drive in the Sharpstown area of Houston.

Expansion, growth, and new ways to serve customers are not at an end, according to president Robert J. Kauffman. Suniland has been a part of Houston's history as one of the city's major retail establishments. With the largest interior design staff in the Southwest, Suniland will always be dedicated to the residents of the area and the creation of beautiful home and office interiors throughout Texas.

WADDELL'S HOUSE FURNISHING COMPANY

The enterprise known today as Waddell's House Furnishing Company was founded in 1881 by Hugh Waddell, an Irish immigrant who came to the United States at the close of the Civil War. The firm's growth was rapid and its original location at 30-32 Main Street quickly became inadequate. A move was made across the street to the Arcade Building in 1887.

In the late 1890s Waddell's purchased a quarter-block at the intersection of Fannin Street and Prairie Avenue and constructed a three-story brick building next door to Christ Church Cathedral. Three additional stories were added in 1905, making it one of the largest structures in Houston at that time. In addition to the downtown display floors, a 105,000-square-foot warehouse/workshop was erected off Harrisburg Road on Sampson Street. That facility is still in use by Waddell's today.

The business was incorporated in 1911 with Hugh Waddell as president; M.R. Waddell, vice-president; and H.K. Waddell, secretary/treasurer. The name became Waddell's House Furnishing Company at that time.

Hugh Waddell set high standards of quality for his business, and his ideals have guided the firm during its more than 100 years of service to the Houston community. Many of Waddell's early clients have enjoyed lengthy, mutually beneficial relationships with the home furnishing firm.

The Bender Hotel was completed at the corner of Walker and Main in 1912, and Waddell's was commissioned to furnish the interior. The following year the first two wings of the Rice Hotel were under construction and Waddell's was commissioned to furnish them upon their completion.

Hugh Waddell died in 1915. M.R. Waddell became president; H.K. Waddell, vice-president; and Earl Wilson, secretary/treasurer. Waddell's was placed under the direction of George A. Rick, general manager.

Success continued for the company. In 1926 the third wing of the Rice Hotel was completed and again Waddell's was commissioned to furnish the interior. The firm was asked to furnish the Lamar Hotel

In 1881 Hugh Waddell founded and became the first president of what is now known as Waddell's House Furnishing Company.

the following year. Other major projects included the Gulf Building, the Texas State Hotel, and the National Bank of Commerce, all in 1929, and Radio Station KTRH.

Waddell's six-story structure was razed in 1938 by a spectacular fire that lasted for many hours. The Great Depression was under way and the store was not immediately rebuilt. Instead, the business was transferred to the warehouse/workshop site.

The outbreak of World War II further lessened the feasibility of rebuilding. The sons of the third generation enlisted in the service and were sent overseas. Both M.R. Waddell and H.K. Waddell died during the conflict and the company remained at

ebb tide until the return of the surviving principals in 1946.

A corporate resurgence began that year with the election of officers. H.K. Waddell, Jr., became president; M.R. Waddell, Jr., vice-president; and John M. Waddell, secretary/treasurer. Under the direction of the new president, a 10,000-square-foot addition was constructed at the Sampson Street location and work began on a warehouse/showroom. That operation became successful as a discount showroom and Houston was introduced to high-quality exclusive lines at reasonable

prices.

In 1950, during the renaissance of Early American furniture, Waddell's opened a South Main location specializing solely in American traditional furnishings. The store, called Waddell's Colonial Shop, enjoyed phenomenal success and once again the company became a major factor in the household furnishing field. No attempt was ever made to reestablish Waddell's commercial division.

A gallery concept store was acquired by merger with Baker's American Heritage House, Inc., in 1970, with V. Truman Baker assuming the corporate reins as general manager and subsequently as president. Current officers of Waddell's House Furnishing Company are Rutherford Waddell, chairman of the board; V. Truman Baker, president; Richard Waddell, vice-president; and Elia Salinas, secretary/treasurer.

V. Truman Baker has been president of Waddell's House Furnishing Company since 1976.

The warehouse crew relaxes beside Waddell's delivery truck, about 1912. The vehicle was chain driven with nonpneumatic tires and one of the first such vehicles in Houston superseding horse-drawn delivery equipment.

EARTHMAN FUNERAL HOMES

In the 19th century there was nothing to compare with today's complex industry of funeral home chains, insurance companies, and cemetery organizations. Undertaking operations usually were sideline occupations. When someone died the local furniture store carpenter often was asked to build a coffin. Then someone had to provide a livery wagon to take the coffin to the cemetery. As a result, undertakers frequently were carpenters or livery stable operators.

James Bradshaw Earthman I, a member of one of the original founding families of Fayette County, was a livery store operator who started a funeral home business in Taylor in 1889. At the time Taylor was a major railroad center in Texas.

Earthman and a good friend, J.C. McCarty, a surveyor for the railroad, often talked about the future of Texas. While Taylor was a busy center of commerce in the late 1890s, McCarty often voiced the opinion to his friend that he felt the major growth of the state would be in the coastal region.

McCarty finally convinced Earthman to move, and they headed for Houston. In 1903 they opened Earthman & McCarty Undertaking Company, Funeral Directors and Embalmers, at 715 Main, with an abundance of enthusiasm and very little cash.

For a short period Earthman was employed at the Stowers Furniture Company. When he received a call to handle a funeral, Earthman would take some time off from work; when the funeral was over, he would return to Stowers. The fledgling business prospered and in 1907 the partners moved their funeral home into a building near the intersection of San Jacinto and Texas Avenue, across from the Christ Church Cathedral.

Robert L. Earthman, grandson of James B. Earthman I and today president of Earthman Funeral Homes, notes that during this period the horses used by his grandfather's company were black. Another funeral home in Houston used white horses. "So the two firms had an agreement to swap out horses, when needed," he recalls. "That way people could have their choice of white or black

James B. Earthman, co-founder of Earthman & McCarty Undertaking Company, in the office on San Jacinto Street.

horses to pull the funeral wagon." Later, Earthman was one of the first Houston funeral homes to use a motorized hearse.

The company moved to 1011 Milam Street in 1914. It remained at that location until 1925, when it moved into its current corporate headquarters at 2420 Fannin. This facility was the first brick building constructed solely for use as a funeral home in the city of Houston. It still serves as a funeral home today, the only downtown funeral home in Houston.

Robert Earthman says, "Many of the people who desire funeral services at the downtown facility are old-time Houston families, or families who are scattered about the city and feel that it is a central location and easy for all family members to reach."

James B. Earthman I died in 1931 and his son, James B. Earthman, Jr., a graduate of Rice Institute and a Houston law school graduate, took over management of the company at that time.

In 1938 he started the Earthman Burial Association, with the help of a group of friends. A small-debit burial organization, it became the predecessor of the Mission Life Insurance Company, which began in 1948. Insurance in force totaled $50 million in 1982. Later, Earthman formed Funeral Services, Inc., a prearranged-funeral company, which today represents some 200 funeral homes in Texas and

surrounding states. In 1982 Funeral Services, Inc., had sales of some $20 million.

The company grew with Houston, opening additional funeral homes throughout the area: Baytown, 1948; Bellaire, 1956; Highlands, 1958; off the Gulf Freeway, 1962; and off the North Freeway, 1968. Earthman Funeral Home at Resthaven Cemetery and the Earthman Funeral Home at Hunters Creek were opened in 1982.

Robert Earthman says, "We will probably stay at about this size for now. We feel that thoughtful service was the foundation of the Earthman Funeral Homes and, as such, we want to continue giving this service to those we serve in the future."

The four family companies, Earthman Funeral Homes, Mission Life Insurance Company, Resthaven Cemetery, and Funeral Services, Inc., are run by family members. Michael R. Earthman is president and Donald E. Earthman is executive vice-president of Mission Life Insurance Company. Bruce Earthman is president of Resthaven Memorial Gardens. James E. Earthman III, a Houston lawyer who served in the Texas legislature for five years, is vice-president

The first motorized hearse in the city of Houston was owned by Earthman & McCarty.

of Earthman Funeral Homes. Two other brothers not directly involved in the business are John A., a partner in the architectural firm of Earthman-Kimbrell; and Dr. Thomas E. Earthman, a medical doctor.

"We brothers visit a lot," says Robert Earthman. "Although we have major family gatherings at Christmas, Easter, and during the summer, it is a rare week that we don't get together two or three times."

The J.B. Earthman Company moved to this new facility in 1925. Located at 2420 Fannin, it is still the corporate headquarters for Earthman Funeral Homes.

RAYMOND INTERNATIONAL INC.

Henry F. LeMieux, chairman of the board and chief executive officer of Raymond International Inc.

R. Nelson Crews, president and chief operating officer of Raymond International Inc.

Raymond International Inc., a worldwide engineering and construction company, was among the first wave of New York-based firms that moved their headquarters to Houston during the early 1970s. The organization has grown and prospered ever since.

Raymond was founded in 1897 by Alfred A. Raymond, inventor of the steel-encased, cast-in-place concrete foundation pile. Originally named the Raymond Concrete Pile Company, the firm maintained its headquarters in New York City for 70 years before moving to Houston in 1972.

In 1911 Raymond became an international corporation by obtaining contracts for construction work in Mexico and South America. That same year, Raymond completed a wharf for the Gulf Refining Company at Port Arthur—one of the first of many jobs in the region.

The company established a district office in Houston in 1924, and has continued to take an active part in the business, civic, and industrial life of the city since that time.

Over the years, Raymond also steadily continued to increase its activities in the international construction market. The name was changed to Raymond International Inc. in 1958. Fourteen years later its entire corporate headquarters was relocated to Houston.

Since that move, the firm has expanded its markets and capabilities. In 1977 Raymond acquired Kaiser Engineers, a California-based engineering company founded by Henry J. Kaiser. This acquisition was important in Raymond's development from primarily a heavy and marine construction corporation into a world leader in most phases of engineering, construction, and construction management.

Raymond International in 1976 established another major subsidiary, Raymond Offshore Constructors, Inc., to manufacture and install offshore oil and gas drilling and production platforms in the Gulf of Mexico.

In 1982 Raymond International's revenues topped $1.6 billion, and ranked sixth in new contracts in its industry. Board chairman Henry F. LeMieux credits Houston with much of his company's success, stating, "The most important thing about our move to Houston is that it put us in an environment where people have the most optimistic, can-do attitude of any place in the country."

THE RUSSO COMPANIES

The Russo Companies commenced business in the late 1960s with two employees. Within 10 years the firm had grown to over 100 employees managing more than $500 million in assets. And— as important as dollar figures—the company represents the new breed of real estate development, combining various areas of investment.

Joe E. Russo, a native Houstonian, is a graduate of the University of Texas at Austin with a degree in engineering through business. After serving as an officer in the U.S. Army Corps of Engineers, he returned to Houston in the late 1950s and entered the commercial real estate field.

Within a year he had organized his own firm, which specialized in commercial real estate brokerage and leasing. A series of partnerships resulted in his company assuming a dominant role in downtown and suburban office building leasing. He represented the Gerald D. Hines and Kenneth Schnitzer development organizations throughout the mid-1960s before deciding to establish his present business.

The firm's projects, which are distinctive in that the architecture expresses a statement of quality, represent more than three million square feet of floor space in a variety of ventures. Notable undertakings of The Russo Companies include a 400,000-square-foot complex at San Felipe and Voss; a 200,000-square-foot facility at 1717 and

Joe E. Russo, president of The Russo Companies.

The Lyric Centre Office Building, a one-million-square-foot office complex being developed by The Russo Companies in downtown Houston.

1770 St. James; a 200,000-square-foot structure at Woodway Centre and Voss; and The Lyric Centre Office Building, a one-million-square-foot downtown office project currently being developed.

The corporation also has expanded its base into financial services and oil and gas ventures. By an affiliation, it acquired a major savings and loan association, and has majority ownership of two national banks.

The Russo Companies' management anticipates a future organization of full financial services, from real estate development to oil and gas properties and banking services. The firm's goal in manageable assets by the end of the 1980s is one billion dollars.

Joe Russo asserts that, "Houston has provided an opportunity for the high-performance company to achieve goals at an accelerated rate. It has, in many ways, allowed the entrepreneur to reach levels of achievements unequaled in any other location in the history of the country."

253

HERMANN HOSPITAL

At the turn of the century Houston was in a state of economic bliss and the population growth was creating a need for bigger and better health care facilities.

No one was more aware of this need than George H. Hermann, who had been forced to seek specialized medical care in the eastern part of the United States before his death in 1914. For years he had dreamed of giving a hospital to Houstonians.

Following the ancient tradition of English common law, Hermann decreed the hospital his "widow" since he left no heirs. According to the old law, as long as "she" (the hospital) continued to exist, she would benefit from his estate.

With the stroke of a pen, Hermann began his hospital gift to Houston and the Hermann Hospital Estate, the perpetual guardian of his dream. The Estate set the wheels in motion, and by 1922 architects had the project under way. Hermann Hospital opened its doors on July 1, 1925.

Isolated on the edge of town, the original Hermann Hospital building graced the horizons of Houston as a great white castle. The ground floor had the appearance of a hotel lobby decorated in faience tile with colors complementing the walls and woodwork. Corridors were spacious and the doorways high and arched. An open patio and flowing water fountain greeted visitors at the main entrance.

One intern who practiced at the hospital during those early years noted that "Hermann was located in a beautiful setting, way out in the country—a far ride by trolley car from downtown Houston. That trolley line ended just across from the hospital where the park is now located on Outer Belt Drive."

The hospital was the first complete unit of a "bacon-plan," or total service medical care, facility. It had its own power, heat, lighting, and refrigeration plant. There were facilities for the Hermann School of Nursing, which also was opened in 1925, and complete quarters for the entire hospital staff. By 1940 Hermann was the only hospital in Houston with three established residency programs—surgery, obstetrics/gynecology, and internal medicine.

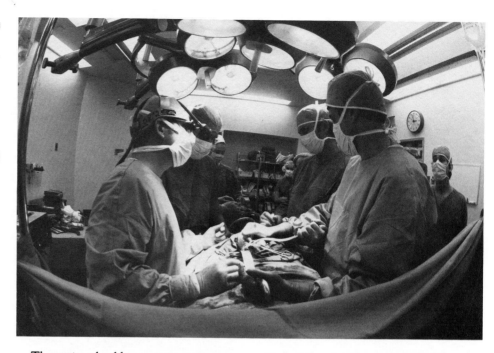

The patient load began to increase as Houston began another population boom in the late 1940s. After World War II the city needed more hospital beds and more doctors capable of providing quality patient care.

Hermann Hospital's parent, the Hermann Hospital Estate, was continuing the guardianship of the founder's dream, and 1949 proved a vintage year for both the hospital and the Estate. The newly

Opened in July 1982, the 53-bed Texas Kidney Institute consolidates Hermann's renal services on the ninth floor of the Jesse H. and Mary Gibbs Jones Pavilion.

formed Texas Medical Center, Inc., selected land adjacent to Hermann as the site for its construction plans. A second Hermann building, which was later rededicated as the Corbin J. and

The Jones Pavilion at Hermann Hospital.

Wilhelmina C. Robertson Pavilion, was opened, adding an additional 400 beds to the original 300 beds. The facility was a modern seven-story structure, one of the first hospital buildings in the United States to be completely air conditioned.

The Hermann Professional Building also went into service in 1949. It offered 15 floors and 120 suites for physician offices. That same year the hospital and the University of Houston jointly began operating the School of Nursing. During the 1950s the hospital gained its reputation as the "baby hospital." By

---

Beginning with one helicopter in 1976, the Hermann Hospital Life Flight Program is now the largest hospital-based and -operated air transport system in the nation.

Hermann Hospital has been affiliated with the University of Texas Medical School since 1968, and serves as the primary teaching hospital for the school.

1956 more than 50,000 infants had been born under Hermann's roof.

The hospital continued its commitment to the teaching aspect of medicine. In 1956 the University of Houston withdrew from the nurse training field, and Hermann announced its plans for expansion of its nursing school. A new nursing building was added to the hospital properties and a new nursing training program, never tried before in Texas, was established. At this same time, the Hermann School of Vocational Nursing opened. The original school for registered nurses would eventually close in 1973, but licensed vocational nurses are still graduating from the hospital's vocational nursing unit at an average of 60 per year.

Modern clinics and outpatient services were developed and expanded in the 1960s. In 1968 the University of Texas System selected Houston, with its Texas

Medical Center, as the site of its new medical school and Hermann Hospital was chosen as its primary teaching hospital.

Upon the approval of the affiliation agreement by the Estate trustees, Hermann Hospital launched a major expansion program in preparation for its role as the primary teaching hospital for the University of Texas Medical School of Houston (UTMSH). The third pavilion, the Jesse H. and Mary Gibbs Jones Pavilion, added 300 more beds to Hermann's patient bed capacity upon its completion in 1977.

The entire Texas Medical Center joined the expansion campaign when more and more Americans began looking to Houston as the place to settle. UTMSH started construction adjacent to Hermann's Jones Pavilion. The original Hermann Hospital building was restored and dedicated as the Hugh Roy and Lillie Cranz Cullen Pavilion in 1973.

The 1970s saw completion of the Mirtha G. Dunn Interfaith Chapel, the Family Center, the Hermann Eye Center, the John S. Dunn Helistop, and other services, including the Life Flight air ambulance program, begun in 1976 and today one of the largest hospital-based and operated air ambulance programs in the nation. It is one of few such programs equipped to fly a physician and a nurse on every mission of mercy. It was also during the 1970s that Hermann's Category I-rated Emergency Center became a major trauma treatment center in the Southwest.

Other innovative programs continued to be added. Hermann provides comprehensive care for burn patients with a 15-bed unit which utilizes the multidisciplinary team approach in the daily treatment of patients. The skin bank, one of the few in the nation, accepts and maintains donor skin for grafting. Opened in 1982, the 53-bed Texas Kidney Institute consolidates Hermann's renal services, including renal transplant, inpatient and outpatient dialysis facilities, and medical and surgical care for renal patients of all ages.

Today Hermann is licensed for 908 beds and has a staff of almost 3,000 employees, and 1,500 active, courtesy, and house staff (resident) physicians.

BROWNING-FERRIS INDUSTRIES

Browning-Ferris Industries (BFI), one of the largest waste service companies in the world, evolved from a small residential waste collection firm, American Refuse Systems, Inc. (ARS), founded in 1967.

However, it was not until the final months of 1969 that the company began a program that would result in the acquisition by the end of 1973 of more than 150 privately owned waste service businesses throughout the United States, Canada, and Puerto Rico.

In the aggregate, these businesses represented approximately one and one-half percent of the estimated 10,000 independent waste service companies operating in the United States at the time. Together, these firms became the nucleus of an international, $700-million, New York Stock Exchange-listed corporation.

Browning-Ferris now provides waste collection, disposal, and resource recovery services through some 150 operation locations in this country, Canada, and Puerto Rico, and has business interests in waste services in South America, Europe, and the Middle East.

Today the company and its affiliates employ approximately 14,000 people, utilize approximately 4,300 collection vehicles, and own or manage 71 sanitary landfills. For the year ending September 30, 1982, revenues totaled $715 million. The firm has approximately 30 million shares outstanding with about

A Browning-Ferris chemical waste truck.

9,000 shareholders of record.

BFI began with the founding of American Refuse by Tom Fatjo, Jr., who provided one-truck garbage collection services to a Houston area subdivision. Fatjo persuaded several of his associates, including Norman Myers, now vice-chairman of the board of directors and chief marketing officer of BFI, to join the fledgling enterprise. In 1968 Louis A. Waters, a fellow Rice University alumnus of Fatjo's and at that time vice-president of a Houston investment banking firm,

The new BFI building—headquarters in Houston for Browning-Ferris Industries' operations.

was retained as financial advisor to American Refuse. Waters guided ARS in raising additional equity capital by offering shares of stock to a group of private investors.

In 1969 American Refuse acquired a controlling interest in the Browning-Ferris Machinery Company, a Dallas-headquartered distributor of heavy construction equipment, changed the name to Browning-Ferris Industries, and made plans to use the venture as the base upon which to build a nationwide operation. That year Waters joined Browning-Ferris as chairman of the board and was instrumental in developing the plans necessary to expand the business by raising capital. The machinery company possessed several key advantages that would make initiation of American Refuse's plans possible. It was an old, established, regional business, publicly held, with its common stock traded on the over-the-counter market.

Patterson Waste Control, Inc., based in Memphis; Houston Disposal Services, Inc., based in Houston; and Waste Control of Puerto Rico, Inc., based in San Juan, were acquired in 1970. The president and majority owner of these companies was Harry J. Phillips, today's chairman of the board and chief executive officer of Browning-Ferris.

Annual revenues of Browning-Ferris climbed to $300 million by 1973, making it the largest waste services company in the world. By the early 1980s its revenues exceeded $500 million.

Browning-Ferris is a leader in seeking to demonstrate that energy can be recovered from waste. BFI of Toronto is now into its second five-year contract with the Ontario Ministry of the Environment to operate an experimental resource recovery plant in Toronto. The company also is licensee in North America for the Deutsche Babcock Anlagen roller grate mass-burning technology, a system used in 50 waste-to-energy plant operations overseas. The first North American application for the technology is expected to be under contract in 1983.

Access to this technology and operating experience will enable BFI to design, construct, and operate plants for municipalities to convert the combustible portion of solid waste to marketable energy products in the form of steam and electricity.

While the company's growth and development in the early 1970s resulted primarily from geographic expansion through the acquisition of waste service businesses, BFI's growth since has resulted from developing and expanding the services offered through existing operating units. Through this shift in emphasis, for example, BFI units that historically had provided waste collection services for commercial and industrial accounts have, in many cases, expanded into residential waste collection contracts in the same communities.

Residential collection services, historically provided exclusively in many areas by municipal sanitation departments, are now often provided by BFI. The company estimates that it currently provides waste collection services for more than 2,660,000 residential customers.

Other growth opportunities for the firm include recent international market development activities. Affiliates of Browning-Ferris already have waste collection, disposal, and street-cleaning contracts in Caracas and Maracaibo, Venezuela; Kuwait Municipality, Kuwait; and Riyadh, Saudi Arabia.

Top:
Today BFI and its affiliates own or manage 71 sanitary landfills.

Above:
From a single truck providing garbage collection to one Houston area subdivision, to an international corporation employing 14,000 people, Browning-Ferris utilizes some 4,300 collection vehicles.

JAMAIL BROTHERS FOOD MARKET

N.D. "Jim" Jamail, founder of Jamail Brothers Food Market.

N.D. "Jim" Jamail, born in a mountain village near Beirut, Lebanon, came to Houston by himself in 1904 at the age of 12 to live with an aunt. By the age of 16 he was in business for himself.

Jamail (when he came to the United States he changed the spelling of his name from Gemayel) began selling produce from a stall in the old City Farmers' Market, a covered facility on the downtown block bounded by Travis, Milam, Congress, and Preston. On the first level of the market, some 50 merchants maintained produce, meat markets, eating establishments, and, off to one side, a fish market. City hall offices were on the second level. Farmers would park on the curb and sell their local fruit and vegetables. The City Farmers' Market was the only shopping area in Houston, which had no suburban stores. The elite area, what is now Montrose, was the limit of the residences.

Jamail established a produce business based on the highest quality and personal service. His motto, "No matter where it grows—we have it," has been carried out throughout the years.

In 1914 his younger brother, Joe D. Jamail, came to Houston from Lebanon, joined the U.S. Army, and served until 1918 when he returned to Houston to join the produce operation. The firm of Jamail Brothers was formed at that time.

A.D. Jamail, a third brother, later joined the firm.

The brothers decided to branch out and joined the ABC Stores chain, which owned some 13 stores in Houston, Galveston, and Beaumont. Around 1934 the old City Farmers' Market was closed, and the brothers concentrated their efforts on the ABC units.

Clarence Jamail joined the business after graduating from Texas A&M in 1938. Then, in 1941, the ABC firm was purchased and the brothers acquired nearly a square block in the 2100 block of South Shepherd. There a grocery store was built to sell only the finest merchandise to its discriminating clientele with emphasis on produce and meat and gourmet items. The brothers brought to Houston a new era in retail grocery marketing by introducing items that were not locally available. The firm was the first to have Pepperidge Farm bread expressed from Connecticut.

In 1946 Fred Jamail joined the firm after his discharge from the U.S. Marines. The second generation of brothers to run the business, Fred Jamail died in 1959.

Two of Clarence Jamail's sons, Edward and Gerald, later joined after graduating from Texas A&M, resulting in the third generation of brothers in the firm. In 1978 Gerald opened Jamail's at Woodlands and four years later he established Jamail's at Kingwood.

In 1944 Jamail Brothers was recognized by *Time* magazine, which named the firm the best grocery store in Houston.

"We are proud that we are a third-generation business and serve many third-generation customers," says Clarence Jamail. "Down through the years we have tried to maintain the type of store that is fast fading in the United States—a neighborhood store that serves its immediate area. We treat our customers as guests and friends, not as numbers."

The old City Farmers' Market where N.D. Jamail began selling produce in 1908.

JoHN W JEWELLER

It was shortly after World War II when Barney and Bunny Walzel opened their first jewelry store in a 1,700-square-foot facility in the 3300 block of Dixie Drive off the Old Spanish Trail.

The Walzels' approach was to offer traditional, not overly expensive, jewelry—known in the trade as traffic items. But their main direction was toward making their store one that provided a great deal of personal attention. Customers almost became family.

Due to tremendous growth in the southwest part of Houston, the Walzels decided to open a new store in the Maplewood area at Beechnut and Hillcroft. Again it was the personalized approach that was emphasized, an approach the Walzels were certain that their children, Cherryll, John, and Robert, understood.

After Barney died in 1970 (Bunny had died about a year earlier), the three children became owners of the jewelry business. Robert was a professional golfer and did not remain active in the company. John, at the time a freshman at Sam Houston State University, returned home to help sister Cherryll run the enterprise.

They decided to move the operation to the just-opened Saks Fifth Avenue Mall, after making two trips to New York to convince the Saks owners that the new store would be appropriate for inclusion in the fashionable facility. John and Cherryll Walzel then opened a 2,500-square-foot store offering fine jewelry.

In 1978 the brother and sister decided to establish separate retail operations, and

John opened a 1,450-square-foot fashion jewelry store in Post Oak Central in the 2000 block of South Post Oak. Cherryll remained at the Saks Mall store.

"Because of the confusion involving two stores with the name 'Walzel' so close to one another, I decided to rename my store John W Jeweller," John says. Since starting his Post Oak Central operation, John has opened a second facility, a 975-square-foot facility at the Warwick Post Oak Hotel.

To enter the Post Oak Central unit, customers push a buzzer and the door is

John W. Walzel opened this 1,450-square-foot fashion jewelry store in Post Oak Central in 1978.

then opened electronically from inside, in what John Walzel asserts is "strictly a safety" feature. "Of course, ours is not what one would call a traffic store. We know 90 percent of the customers who push that buzzer. And most are Houstonians."

As to the future, John Walzel says he may open new hotel units in the future, and is considering expanding to other Texas cities.

LINBECK CONSTRUCTION

The story behind Linbeck Construction's emergence as one of the country's premier general contractors began in an obscure Arkansas town in the late 1920s. There in Subiaco, Leo Linbeck pursued his dream of becoming a builder, learning from the age of 15 the trades of carpentry, electrical wiring, plumbing, and cement finishing. The drive to excel was evident early. After building homes in the Arkansas countryside for a number of years, he left for Tulsa, Oklahoma, in 1930. In Tulsa, then (as now) an oil boom town, Linbeck worked on his first high-rise construction project and soon was in charge of many of the on-site construction operations, working in some dozen midwestern states over the next several years.

Leo Linbeck was well suited to these tasks and ready for the challenges ahead. While working on a building project in Dallas, Linbeck accepted a local firm's offer to become its general superintendent. The firm promptly sent him to Houston to oversee the successful completion of a 90-day construction

Linbeck Construction was the general contractor for St. John's School in Houston.

project, and Linbeck, as he later said, "never got around to leaving . . . I decided to go into business for myself, and opened a two-room walk-up office on Main Street. We had one employee." The year was 1938, and Linbeck Construction was off and running.

Within two weeks the fledgling company had secured its first job. During the first few years, growth was rapid but carefully controlled. Controlled expansion was to be a Linbeck hallmark. By 1941 the firm had relocated, building its own offices and equipment warehouse on Peden Street. This property later was sold to Miner-Dederick Construction Company, and the Linbeck operations moved to Saint Street.

To complement the construction firm's accelerated growth, Linbeck in the early 1950s formed P & L Equipment Company, Inc. The board of directors— Linbeck, his wife Patti Ruth, and their three children—handled P & L's accounts for heavy construction work on such projects as underpasses, elevated roadways, flood-control structures, and bridges.

The company continued to expand, and in 1956 Linbeck Enterprises was

Leo Linbeck, Sr., the founder of Linbeck Construction.

chartered under the same board and management. Initially providing bulk storage for wheat, rice, milo, and fertilizer, the company (since renamed Distribution Services, Inc.) now offers general

Built in 1939, Avalon Alley's Duckpin Bowling Lanes was Linbeck Construction's first project.

warehousing and distribution services in the Houston market.

From the start, all of the Linbeck businesses had been family directed. Accordingly, Leo Linbeck, Jr., joined the firm in 1957 after completing his studies at the University of Notre Dame and the University of Texas. He spent the next nine years working in the field and in the Linbeck offices, and in 1966 was elected president and chief executive officer. At that point, Leo Linbeck, Sr., assumed the position of chairman of the board.

As the construction industry changed, the Linbeck organization responded. The company was restructured in 1973 with the formation of the Linbeck Corporation (formerly Linbeck Enterprises) and its wholly owned subsidiaries: Linbeck Construction Corporation, Urban Construction Company, P & L Equipment Company, Inc., Distribution Services, Inc., and Linbeck International Company. The board of directors, then comprised entirely of family members, also was reorganized that year. Mrs. Leo Linbeck, Sr., Mrs. Peter G. Doyle (Poppy Linbeck Doyle), and Mrs. F. Fisher Reynolds, Jr. (Suzanne Linbeck

Reynolds), resigned from the board, and three independent outside directors were appointed. The family had decided that the next phase of Linbeck's development could be assisted by the perspectives of business leaders from outside the family structure, and indeed outside the construction industry. Although the company remained privately held, the directors were given the authority associated with publicly held companies. The new board structure would help Linbeck become an even more dominant force in the construction industry. Since the 1973 reorganization, the corporation has grown at a compounded rate of 25 percent per year. During this period, additional operating units were incorporated in order to further broaden the capabilities of the company. Helena Inc. erects structural steel. Lucia Inc. encompasses a full range of masonry skills, including precast architectural concrete erection.

Leo Linbeck, Jr., was appointed chairman of the board in 1975 and his father was elected senior chairman. Both have served as president of the Associated General Contractors of America, Houston Chapter. In addition, Leo Linbeck, Jr., has served as building division chairman of the National Associated General Contractors

of America and he currently is a member of the executive committee and is a life member of the board of directors. Other senior officers of Linbeck Construction are Peter G. Doyle, who in 1973 opened Linbeck Construction's Dallas office and was elected president and chief operating officer in 1982, and Glenn D. Graff, executive vice-president and chief financial officer. In addition, the parent Linbeck Corporation lists Glenn Graff as executive vice-president and chief financial officer and F. Fisher Reynolds, Jr., as vice-president, property management.

Today the Linbeck corporate offices are located at 3810 West Alabama in a two-story structure the firm constructed. The company operates additional offices in Dallas, Fort Worth, Tulsa, and Beaumont. From a staff of 30 in its first year of operations in 1938, Linbeck Construction now employs 200 salaried professionals and as many as 2,000 construction craftsmen. The company is ranked by *Engineering News Record* as the 63rd largest contractor in the United States, based on 1982 contract volume figures.

Another Linbeck undertaking of note is the 40-story Dresser Tower. Built in 1973, it is situated in Cullen Center in downtown Houston.

RALPH RUPLEY FURRIERS

Ralph Rupley, Sr., born in Victoria, moved to Houston around the turn of the century with his family. Among his first jobs, in addition to schoolwork, was lighting the gas lamps in downtown Houston in the early 1900s. While still in high school, he delivered the *Houston Post* via horse and buggy.

After serving in the U.S. Army during World War I, he returned to Texas and attended Texas Christian University in Fort Worth, where he worked in a dress shop. Thus began his interest in the retail business.

Moving to Houston in 1923, Rupley and his wife Mildred opened their first fur company in a second-story room over the old Queen Theater on Main Street. It was the style of the day to wear silver fox skins rounded rather than flat, with a silk lining. The Rupleys, who by now had two infant children who often slept in tissue-lined shipping boxes, began sewing the fox fur pelts together while stocking their first fur pieces.

Two German immigrants, Carl and George Stephanow, joined the Rupleys in 1929 and remained with the organization for more than 40 years.

Following World War II Ralph Rupley, Jr., joined the furrier upon his graduation from Rice Institute. The store property was purchased by the First City Bank in 1958, and the company moved to the C&I Building at Main and McKinney. Operations continued there until Ralph

Rupley Furriers relocated to a new store built on a tract that is now adjacent to the present Post Oak Central Building.

As the Post Oak area grew in size and

For many years the downtown location of Ralph Rupley Furriers was at Main and McKinney.

importance, the downtown store was closed, and the cold-storage vault was moved to a business park to accommodate the more than 8,000 customers using the facility. The Post Oak property was sold in 1981 and the store moved across the street to the 2300 block of Post Oak.

Ralph Rupley, Sr., died in 1967; the firm's operations have been managed since that time by Ralph Rupley, Jr., an attorney, with the assistance of his younger brother, Bob Rupley.

Today Ralph Rupley Furriers is one of the few large retail operations still controlled by the original family.

Ralph Rupley, Sr., and his wife Mildred opened their first fur company over the old Queen Theater on Main Street.

C.O.D. CONCRETE, INC.

The history of a company often is revealed by its sights and sounds. If you had stood outside the C.O.D. Concrete yard in 1972, for example, you might have seen a pair of old mixers sitting lazily in the hot Houston sun. The mixers' steady grinding and an occasional ringing telephone from the nearby offices would have been the only sounds.

But just 11 years later these lonely images have become memories, nostalgic echoes of the past. If you were to drive up to the C.O.D. plant today, you would be met with quite a different sight—a dynamic 4.5-acre plant bustling with the activity of 140 employees. Instead of the two dilapidated mixers, you would see a fleet of 70 trucks. You might even hear the engines of the company helicopter as it took off for a site inspection or to deliver personnel to the field. Inside the plant the sporadic rings of the lone office phone have been replaced by the conversations of the large C.O.D. sales staff, who try to keep up with the firm's diversified projects.

The main link between the past and present—and the painter of C.O.D.'s changing "mural"—has been Milton P. Koy, the founder of the company and now its president. While working for another Houston concrete firm, he and Richard Mitchell conceived the idea for the business and bought the two mixers with $6,000 in loans. Initially, the partners intended to specialize in residential jobs, such as patios, driveways, and the like, which were commonly turned down by the larger concrete companies. During the 1973-74 recession, however, many larger firms were forced to enter this market, and as the competition became more fierce, Koy decided to explore the commercial side of the concrete business.

It turned out to be a fortuitous decision. In the mid-1970s the Houston business community began to explode and the construction trades grew along with the city. With consistent dedication to providing the highest-quality concrete materials and service, C.O.D. became one of the leaders in the city's expansion. Today more than 80 percent of C.O.D.'s business comes from the commercial sector.

Milton P. Koy, owner and president of C.O.D. Concrete, Inc.

C.O.D. not only has contributed a great deal to the city's physical growth, it also has been an innovator within the construction industry. Koy's plant, located at 9500 Harwin Street, was one of the first to institute testing laboratories, computerized systems for concrete batching, and air-conditioned trucks. As many people already know, the C.O.D. trucks—which are designed to resemble the Houston Oilers and Rice University Owls football teams, the Houston Astros, Hunt's Catsup, French's Mustard, Lone Star Beer, and various Walt Disney characters—have proved to be a clever and delightful promotional gimmick.

In the future, the sights and sounds of C.O.D. Concrete will continue to change, as the company proceeds with plans to expand into the San Antonio area and the Rio Grande Valley. But one "scene" will never change: C.O.D.'s firm commitment to providing the best in concrete products and services to all its individual and commercial clients.

Several of C.O.D.'s trucks have been decoratively painted, such as this one embellished as a football.

TEAS NURSERY

John C. Teas always liked to plant things, especially apple trees. In fact, as he was growing up in the early 1800s, in the Philadelphia area, the Teas' backyard was full of apple seedlings.

The neighbors and even some family members told young Teas there just wasn't much future in apple trees. But his father, Thomas Teas, a builder of lumber and flour mills, encouraged his son's horticultural activities, and the yard filled with trees.

In 1843 John, along with his brother, E.Y., started Teas Nursery in Raysville, Indiana, a small Quaker community. John moved to Carthage, Missouri, where he obtained 200 acres of land and became one of the most famous horticulturists of the era. Not surprisingly, the nursery had some 100 varieties of apple trees.

In Carthage, John specialized in landscape engineering and developed many of Teas' own hybrids, including the Teas Weeping Mulberry. He also introduced the white-flowering redbud and developed several varieties of the catalpa tree, peonies, and apples.

Edward Teas (John's son) opened an expansion operation in Joplin, including three greenhouses spanning nearly a city block. One greenhouse held nothing but ferns and other greenery used to fill out floral arrangements. Teas also was the leading landscape architect in Joplin.

In 1906, during an especially severe winter storm in Missouri, Teas and a few others were discussing the warmer temperatures down South, and someone mentioned a small, but growing, town called Houston. The more they talked the more Teas wanted to visit the city on the Texas Gulf Coast.

At the time, much of the area now known as Pasadena was planted in citrus trees. Teas decided to visit the Houston vicinity. When he left Joplin, the temperature was around zero. When he arrived in Houston, trees still had most of their leaves. And when he saw the abundance of orange and grapefruit trees, as well as large fig orchards and tremendous patches of strawberries and vegetables, he was so impressed that he purchased several tracts of land where the Houston Lighting and Power Company

In 1913 Teas' employees cultivate an orange grove in Bellaire.

Plant now sits in Pasadena and developed a citrus orchard.

Teas went to work developing the orchard and nursery operations. Soon the venture had some 250,000 fruit trees under contract and ready for delivery (they had not been paid for), when a hard freeze hit the area. Every tree died.

Edward Teas, Jr., recalls that his father "was in the bank one day trying to get a loan to start over. One of the bankers overheard him say something about landscaping and asked Dad if he would do his lawn. He gave Dad $500 to do the job, others saw what Dad was doing at the banker's yard, and he was busy with landscape work for the rest of his life."

In 1908 Edward Teas, Sr., met W.W. Baldwin, who was developing

Westmoreland Farms with Bellaire as its townsite. Baldwin sold Teas a tract of land in 1910, land that today fronts Bellaire Boulevard. Teas decided to bring his family to Houston.

"Dad first settled us in Mother Case's Boarding House, then we moved into the old Anderson place until they completed our home on land purchased from Baldwin," recalls Edward Teas, Jr., who spent 23 years as president of Teas Nursery Company and remains active on its board of directors.

One of the early modes of transport used by Teas Nursery was this 1914 chain-driven Ford "Model T."

That original Teas home in Bellaire is still used by the firm in its nursery operations. And many of the original pieces of furniture in the home are still in use today. The Teas Nursery Company is believed to be the second oldest business establishment in the Southwest that is still operated by the original owners.

Mr. and Mrs. Edward Teas had six children. In addition to Edward Jr., there were the twins, Fred and Paul, and Josephine, Ruth, and Ben. All four brothers became involved in horticulture and landscaping.

After World War II, Ben and Edward Jr. opened a second location in Spring, which served as the growing operation for the Bellaire store and for years supplied 90 percent of all stock sold by the Teas Nursery Company. Teas' Spring location has expanded to a thriving garden center, greenhouse, and landscape operation.

John Fred Teas has been working in the family business since his graduation in nursery management from Texas A&M

Edward Teas, Sr., developed the firm's first orchard and nursery operation in the area that is now Pasadena.

Today Thomas S. Teas (right) and John F. Teas (left) are president and vice-president, respectively, of Teas Nursery Company, Inc.

University in 1957; he currently is vice-president of the Bellaire nursery. Thomas S. Teas, who holds a degree from the University of Houston, joined the organization in 1977 and currently is its president and board chairman. B. David Teas is landscape manager of Teas Nursery's Spring Landscape Department and is on the board of directors. Daniel Teas is plant buyer for both locations. Diann Teas, wife of Tom Teas, joined the corporation in 1978 and serves as treasurer and director of advertising.

Among its many projects, Teas Nursery Company has landscaped Trees of Main Street; The American Productivity Center; building projects for Trammell-Crow, Shell Development, and Texaco Research; and much of the Montrose and River Oaks areas. In addition, Teas landscaped Rice University, considered to be one of the most beautiful college campuses in the country.

Edward Teas, Jr., is past president of the Houston Landscape and Nurserymen Association and of the National Landscape Association; he is past director of the Texas Association of Nurserymen. Among Tom Teas' posts are service as a director of the Texas Association of Nurserymen and as a director of Interfirst Bank, Southwest Houston, N.A. John Teas is director of the Garden Centers of America. David Teas is current president of Houston Landscape Association. All four men hold an impressive number of civic and business directorships and memberships.

ROBIN ELVERSON REALTORS

Growing up in England prior to World War II, Robin Elverson spent as much time as possible in the field hunting game birds in the Wiltshire countryside near Marlborough.

Today the Houston real estate broker still finds time to hunt ducks, geese, quail, dove—and an occasional wild turkey—in Texas. Two sides of his River Oaks office are covered with displays of hand-carved decoys, and he even tries to hunt pheasant and grouse in England and Scotland each year.

What's surprising is that he finds the time to hunt. In addition to heading a major real estate firm, he has served or is presently serving on the boards of the Houston Symphony Society, the Museum of Fine Arts, Bayou Bend, the Winedale Council, the March of Dimes, the Houston Board of Realtors, the Texas Real Estate Association, River Oaks Bank & Trust, and as a member of the Condominium Subcommittee of the National Real Estate Association.

Elverson was born in Manchester, England, and moved to Marlborough with his family at the age of two. In 1940 he joined the Royal Air Force and spent some time in the United States during World War II as a flight instructor for the

Robin Elverson, in addition to heading the realty firm that bears his name, is well known in the Houston area for his many civic involvements.

An avid sportsman, Robin Elverson travels to England and Scotland nearly every year to hunt pheasant and grouse.

United States Army Air Corps. He then returned to England to finish the war as a fighter pilot.

When the war was over Elverson returned to the United States and to Houston, where his sweetheart, Virginia Thompson, was attending Rice University. They soon were married.

Elverson was employed during the latter 1940s by an air conditioning and appliance firm which also had substantial real estate holdings. He persuaded his employer to become more involved in the real estate aspect of the business, and everyone prospered. In 1950 Elverson took the plunge, formed his own

company, and one of Houston's top third-party real estate firms was born. Although the organization now has more than 20 agents, Elverson maintains the same personal touch, still overseeing each transaction.

Robin Elverson was recognized as the 1981 Realtor of the Year by the Houston Board of Realtors. In 1982 he received the John E. Wolf Citzenship Award for his prominent role in civic involvement and accomplishments.

LOCKWOOD, ANDREWS & NEWNAM, INC.

On June 1, 1982, Lockwood, Andrews & Newnam, Inc., moved into its corporate headquarters at 1500 CityWest Boulevard in West Houston—a 10-story office building which the firm designed, developed, and owns in a joint venture.

architecture, planning, and project management. The Geogram Corporation, acquired by LAN in 1963, provides surveying services. Carter Engineers, acquired in 1980, provides a full range of services in California.

From its humble beginnings, the firm's practice eventually grew to include work on such projects as the Harris County Domed Stadium, Houston Intercontinental Airport, the Houston Ship Channel, NASA, and the Texas Medical Center.

Following completion of its first large assignment in 1941—the San Jacinto Ordnance and Shipping Depot—LAN began to grow rapidly after World War II. Major activities included port design and award-winning master planning for the Port of Houston and major expansions for the Hughes Tool Company and Cameron Iron Works.

As the managing firm in the joint venture Engineers of the Southwest since 1960, LAN has provided engineering services for Houston Intercontinental and William P. Hobby airports. The company was awarded one of its largest projects—the 69th Street Wastewater Treatment Complex—in 1975. When completed, it will service the northern half of the city of Houston.

Frank H. Newnam, Jr., joined the firm as a partner in 1946. His name was added to the corporate title in 1956, and LAN was incorporated six years later. The firm merged with Koetter Tharp Cowell & Bartlett, Architects, in 1977, thus blending the strengths of two prestigious Houston entities within one organization.

Continued success and expansion led to moves to more spacious quarters at 1010 Waugh Drive in 1956, and to 1900 St. James Place in 1974. LAN now occupies its own 10-story office tower at 1500 CityWest Boulevard. The firm also has offices throughout Texas, with major branches in Brownsville, Dallas, and San Antonio.

Lockwood, Andrews & Newnam, Inc. (LAN), founded in 1935 by Mason G. Lockwood and William M. Andrews to provide civil engineering services, has grown into the nation's 59th largest design firm.

Today LAN and its two subsidiaries provide a complete range of professional services in all fields of engineering,

The 70-acre 69th Street Wastewater Treatment Plant will serve half the city of Houston by the year 2000. Lockwood, Andrews & Newnam, Inc., provided complete architectural and engineering services for the complex.

PILGRIM ENTERPRISES, INC.

In the early 1900s a strong back was a good deal more important than a college degree for a deckhand aboard the ore ships working on the Great Lakes. For 16-year-old C.J. Robertson, out on his own in 1913 after being in a Springfield, Ohio, orphan's home since the age of five, a deckhand job on one of Pittsburgh Steel's steamships provided enough for room and board and a little extra.

Robertson, now retired in Houston, recalls, "The job provided enough money. In fact, I even had the captain take some out of my pay for a Liberty Bond."

After serving in the U.S. Army until the end of World War I, Robertson says, " I followed the work. For awhile I worked in the oil fields of Ohio and Oklahoma, then went to California for a period. I hitched a ride with a man driving a fruit truck and ended up in Miami, Florida.

"Because I had some experience working at the laundry shop in the orphan's home, I acquired a job at the Nu-Way Laundry in Miami. The laundry had a fleet of trucks, and they had to give me the biggest truck because I had the most business.

"In those days laundry was picked up and delivered by truck drivers. Unfortunately, the big land boom that was going on in Florida at that time went flat, and the laundry went out of business."

While working at Nu-Way, Robertson

met, fell in love with, and married a fellow employee, Ruby Wallace, who had come to Miami from Atlanta. They decided to return to Georgia, and in 1930 opened Bob's Laundry on Peach Tree Road. Believed to be the first cash-and-carry laundry and cleaning operation in the country, the venture came about somewhat by accident.

"Ruby and I were starting up this very small firm, and because everything was delivered in those days, we bought a truck and were having it painted when the painter and truck both disappeared.

"So we were faced with coming up with some way to do without a truck or go out of business. We decided to offer laundry and cleaning services at a discount for those people who would bring the clothes by and would then later pick them up.

"We lived across the street from the cleaning shop, and Peach Tree was a very busy street. So we decided to have a drop station near the house. On their way to work, customers could drop off their clothes at the station and not have to go through traffic. They could pick them up on the way home."

The idea worked. While many businesses were failing during those bleak economic times, the Robertsons' company grew and expanded. Not everyone was happy with the development, however. The local laundry association, says

C.J. Robertson, now retired, purchased the Pilgrim Steam Laundry in 1945.

Robertson, "kicked me out because they said I was putting drivers out of business."

Eventually he sold the Atlanta unit for $100,000, and ended up in Texas. A salesman mentioned to Robertson that there was a laundry for sale in Houston. Robertson scheduled a stop in Houston, saw the laundry, a small facility near the intersection of Almeda and Isabella, and decided to stay in Houston. Pilgrim Steam

The first Pilgrim laundry plant was in this building at Almeda and Isabella, Houston.

real estate field by developing office/warehouses and self-service storage warehouses. At the current time it has over 3.3 million square feet of warehouse space in Houston, Dallas, Fort Worth, Atlanta, and Indianapolis.

C.J. and Ruby Robertson had a son, Guy J. Robertson, Sr., and a daughter, Nancy Robertson Schissler, wife of Richard Schissler, Jr. Today Guy Robertson, Sr., and Richard Schissler, Jr., oversee the company, which currently includes over 250 laundry and dry cleaning locations throughout Houston and San Antonio, as well as the strip centers and warehouses. The day-to-day operations are handled by an experienced and well-qualified management team. The firm also has been active in several area banks, equipment leasing, and real estate management. As with most successful businesses, Pilgrim attributes much of its growth to the loyalty of its employees, and to the dynamic growth of the Houston area. Pilgrim currently has over 900 employees, some of whom have been with the company for more than 20 years. Pilgrim takes a great deal of pride in its employees and in its contribution to Houston's growth.

Laundry, founded on November 30, 1928, was purchased by Robertson on July 2, 1945, for $73,000. By 1957 Pilgrim had some 20 units, mostly in small strip shopping centers in the Houston area.

Pilgrim's rapid expansion in the Houston area led to its entrance into the real estate field. In the late 1960s Pilgrim

As noted in this advertisement from the Houston Post, Pilgrim had grown to 20 plants by 1957.

began to develop its own strip centers, where it would locate one of its own laundry and dry cleaning operations. Pilgrim has developed more than 50 such centers since that time. In the early 1970s the company expanded its interest in the

Pilgrim Enterprises, Inc., 6723 Stella Link, Houston, now has over 250 laundry and dry cleaning locations plus banking, real estate, and equipment leasing interests.

STARBUCK, INC.

Just prior to the outbreak of the Spanish-American War, R.M. Starbuck, Sr., a middle-aged plumbing contractor, and his son, R.M. Starbuck, Jr., decided to move their operation from Worcester, Massachusetts, to Hartford, Connecticut.

Joseph H. Starbuck, father of R.M. Sr., had been a plumber on Nantucket Island, and apparently had been a good teacher. His descendants had learned their trade well. However, R.M. Starbuck, Jr., was concerned in the late 1800s about the quality of training being given to apprentice plumbers. He decided to do something about it, and during one of the times when business was down—plumbing contractors often had extended periods of no work during winter months—he decided to write a plumbing textbook, *Questions and Answers on the Practice & Theory of Sanitary Plumbing,* first published in 1900. Today, some 83 years

later, the Starbuck company is still publishing versions of that same textbook.

Also around the turn of the century the family, through their firm, R.M. Starbuck & Son, began the sale and manufacture of plumbing tools at a facility in Hartford. During the period between 1900 to 1953 the Starbucks invented a number of tools for their trade, many of which are still in use today.

R.M. Starbuck, Jr., died in 1953 and Alfred Joy, a son-in-law, and Marion Saling, a daughter of R.M., ran the firm until 1976 when it was acquired by Paul W. Garvis. He moved the company's headquarters to the Houston area in 1981, and has since begun construction work on a second tool manufacturing and distribution facility near Humble. Garvis also has doubled the size of the Hartford plant and has developed an international sales, licensing, and distribution operation. Starbuck markets its tools through manufacturers' and factory-direct representatives to a network of wholesale

and retail plumbing distributors throughout North America.

Starbuck will publish five new plumbing textbooks in 1983 to expand upon the 12 previously published volumes. The five upcoming books will be *Introduction to Sanitary Plumbing, Drain-Waste-Vent Systems for Sanitary Plumbing, Hot & Cold Water Systems for Sanitary Plumbing, Hotwater Heating and Other Practical Plumbing Applications,* and *The Business of Plumbing.* These new publications will be marketed by means of direct mail, as well as to bookstores and vocational technical schools throughout the world.

"We plan that Starbuck, which traces its roots back to Joseph H. Starbuck's operation in 1840 on Nantucket Island, will have three operating divisions—tools, books, and educational—by the end of 1983," Garvis asserts.

Paul W. Garvis, chairman of the board and chief executive officer of Starbuck, Inc.

Lorelei T. Garvis, the firm's executive vice-president.

HORLOCK BEVERAGE COMPANY

Frank Horlock was destined to be associated with ice-cold beer for most of his life.

Born in Navasota in 1925, Horlock worked in the family business early on. And the family business was ice, with facilities in Houston, Navasota, and Bryan. His grandfather, R.W. Horlock, was considered by many to be the largest independent ice manufacturer in Texas during the early 1950s. And, because ice and beer tended to go hand in hand, it was natural that some of the operations would include beer distribution.

By the age of 13 Frank Horlock was driving his grandfather on his rounds during summer school break. At 17 he joined the U.S. Air Force. Then, in 1946, Horlock came to Houston to open a convenience store on Almeda Road. Two years later he decided to enter the real estate business.

But the real estate business was not booming in Houston during the late 1940s, at least not like it would be a decade later. Horlock mentioned to Marvin Hurley, then executive head of the Houston Chamber of Commerce, that he was looking for something else.

Shortly after their conversation, Hurley made a speech at a U.S. Chamber of Commerce meeting in St. Paul, Minnesota. His seatmate on the flight back to Houston was James Kelley, a member of the family that controlled Hamm's Brewery. Kelley told Hurley that he was coming to Houston to find a bright young man to help Hamm's break into the Houston market, then held largely by local brands such as Grand Prize, Falstaff, and Southern Select.

Hurley mentioned Horlock, and the next morning, a Saturday, Kelley met the young man at the Lamar Hotel. They talked for nine hours, made a deal, and Frank Horlock was in the beer business. His new enterprise was called Hamm-Tex, based in an old tin building on Washington Avenue. Eight years later, after Horlock had purchased all of the firm's stock from Hamm's, the name was changed to the Horlock Distribution Company.

Pearl Brewery decided to break the Houston area market into three sections in 1961 and Horlock ended up with the area south of Buffalo Bayou. He also moved the venture to new facilities at 301 North Main, the old Katy Terminal.

When Southdown purchased the Pearl Brewery in 1969, Horlock was asked to take over the subsidiary as board chairman. In 1976 he resigned that post, and acquired the Miller distribution for part of Houston.

Walt Fabian is president and chief operating officer of Horlock Beverage Company, which has 120 employees. Horlock, active in community affairs, is board chairman. Horlock Beverage has been awarded the Miller Masters for the past six years. This coveted award is given to 15 distributors out of 900 wholesalers in the United States.

The company purchased a four-acre tract fronting Loop 610 in 1966 and moved into a new 40,000-square-foot building on the site two years later. It was expanded in 1975, 1978, and 1982, and today has 90,000 square feet of space.

Frank Horlock is board chairman of the Horlock Beverage Company.

RANDALL'S FOOD MARKETS, INC.

On July 1, 1966, Robert Onstead, Randall C. Barclay, and Norman Frewin, Sr., formed a new grocery company with the purchase of two small stores, one near the intersection of 43rd Street and Mangum Road, and the other near the corner of Tidwell and the North Freeway.

All three men had worked for Onstead's father-in-law, Blocker Martin, who with E.K. Atwood had developed a grocery store chain called Randall's Inc. The firm was dissolved in 1964 when it was merged into an El Paso chain.

"After a few years with this chain, the three of us decided to try it on our own," Onstead says. "We gave the matter a lot of study, and were leaning toward opening stores in Central Texas, around Temple, when a representative of the Fleming Company told us about the two small grocery stores for sale in Houston. We decided to stay in Houston, and a very wise decision it turned out to be."

At the time of the purchase the two small stores were grossing about $18,000 a week, recalls Barclay, president and chief operating officer. Within three months that weekly figure had climbed to $38,000. Today the company has an annual volume of over $300 million. A 60,000-square-foot warehouse on Telge Road at Highway 290 was constructed in 1983 for the distribution of meat, produce, dairy, and floral products.

Onstead, born near Ennis and a graduate of North Texas State, and his wife Kay moved from Dallas to Houston in 1955 to work for his father-in-law.

The founders of Randall's Food Markets, Randall C. "R.C." Barclay (left), Robert R. "Bob" Onstead (second from right), and Norman Frewin, Sr. (right), meet with their produce buyer, Tony Ferro (second from left) back in the early days.

Frewin, a native of Canada, joined the old Randall firm in 1958. He recently retired from Randall's Food Markets. Barclay, born at Pineland near Jasper, moved to Houston in 1939, worked at and owned several grocery stores before joining a Houston bakery firm, and joined the old Randall firm in 1957.

Competition in the grocery business was tough in 1966. From its initial two-store operation that year, Randall's has grown to be one of the top food chains in Houston. Onstead, the company's board chairman and chief executive officer, asserts that the firm plans to remain in the Houston area and, in fact, one of Randall's biggest problems is "keeping up with the city's growth. There are areas around Houston where we do not have stores. We plan to change that."

The firm has been in the forefront of a number of changes: It was one of the first to offer floral products; it pioneered separate produce rooms in each store; it was one of the first to offer decor such as ruddy brick walls decorated with photos or paintings by local artists, arched doorways, and Mexican-tile floors in its produce departments; and it was one of the first in the area to computerize. One aspect that is not likely to change at Randall's Food Markets, though, is its congenial family atmosphere: Each of the three founders has a son in a top-management positon.

Randall's first food market was located at 4615 Mangum, Houston.

CRH ASSOCIATES

CHARLES R. HAILE ASSOCIATES, INC.

Charles R. Haile had been the county engineer of Harris County for eight years when he retired from public service and established a private consulting firm. His first office in the Scanlan Building became too small when Robert J. Blair and T. Spencer Love joined him in 1939, prompting the three men to move the operation to a facility of their own design at 2801 San Jacinto.

Today the engineering firm, which has aided in the growth of Houston by designing major water, wastewater, street, storm drainage, and other essential public works projects, has more than 100 employees in five offices and operates along the entire Texas Gulf Coast. It has just concluded design for the expansion of the City of Houston's Northwest Treatment Plant.

Love, who had been with the Harris County Engineering Department in the late 1930s when Haile served as county engineer, was first employed by the State Road Department of Florida after studying at the University of Florida. He joined Haile in 1939, serving as president and chief engineer of the firm before retiring in 1973.

Blair and Love joined the Armed Forces in 1942. When World War II ended the two men returned to the company; it was renamed Charles R. Haile and Associates at that time.

The postwar years brought both internal and external expansion. Katherine de Geus joined the firm as a secretary in 1947, after a tour of duty in the U.S. Navy. She went on to serve as senior vice-president and secretary/treasurer until her retirement. Haile died in 1955, bequeathing his shares to Ms. de Geus. The company acquired its present name—Charles R. Haile Associates, Inc.—after his death.

David C. Perrell, who joined the firm in 1953, became resident engineer for the Nederland office when it opened in 1961. He moved to Houston in 1981 as a member of the board of directors and a vice-president, and he was elected president in 1982.

Stanley G. Newsome, Jr., who joined Charles R. Haile Associates, Inc., in 1968, serves as senior vice-president and manager of the Nederland office. David E.

David C. Perrell was elected president of the firm in 1982.

LaCombe is currently executive vice-president and secretary/treasurer.

The Texas City wastewater treatment plant was designed by Charles R. Haile Associates, Inc.

HOUSTON POST

The *Houston Post,* as a continuously published newspaper, officially began on April 5, 1885, when two small papers were merged to form the *Houston Daily Post.* However, the *Post* can trace its lineage back to the very beginnings of the Republic of Texas.

In 1835 Gail and Thomas Borden formed the *Telegraph and Texas Register* in San Felipe de Austin, a Brazos River community some 50 miles from the Gulf of Mexico.

When General Sam Houston retreated through San Felipe from Santa Anna's army, the Bordens moved their operation to Harrisburg on Buffalo Bayou. As Santa Anna closed in on Harrisburg in the spring of 1835, the Bordens dumped the presses into the bayou and escaped with top Texas government officials to Galveston.

After the Battle of San Jacinto one week later, the presses were retrieved from the bayou and the Bordens set up again, this time at Columbia. Some 12 months later the steamship *Yellowstone* carried the presses to Houston, and on May 2, 1837, the first Houston edition was published.

The newspaper was published for the next 36 years, but in 1873 it collapsed when Nelson Davis foreclosed on a $2,587 debt. It began again one year later under A.C. Gray, but he lost it after just three years. The paper's assets were then taken over by its employees, but in 1880 it foundered again.

Gail Borden's son-in-law, J.W. Johnson, a West Virginian, purchased the paper's stock through his son, Gail Borden Johnson, at a foreclosure sale on February 19, 1880. In March it became the *Houston Daily Post.* For six months in 1884 and the first part of 1885, the *Post* did not publish. On April 5 of that year it was reorganized, and has appeared regularly ever since.

The *Post* drifted along with occasional changes in management, including Julius L. Watson, who had been a trader aboard a raft on the Mississippi River. The paper was incorporated in 1886 and William C. Brann, later known as publisher of the *Iconoclast,* was hired at that time. When he left, a young writer by the name of William Sidney Porter, who later became famous as O. Henry, joined the *Post.* In

The first home (1885-1896) of the *Houston Post* was in this building on Congress Avenue opposite the courthouse. During this time a young writer named William Sydney Porter worked for the newspaper. He later became famous as O. Henry.

1895 a 17-year-old clerk was hired to work in the circulation department. His name was William Pettus Hobby.

The *Post* continued to grow, and in 1896 it moved from the Larendon Building at 1111 Congress (which also had served as base for the old *Telegraph and Texas Register*) into new quarters at Franklin and Fannin. Watson died in 1907 and left the company to a trust until his son, Ray Garrett Watson, reached his 25th birthday in 1917.

Will Hobby purchased 10 shares of stock in the newspaper about 1900. A year later he asked to be moved to the editorial department, where he became a reporter, business editor, city editor, and, in 1905, managing editor. He left the *Post* in 1907 to become editor, manager, and

principal owner of the *Beaumont Enterprise.*

Before Hobby returned to the *Post* in 1924, he set up the Texas Election Bureau, became president of the Texas Associated Press Managing Editors' Association, established in Beaumont the first combination morning and afternoon paper in the nation, led the fight to make Beaumont a major port, and, in 1914, was elected lieutenant governor of Texas. He became governor in 1917 when James E. Ferguson was impeached.

At the *Post,* young Ray Watson took

over. He came out in favor of Prohibition, woman suffrage, and Woodrow Wilson. Watson sold the paper to Ross Sterling in 1924 for $1.15 million.

Sterling combined the *Post* with the *Dispatch,* another Houston newspaper he owned, and asked Hobby to return to Houston to help run the operation. The paper moved again, this time to the northwest corner of Polk and Dowling.

When Sterling was elected governor in 1930, Hobby assumed direction of the organization. Circulation jumped to 71,000 in 1931. That same year Hobby married Oveta Culp at the bride's home in Temple.

Sterling suffered heavy financial losses the following year and, in addition, was defeated for reelection. On December 8, 1932, J.E. Josey assumed control of the enterprise. Hobby, who became publisher, renamed the paper the *Houston Post.* The Hobbys purchased control of the enterprise in 1939.

The advent of World War II posed many challenges for the paper. A shortage of newsprint resulted in some adless days, and many members of the staff went off to war. Mrs. Hobby accepted a one-dollar-a-year position with the War Department as chief of the women's-interest section, and later became commander of the Women's Auxiliary Army Corps. By 1943 the WAAC had become the WAC and Mrs.

Hobby was commissioned a colonel to command the corps. She returned to Houston in 1945. In 1953 Mrs. Hobby once again was off to Washington, this time as the first Secretary of Health, Education and Welfare, a position she held for 31 months.

The *Post,* meanwhile, had outgrown its quarters and in 1955 expanded to a new facility across Dowling Street, adding three folders and 15 units to letterpress capacity. Circulation climbed past the 200,000 mark. In 1960 the paper again expanded press capacity, adding two folders and 14 units. The following year, in conjunction with a major expansion project, another folder and 10 new units were added.

Will Hobby died on June 7, 1964, and the responsibility of running the company passed to his family. Mrs. Hobby became chairman of the board and editor.

The organization broke ground for a new office building/printing plant complex at the intersection of Loop 610 and the Southwest Freeway in 1968. The 7.5-mile move to the new complex began on December 29, 1969, and was completed by January 12, 1970. A folder and 10 new units were added to press capacity in 1973. The newspaper added three folders and 26 units (offset) at the Southwest Freeway printing operation in 1980. The project also included an additional building.

Today's *Houston Post* is produced with the most modern technology available, most of it developed within the past decade. An optical character reader was installed in 1973, followed one year later by a "third-generation" photo-typesetter. In 1975 video display terminals were placed in the newsroom as part of an editing system developed by Tal-Star. The use of metal type was ended, and the resulting error rate dropped to approximately one character in every 25,000.

The Tal-Star system was scrapped in 1982 and an entirely new newsroom was built on raised floors, using a more sophisticated editing system designed by ATEX, a system that provides video terminals for all reporters and editors.

Post officers, in addition to Mrs. Hobby and Lieutenant Governor Hobby (president, on leave of absence), include Jessica Hobby Catto, vice-president; M.B. Womack, executive vice-president and general manager; Harry E. Hayes, vice-president for sales and marketing; Roger Small, vice-president for production; James E. Crowther, executive vice-president and general counsel; and George A. Butler and Diana Hobby, directors.

Today the *Houston Post* is in this office building/ printing plant complex at the intersection of Loop 610 and the Southwest Freeway.

KPRC RADIO COMPANY

In 1925 radio broadcasting of programs designed for a general audience usually was regarded as a tinker's plaything, even though Morse code short-wave transmissions from ship to shore and from ship to ship had become commonplace.

But a number of forward-looking businessmen and community leaders, among them William P. Hobby, former governor of Texas and president of the *Houston Post-Dispatch,* saw in the new medium an opportunity for wider public service as well as a potential for business.

Thus, on May 9, 1925, Hobby dedicated KPRC, licensed by the United States Department of Commerce, Bureau of Navigation, to broadcast "entertainment and like matter, also weather forecasts"; the license was signed by Secretary of Commerce Herbert Hoover.

The new station, the first in Houston and one of just a few in the country, undertook as a public service an effort to supply radio receivers (as rare then as the early television sets were to be three decades later) to the prisons and prison farms operated in the area by the state.

G.E. "Eddie" Zimmerman, the station's first manager, also proposed that the KPRC facilities be used, during the hours it was not broadcasting programs to the general public, for the transmission of messages by the Houston police department to police vehicles in the field concerning "stolen property, robberies, etc."—an imaginative forerunner of today's sophisticated police communications systems.

Over the years KPRC kept pace with the development of radio broadcasting's "state of the art," increasing its power from 500 to 1,000 to 5,000 watts; designing and building successively new and more modern studios, first in the Post-Dispatch Building in downtown Houston, then in the Lamar Hotel, then in its own facility in southwest Houston just south of the Galleria, and finally on the Southwest Freeway site it occupies today.

KPRC also was a pioneer in broadcast journalism, establishing its own news department shortly before World War II, and providing assistance to its sister stations around the state in a series of news seminars. Its first full-time news director was Pat Flaherty, a veteran network news correspondent, followed by Ray Miller, also known for his *Eyes of Texas* travel books.

The station faced its largest challenge on April 16, 1947, when Texas City was rocked by a series of explosions along its waterfront. Flaherty and his crew kept the country informed through a three-day series of news broadcasts from the disaster scene.

KPRC has had a bare minimum of managers: Zimmerman was succeeded in 1935 by Kern Tips, who also became the dean of Southwest Conference football broadcasters; and Tips was succeeded in 1947 by Jack Harris, whose wartime career included service as deputy director of the United States War Department radio section and chief of radio and press communications for General Douglas MacArthur at the Japanese surrender on the deck of the battleship *Missouri.* Harris, now in his 37th year with KPRC, is still its president.

Houston's first radio station is one of a handful across the country still operating under its original ownership.

KPRC, the first radio station in Houston, was dedicated on May 9, 1925. Its license was signed by Herbert Hoover, Secretary of Commerce. It is now located in this building off the Southwest Freeway.

WICKS 'N' STICKS

Few people in Warren, a small town in the oil fields of Tyler County, were surprised when Harold Otto decided to attend Texas A&M University and major in engineering.

And it wasn't too astonishing when the young man decided to try sales. By 1968, at the age of 27, he was a relatively successful electrical equipment salesman. But what has the folks now shaking their heads is that the horse-loving Texan is making a successful career of candles.

During a walk through a Houston shopping center, Otto noticed a small candle shop, went in, and talked to the owner about how candles were marketed. It seemed like an interesting way to make money in his spare time.

Otto's research showed that it would take $20,000 in initial capital to open a candle shop. Otto and a partner, who since has sold his interest in the venture, each borrowed $4,000 on their own at the bank, and added that to a $12,000 Small Business Administration loan at an interest rate of 5.25 percent. They opened the store in Houston's Almeda Mall in 1968 as the first of many franchised locations.

In response to the enthusiasm of the mall leasing agent, a second store was opened almost simultaneously in Northwest Mall in Houston. Today the two-retail-outlet operation has grown to include some 274 specialty retail stores conducting business in more than 39 states. Annual sales total approximately $65 million.

More than 90 percent of the stores are franchise operations. Before choosing a franchisee, a Wicks 'N' Sticks management team finds a regional mall, secures the store location within the center, then builds the store and stocks it. From then on, franchisees purchase directly from the 90 manufacturers that supply the company.

Initially, Wicks 'N' Sticks bought all candles from outside suppliers, but with the growing demand for the basic wax products—pillars and votives—the firm began to manufacture its own line. The company now produces 20 percent of its

Wicks 'N' Sticks and Deck the Walls are franchised candle shops and wall decor stores located in 39 states.

Harold R. Otto founded Wicks 'N' Sticks and is president and chairman of the board.

candles at its 80,000-square-foot Houston complex.

Wicks 'N' Sticks acquired a chain of 12 frame stores in Texas and Louisiana in 1978. The wall decor business has expanded from the initial dozen stores to some 60 locations now operating under the name Deck the Walls.

KICKERILLO COMPANY

Vincent D. Kickerillo, founder and chairman of the board of the Kickerillo Company.

Vincent D. Kickerillo (standing) with his wife Mary, who is vice-chairman of the board of Kickerillo Company, and their daughter Sara-Kelli.

In 1943 Vincent Kickerillo, the son of an Italian sharecropper in the Brazos River bottom near Bryan, quit the farm at the age of 13 and came to Houston to seek his fortune.

Born in Bryan, the youngest of 14 children, Kickerillo, at 13, already had three years of farming, and it did not look prosperous.

Today this multimillionaire heads a massive banking and real estate empire. Over the years he has developed some 5,000 lots and built more than 2,000 homes, almost all in the premium-price category. He also has generated approximately 1,000 acres of commercial property.

Kickerillo acquired his first bank, a Raymondville, Texas, institution, in 1964. Since that time he has owned or controlled over 20 banks in Texas. The company now has four operating banks in Harris County and others throughout the state. In October 1983 the firm and Kickerillo's lead bank, Unitedbank-Houston, will move into Unitedbank Plaza, a 45-story office tower under construction in the 1400 block of Louisiana.

This is an impressive record of accomplishments for a young man who only had a few dollars in his pocket when he arrived in Houston 40 years ago. His first job was as a laborer with the Hughes Tool Company. Three years later, at the age of 16, he joined the Merchant Marines, shipping out mainly on oil tankers, and worked his way up to second engineer during the next 12 years as he traveled around the world.

In 1958, by a quirk of fate, the sailor became a home builder. At home during a break in shipping tours, he decided to build a garage apartment for his father next to his one-story, three-bedroom house in the southeast part of town.

However, building restrictions and other delays became hurdles difficult to overcome. So Kickerillo decided to do his own construction—on the west side of Houston in the Spring Branch area. Never was the move to "Go west, young man" more profitable.

He became excited about building, and with a small bankroll from shipping savings, Kickerillo, along with a partner, built two more houses. He was on his way.

He formed the Kickerillo Company in 1960 and created an integrated home-building operation to include air conditioning, furniture, decorating, carpeting, and other finishing aspects.

In 1961 Kickerillo purchased the first tract of land that he was to develop. His first project was Fonn Villas, on Memorial Drive on the then western fringe of Houston. His next subdivision was Nottingham, a development in the Memorial area. Then came Nottingham Forest; Nottingham Forest, Section 8; and Ponderosa Forest, the second major residential development along FM 1960 in what became known as the Champions area.

The first sales office of the Kickerillo Company.

Kickerillo then began development of Greenwood Forest in the 1960 area. Both Greenwood Forest and Ponderosa Forest were 640-acre projects. Also , at one time, Kickerillo owned the land that is now Oak Creek Village and Northchester.

In 1971 the builder of custom homes added to his projects land along the Katy Freeway, or Interstate 10, off Fry Road in the fast-growing Katy area west of Houston. There he began development of Nottingham Country, a 2,000-acre multi-use subdivision. Fleetwood was started in 1972, and it soon became the last prestigious subdivision on Memorial Drive.

Kickerillo started development of the Kleinwood Subdivision north of 1960 in 1973, and three years later sold the first lots in nearby Olde Oaks, another FM 1960 custom-home project.

He decided to get out of the home-building business in 1976. At that time, Kickerillo was partner with a number of builders. He bought out their interests, and the builders, many of whom still buy lots from Kickerillo, formed new companies.

He ventured into the commercial sound and production business in 1976 and two years later built a recording studio fronting Memorial Drive. The firm is called Inergi Productions, Inc.

Kickerillo, who believes that loyalty and integrity are the premium qualities needed for success, was told in 1975 that he should go public with his company. He decided to stay private. His advice is "never go into a deal unless you can end up as the controlling party."

At present, he owns some 95 percent of all his bank operations and, in addition to his subdivision development activities, is one of the largest individual bankers in the United States.

The three men having the biggest impact on the firm, other than Kickerillo, were Henry C. King, Jr., president of the firm for 12 years until his death in 1977; T.D. Smith, a Houston attorney; and S.W. Scurlock, Jr., C.P.A., of Houston.

Walter M. Mischer, of Allied Bank of Texas; J.A. Elkins, Jr., of First City National Bank; and Gene H. Bishop, of the Mercantile Bank of Dallas, also were instrumental in the development of Kickerillo Company.

Officers of Kickerillo Company today are Vincent Kickerillo, board chairman; his wife, Mary, vice-chairman of the board; W. Philip Conway, president; and Jim A. Miller, executive vice-president.

The new headquarters of the Kickerillo Company and Unitedbank-Houston are located in Unitedbank Plaza.

DON'S WESTERN WEAR

The Huntsville merchant had watched Don Murphy, just out of the eighth grade and working at a sidewalk fruit stand, operate for some time before he walked over and predicted that someday the young salesman would see his name on a storefront. The year was 1942.

Few people passing the fruit stand then would have been able to foresee just how widespread would be the name of Don Murphy. For in the early 1940s Murphy was poor, very poor. In fact, his first boots were paid for by the Lions Club.

"It was around 1939, when a bookkeeper at the sawmill where my father worked called me over to the porch and noted that I was running around barefoot," Murphy recalls. "It was a pretty cold day. He told me to go down to the Grand Leader Department Store in Huntsville and pick up the boots."

Years later, when Murphy became a member of the Lions Club chapter, he found out that the organization had been responsible for the boots. Since that time he has remained active in the Lions, and estimates that he has helped to provide 10,000 pairs of shoes for needy children.

Following his stint at the fruit stand, Murphy delivered ice to Huntsville residents before joining the service for three years. After the war, while working on a seismograph crew, he met and married the former Theda Rogers, an East Texas schoolteacher, in 1945. Four years later they moved to Houston, where Murphy went to work in a warehouse for 75 cents an hour. Within three years he was the company's purchasing agent.

"When we arrived in Houston, Theda and I decided to move into the Denver Harbor district to be close to work," Murphy says. "At first we rented, then we purchased the house. I had to borrow $100 from my boss to have enough for the earnest money."

During the next few years Murphy made many friends in the neighborhood. One of those friends owned a vacant building on Lyons Avenue and offered to rent it to Murphy for $100 a month. By taking out a loan on their home, the Murphys opened a liquor store in November 1953 with $1,500 in inventory. By January 1, 1954, that

Don H. Murphy, founder and owner of Don's Western Wear.

inventory total had soared to $5,500.

Murphy decided to expand, and when a tract across the street became available he and a friend purchased it and erected a duplex-type building to house a liquor store on one side and offices for a doctor and dentist on the other.

On the Saturday before Easter in 1955, Murphy took his two small sons out to purchase new shoes. He ended up standing in line for 30 minutes and had to pay $6.95 a pair. "I told Theda that I should be in that line of work," he says. "I later found out that the markup on shoes was 40 percent, compared with 20 percent in the liquor business. I contacted my brother-in-law, an attorney, to write a letter to the International Shoe Company inquiring about purchasing shoes. Of course, I didn't have any money."

The next day at a Lions Club meeting a friend asked Murphy what his plans were, and he mentioned the shoe business idea and his lack of cash. The following

morning the friend walked into the liquor store and handed Murphy a check for $4,000, with "no-interest, pay-me-back-as-you-can" terms.

However, another roadblock to his shoe business start-up was still ahead. With the $4,000 in hand, Murphy contacted two representatives of the International Shoe Company to acquire the needed inventory. After an all-night meeting with two of the firm's sales representatives, it was determined that it would take a $16,000 inventory to set up the store. Fortunately, the salesmen underwrote the order. Two other shoe companies soon followed International's lead, and the Murphys were officially in the shoe business.

Over the years Murphy expanded the operation several times, adding a men's shop and a ladies' dress shop. During this

period, he also earned extra money by working as a comedian and emceeing parties throughout Houston.

In 1970 the Murphys' daughter Patricia, noting the growing popularity of western wear, suggested to her father that he enter that aspect of the business. Murphy, who was involved with the Harris County Mounted Sheriff's Posse and the Houston Fat Stock Show, was enthusiastic. He received approval for a bank loan and opened a western wear store near his other businesses on Lyons Avenue.

Don's Western Wear grossed $174,000 its first year. The following year sales climbed to $300,000 and Murphy knew he had found his niche.

When a site became available on Interstate 10, he got his bank's approval and bought it for $28,000. In 1974 he moved into the store. Within three years the company's sales climbed to one million dollars; in 1979 sales totaled $1.6 million at the freeway store. Murphy opened Don's Western Wear No. 4 in 1979 and No. 5 in 1980. Don's Western Wear No. 6 and No. 7 were opened in

Don's Western Wear No. 3, 10901 Katy Freeway, Houston, is one of seven in the chain with three additional stores in the planning stage.

1982.

Sales of the seven-store western wear chain totaled $20 million in 1982, with one unit, the Southwest Freeway store, having sales of some $400 for every square foot of retail space.

Murphy also had three additional stores on the drawing boards. "Things have just fallen into place for me," Murphy says. "I am sure the Lord has more planned."

281

PALAIS ROYAL

Isadore and Moselle Erlich, married in 1935, decided to move from Dallas to Houston a year later to become more involved in the operation of their downtown women's specialty store at 706 Main. And become more involved they did.

"From the start, Isadore and I felt we should do everything we could to offer fashion and quality merchandise at affordable prices," Moselle says.

"In fact, our daughters, Joan, Judy, and Phyllis, were partly raised in the business. The twins, Judy and Phyllis, were born the day before we started our annual Easter season two-for-one sale in 1940."

Over the years the downtown operation relocated several times, and in 1969 the store moved to the historical Kirby Building, erected in 1926 by the Kirby Lumber Co. Today the 22-unit fashion specialty store is headquartered in a 130,000-square-foot service center at

Moselle Pollack, formerly Mrs. Isadore Erlich.

Isadore Erlich.

Opening day at Palais Royal's store at 706 Main Street in the late 1920s.

10201 South Main. Besides the corporate offices, the $7-million facility contains the distribution center, data-processing, credit, financial, advertising, merchandising, and human resource divisions.

The Erlichs already were leasing ready-to-wear departments in several cities, including Dallas, Oklahoma City, Kansas City, Little Rock, and Wichita, when they moved to Houston in 1936. Since then the firm has concentrated on expanding in the Houston area, with the exception of stores in Beaumont and Orange.

Palais Royal, foreseeing the future growth of Houston, opened its first suburban store in 1950 in the Village, near Rice University.

After Isadore Erlich died in 1968, Moselle, now Mrs. Milton Pollack, remained active in the business and today is chairman of the board.

She recalls that the firm was "one of the first Houston stores to purchase merchandise in the European market. I remember going over on a ship soon after World War II to buy fine laces, dresses, hand-woven materials, and display pieces. It was very difficult getting around in the bombed-out areas."

Palais Royal, pioneering many retail innovations in Houston four decades ago, was one of the first ready-to-wear firms in the city to install air conditioning, to offer a full children's department, and to offer art objects and paintings as part of the retail operation.

Mrs. Pollack, who said the firm owed much to Jesse A. Jones for his interest and involvement in its early days, noted that Palais Royal "always has been people-oriented. Our associates are like family."

PORTA-KAMP MANUFACTURING COMPANY, INC.

Porta-Kamp Manufacturing Company, Inc., a Houston firm that manufactures remote-area housing for shipment worldwide for the oil and construction industries, was founded a little more than two dozen years ago by a man with a concept for more flexible living accommodations.

After a trip to the beach at Galveston in the summer of 1955, Floyd E. Bigelow, Jr., then involved in title work in the Houston area, decided to build a camping unit that could be carried on top of a car, and that could be handled by two people.

The camper unit was the subject of much interest, so much so that he decided to exhibit it in a boat show in Houston that year. During the show, he got into a discussion about the difficulty of shipping living units overseas.

The portable structure folded into a box which not only served as the unit's flooring but also as the shipping crate for the entire package, just right for loading aboard ships.

The design was a success, and Bigelow has been building portable living units ever since. He has more than 60 patents as a result.

The firm began in an old washateria facility on Fulton Street, then a year later moved to a building on 16th. Porta-Kamp moved to the 3600 block of West 12th Street in 1959, and the present offices were built the following year.

The company purchased a facility at Jacintoport as a manufacturing base to build multistoried offshore units in 1970. It was the first firm to build the huge offshore units completely under roof, drastically reducing construction time of the units.

Porta-Kamp expanded its Jacintoport plant, using assembly line procedures that produced some 20 module camping units per day, while simultaneously constructing offshore units on the other side of the plant.

In 1977 Porta-Kamp acquired land for its Gellhorn plant. Full production began in the fall of 1978, with two assembly lines with a total capacity of some 40 modules per day. The facility at 555 Gellhorn has 250,000 square feet under roof sitting on 50 acres of land.

Bigelow is assisted by his two sons, William H. and F.E. (Bo) Bigelow. The privately held firm has an average payroll of some 300 persons.

Today Porta-Kamp sells its units around the world, with 90 percent of its sales overseas. However, the firm intends to

Floyd E. Bigelow, Jr., founder and president of Porta-Kamp Manufacturing Company, Inc.

expand its domestic operations and has formed a new division, Great Texas Homes, headed by William Bigelow. It plans to offer single-family residential units at moderate prices, available completely furnished or unfurnished.

The Porta-Kamp facility on Gellhorn Street in Houston.

SHIPCO, INC.

Norman R. Wittkamp has been interested in the freight-forwarding business since 1947. Starting out in the Midwest, Wittkamp was one of the first in the industry to recognize the advantages of using the computer. Today his firm, Shipco, Inc., is a world leader in real-time computer operations for the maritime field.

Moving to Houston from Chicago in the mid-1960s, Wittkamp sold his small freight-forwarding venture to another Houston company. And without even an office (he was working out of his residence near Hobby Airport) he started another firm to handle certain logistics services.

"I remember that first piece of business back in 1966," Wittkamp says. "I was going through Longview and received a promise of an order from a representative of Letourneau (now Marathon Letourneau). Before I could get back home the order had arrived in Houston."

The orders kept coming in, and in 1968 the firm was incorporated. Today Shipco, with some 250 employees worldwide, offers single-source responsibility and single-source control in all areas of routine and critical materials flow.

The firm, one of the first in the world to offer international logistics service with real-time computerization, has divisions and subsidiaries that can provide worldwide mobilization; demobilization; international ocean and air freight forwarding; aircraft, ship, and bulk tanker chartering; crew changes; purchase order writing and control; export crating and boxing; inventory control; order status reporting; customs house brokerage; and international procurement services.

The SECAB (Shipco Export Crating and Boxing) division recently leased from the Port of Houston two large buildings, formerly known as the Dickson Gun Plant, to provide 6.5 acres of covered storage and 20 acres of outside storage, just to the rear of Dock 32, near Loop 610. Included are 14 overhead cranes with a 30-ton capacity each.

With the 1982 move to the Houston Ship Channel operation, which includes a major crating unit, Shipco closed its Hobby Airport facility. The firm still maintains a major unit at Houston Intercontinental Airport.

"We are glad to be near the new Port of Houston docks," Wittkamp says. "We feel that our presence will help make the port a great deal more competitive. We expect to attract a number of large-type movements, such as equipment and machinery for multibillion-dollar overseas refinery and airport projects."

In addition to its Houston base, Shipco has offices in New York City; Los Angeles; New Orleans; Greenwich, Connecticut; Stavanger, Norway; La Paz, Bolivia; Lima, Peru; Santiago, Chile; and a number of other countries.

Norman R. Wittkamp, founder and president of Shipco, Inc.

Shipco, Inc., is ideally located in these spacious dockside facilities at the Port of Houston.

STRAKE FOUNDATION

By the time he was 28, George W. Strake had amassed a fortune of $250,000 in Mexican oil ventures, lost most of it in a Hupmobile car agency and unfortunate investments in Cuba, and found himself in Houston in 1927 with little left but his love of God, family, and the oil business.

Strake decided to try buying and selling oil leases in Louisiana and Texas to mark time and keep what money he had left moving. Along with his business deals, he enjoyed exploring lands that others had passed over in the two states.

It was on one of these excursions near Conroe, Texas, along the side of the creek that recently had overflowed its banks that he noticed a shelf of rock that looked familiar from his experience in Mexico. "There was no doubt; it was Lagarto-Reynosa contact," Strake recalls. These oil and gas seeps are a good indication of the presence of oil.

He wanted to drill a well, but raising money in 1931 in Houston was all but impossible. So Strake drew on a small nest egg he had kept hidden away, rented a rig, and began drilling on a shoestring. By October 13, 1931, he had cored a shale which had a slight show of oil and gas. On December 13 the well came in, flowing primarily gas and some oil.

But Strake was worried. Millions of cubic feet of gas was being flared in the area, and he was concerned about the possibility that the Texas Railroad Commission, which had taken stern measures to control the East Texas field, might move in and close him down. He decided to create a market for his production.

A small refinery was established fronting the highway, connected to the well by a three-mile pipeline, to sell very high-octane gasoline to tank trucks to be hauled away to larger refineries to blend with cheaper gasoline.

His second well in the Conroe field came in on June 5, 1932. The rest is history. A year from the date of the first

George W. Strake (left), developer of one of the largest oil fields in the United States and benefactor, along with his wife Susan Kehoe Strake (right), to the many charitable works carried on by the Strake Foundation.

discovery well, there were 431 producing wells and 65,102 barrels of oil being produced daily from the field, today one of the largest in the United States.

Strake, prior to his death in 1969, together with his wife Susan Kehoe Strake, was active in numerous civic and charitable events. An ardent Catholic, he has made many bequests to the Church and to other organizations, including the 2,700-acre Camp Strake, near Conroe, to the Boy Scouts of America. In 1946 Pope Pius XII decorated Strake, making him a Knight, Grand Cross, of the Order of St. Sylvester—the oldest and most prized of the Papal Orders. While in Rome in 1950, Strake was given the rank of Supernumerary Private Chaplain of the Cape and Sword, one of the highest honors ever conferred on an American layman of the Church.

The Strake buildings at St. Joseph Hospital in Houston were erected through their generosity and Strake Jesuit College Preparatory in Houston bears his name. Strake Foundation carries on the charitable work started by George and Susan Strake.

PATRONS

The following individuals, companies, and organizations have made a valuable commitment to the quality of this publication. Windsor Publications and the Harris County Historical Society gratefully acknowledge their participation in *Houston: A Chronicle of the Supercity on Buffalo Bayou.*

A & M Pump Company
Adams & Porter Associates, Inc.*
Clara Elisabeth Bates-Nisbet
Baxter and Swinford Inc., Realtors*
Bering's*
Browning-Ferris Industries*
James Bute Paint Company*
C.O.D. Concrete, Inc.*
Lily & Ralph Carrigan
Charter Bank-Willowbrook
Denton A. Cooley, M.D.
Cooper Industries*
CRH Associates
    Charles R. Haile Associates, Inc.*
Cullen Center, Inc.*
Deloitte Haskins & Sells
Don's Western Wear*
Mr. & Mrs. Ben C. Duffie
Earthman Funeral Homes*
Robin Elverson Realtors*
Finger Furniture Company, Inc.*
Fisk Electric Company*
Forest Park Cemeteries & Funeral
    Homes
Geosource Inc.*

Mr. & Mrs. A.C. Golden
Lindi Goree
Gulf Resources & Chemical
    Corporation*
The Hale Investment Group, Inc.
Harrington Homes
Harris County Heritage Society
Heitmann, Bering-Cortes Company
    Wholesale Hardware and Industrial
    Supplies*
Hermann Hospital*
Horlock Beverage Company*
The Horne Company, Realtors*
Houston Post*
Jamail Brothers Food Market*
James Original Coney Island*
John W Jeweller*
Kickerillo Company*
Koomey, Inc.
KPRC Radio Company*
Linbeck Construction*
Lockwood, Andrews & Newnam, Inc.*
McCormick Oil & Gas Company*
K.L. McGuirt & Company*
National Convenience Stores
    Incorporated*
Pakhoed USA Inc.*
Palais Royal*
Payne & Keller Corporation
Pilgrim Enterprises, Inc.*
Port of Houston Authority*
Porta-Kamp Manufacturing Company,
    Inc.*
Randall's Food Markets, Inc.*
Raymond International Inc.*
Renfro Corporation
John Tryon Robinson
Ralph Rupley Furriers*
The Russo Companies*

Sakowitz*
San Jacinto Museum of History
Shipco, Inc.*
Shippers Stevedoring Company*
Martha Francis Singleton
Spaw-Glass Inc.*
Starbuck, Inc.*
Stewart & Stevenson Services, Inc.*
Strake Foundation*
Suniland Furniture*
Teas Nursery*
Texas Western Mortgage Company*
Dr. & Mrs. William L. Van Pelt
Waddell's House Furnishing Company*
Wald Transfer & Storage Co.
Owen Heywood Walker
Wallisville Heritage Park
Western Oceanic, Inc.
Westheimer Companies*
Westheimer Rigging & Heavy Hauling
    Co., Inc.
    Houston, Texas
Westheimer Transfer & Storage Co.,
    Inc., Houston, Texas
    "Since 1883"
Wicks 'N' Sticks*
Williams Brothers Construction
    Company*

*Partners in Progress of *Houston: A Chronicle of the Supercity on Buffalo Bayou.* The histories of these companies and organizations appear in Chapter 10, beginning on page 209.

286

BIBLIOGRAPHY

Articles

Barker, Eugene C. "The United States and Mexico, 1835-1837," *Mississippi Valley Historical Review*, I (1914).

_____ . "Notes on Early Texas Newspapers, 1819-1836," *Southeastern Historical Quarterly*, XXI (1917).

Barr, Alwyn. "Sabine Pass, September, 1893," *Texas Military History* (1962).

_____ . "Texas Coastal Defense, 1862-1865," *Southwestern Historical Quarterly*, XXXVII (1961).

Drummond, Lorena. "Five Texas Capitals: An Account of the Seats of Government in Texas Since the Adoption of the Declaration of Independence," *Texas Monthly Magazine*, V (1930).

Gillette, Michael L. "The Rise of the NAACP in Texas," *Southwestern Historical Quarterly*, LXXXI (1978).

Hendricks, Pearl. "Builders of Old Houston," *Houston*, XII (1941).

Hine, Darlene Clark. "The Elusive Ballot; The Black Struggle Against the Texas Democratic White Primary, 1932-1945," *Southwestern Historical Quarterly*, LXXXI (1978).

Lang, Aldon S. "Financial Aspects of the Public Lands in Texas," *Southwestern Political and Social Science Quarterly*, XIII (1932).

Ledbetter, Nan Thompson. "The Muddy Brazos in Early Texas," *Southwestern Historical Quarterly*, LXIII (1959).

Looscan, Adele B. "Harris County, 1822-1845," *Southwestern Historical Quarterly*, XVIII (1914).

McCraven, William. "On the Yellow Fever of Houston, Texas, in 1847," *New Orleans Medical and Surgical Journal*, V (1848-1849).

Muir, Andrew Forest. "The Destiny of Buffalo Bayou," *Southwestern Historical Quarterly*, XLVIII (1943).

_____ . "Railroads Come to Houston, 1857-1861." *Southwestern Historical Quarterly*, LXIV (1961).

_____ . "Railroad Enterprise in Texas, 1836-1841," *Southwestern Historical Quarterly*, XLVII (1943).

_____ . "William Marsh Rice, Houstonian," *East Texas Historical Journal*, II (1964).

_____ . "Diary of a Young Man in Houston, 1838," *Southwestern Historical Quarterly*, LIII (1950).

_____ . "The Free Negro in Harris County, Texas," *Southwestern Historical Quarterly*, XLVI, (1943).

_____ . "The Mystery of San Jacinto," *Southwest Review*, XXXVI (1951).

Oates, Stephen B. "NASA's Manned Spacecraft Center at Houston, Texas," *Southwestern Historical Quarterly*, LXVII (1964).

Porter, Eugene O. "Railroad Enterprises in the Republic of Texas," *Southwestern Historical Quarterly*, LIX (1956).

Reese, James V. "The Early History of Labor Organizations in Texas," *Southwestern Historical Quarterly*, LXXII (1968).

Stratford, James. "Behind the NASA Move to Houston, Texas," *Texas Business Review*, XXXVI (1962).

Suman, John R. "Importance of the Oil and Gas Industry to Houston," *Houston*, VI (1935).

Swenson, Loyd S. Jr. "The Fertile Crescent: The South's Role in the National Space Program," *Southwestern Historical Quarterly*, LXXI (1968).

Thompson, Charles H. "Separate But Equal; The Sweatt Case," *Southwest Review*, XXXIII (1948).

Winkler, Ernest W. "The Seat of Government in Texas," *Quarterly of the Texas State Historical Association*, X (1906).

Wooster, Ralph. "Foreigners in the Principal Towns of Ante-Bellum Texas," *Southwestern Historical Quarterly*, LXVI (1962).

Wrightman, Francis. "Alley-Theater Unusual," *Houston*, XXII (1948).

Books

Agatha, Sister M. *History of the Houston Heights, 1891-1918*. Houston: Premier Printing Company, 1956.

Alexander, Charles C. *Crusade for Conformity: The Ku Klux Klan in Texas, 1920-1930*. Houston: Texas Gulf Coast Historical Association, 1962.

Barker, Eugene C. *Mexico and Texas, 1821-1835*. Dallas: P.L. Turner Company, 1928.

Barr, Alwyn. *Black Texans: A History of Negroes in Texas, 1528-1971*. Austin: Jenkins Publishing Company, 1973.

Bartholomew, Ed. *The Houston Story: A Chronicle of the City of Houston and the Texas Frontier from the Battle of San Jacinto to the War Between the States, 1861-65*. Houston: Frontier Press, 1954.

Baughman, James P. *Charles Morgan and the Development of Southern Transportation*. Nashville: Vanderbilt University Press, 1968.

Brophy, William Joseph. *The Black Texan, 1900-1950*. Ann Arbor: University Microfilms, 1974.

Buchanon, James E. (ed.) *Houston: A Chronological and Documentary History, 1519-1970*. Dobbs Ferry, New York: Oceana Publications, 1975.

Chandler, Charles Ray. *The Mexican-American Protest Movement in Texas*. Ann Arbor: University Microfilms, 1968.

Conner, Seymour V. *Texas: A History*. New York: Thomas Y. Crowell Company, 1971.

Daniels, Pat. *Texas Avenue at Main Street*. Houston: Allen Press, 1964.

Dresel, Gustav. *Houston Journal: Adventures in North America and Texas, 1837-1841*. Trans. by Max Freund. Austin: University of Texas Press, 1961.

Frantz, Joe B. *Texas: A Bicentennial History*. New York: W.W. Norton & Company, 1976.

————. *Gail Borden, Dairyman to a Nation.* Norman: University of Oklahoma Press, 1951.

Friend, Llrena. *Sam Houston: The Great Designer.* Austin: University of Texas Press, 1954.

Fuermann, George. *Houston: Land of the Big Rich.* Garden City: Doubleday, 1951.

————. *Reluctant Empire: The Mind of Texas.* Garden City: Doubleday, 1957.

Gallegly, Joseph. *Footlights on the Border: The Galveston and Houston Stage Before 1900.* The Hague: Mouton and Company, 1962.

Garwood, Ellen Clayton. *Will Clayton: A Short Biography.* Austin: University of Texas Press, 1958.

Giesberg, Robert I. *Houston Grand Opera: A History.* Houston: Houston Grand Opera Guild, Inc., 1981.

Gray, Kenneth E. *A Report on the Politics of Houston.* Cambridge, Massachusetts: Joint Center for Urban Studies for the Massachusetts Institute of Technology and Harvard University, 1960.

Hatch, Orin Walker. *Lyceum to Library: A Chapter in the Cultural History of Houston.* Houston: Texas Gulf Coast Historical Association, 1965.

Haynes, Robert V. *A Night of Violence: The Houston Riot of 1917.* Baton Rouge: Louisiana State University Press, 1976.

Hogan, William Ransom. *The Texas Republic: A Social and Economic History.* Norman: University of Oklahoma Press, 1946.

Holmes, Ann. *Houston and the Arts: A Marriage of Convenience That Became a Love Affair.* Houston: Houston Chamber of Commerce, 1970.

Houston: A History and Guide Compiled by Workers of the Writers Program of the Works Progress Administration in the State of Texas. Houston: Anson Jones Press, 1942.

Hurley, Marvin. *Decisive Years for Houston.* Houston: Houston Magazine, 1966.

Iscoe, Louise Kosches (ed.) *Ima Hogg: First Lady of Texas.* Houston: Hogg Foundation for Mental Health, 1976.

James, Marquis. *The Raven: A Biography of Sam Houston.* Indianapolis: The Bobbs-Merrill Company, Inc., 1938.

————. *The Texaco Story.* New York: The Texas Company, 1953.

Johnston, Marguerite. *A Happy Wordly Abode: Christ Church Cathederal, 1839-1864.* Houston: Cathedral Press, 1964.

Jones, Anson. *Memoranda and Official Correspondence Relating to the Republic of Texas, Its History and Annexation — Including a Brief Autobiography of the Author.* New York: D. Appleton & Company, 1859.

Justice, Blair. *Violence in the City.* Fort Worth: Texas Christian University Press, 1969.

King, John O. *Joseph Stephen Cullinan: A Study of Leadership in the Texas Petroleum Industry, 1897-1937.* Nashville: Vanderbilt University Press, 1970.

Larson, Henrietta M. and Porter, Kenneth W. *History of the Humble Oil and Refining Company: A Study in Industrial Growth.* New York: Harper, 1959.

Lasswell, Mary. *John Henry Kirby: Prince of the Pines.* Austin: Encino Press, 1967.

Lubbock, Francis R. *Six Decades in Texas.* Edited by C.W. Rains. Austin: Ben C. Jones & Company, 1900.

McComb, David G. *Houston: The Bayou City.* Austin: University of Texas Press, 1969.

Mann, Dene Hofheinz. *You be the Judge.* Houston: Premier Printing Company, 1965.

Maxwell, Robert S. *Whistle in the Piney Woods: Paul Bremond and the Houston East and West Texas Railway.* Houston: Texas Gulf Coast Historical Association, 1963.

Oates, Stephen B. *Visions of Glory: Texans on the Southwestern Frontier.* Norman: University of Oklahoma Press, 1970.

Reed, S.G. *A History of Texas Railroads.* Houston: St. Clair Publishing Company, 1941.

Rister, Carl C. *Oil: Titan of the Southwest.* Norman: University of Oklahoma Press, 1949.

Rose, Warren. *The Economic Impact of the Port of Houston, 1958-1963.* Houston: University of Houston, 1965.

Roussel, Hubert. *The Houston Symphony Orchestra, 1913-1971.* Austin: University of Texas Press, 1972.

Sibley, Marilyn McAdams. *The Port of Houston: A History.* Austin: University of Texas Press, 1968.

Siegel, Stanley. *A Political History of the Texas Republic, 1836-1845.* Austin: University of Texas Press, 1956.

————. *The Poet President of Texas: The Life of Mirabeau B. Lamar, President of the Republic of Texas.* Austin: Jenkins Publishing Company, 1977.

Spratt, John S. *The Road to Spindletop: Economic Change in Texas, 1875-1901.* Dallas: Southern Methodist University Press, 1955.

Thompson, Craig. *Since Spindletop: A Human History of Gulf's First Half Century.* Pittsburg: 1951.

Timmins, Bascom. *Jesse H. Jones.* New York: Henry Holt & Company, 1956.

Warner, C.A. *Texas Oil and Gas Since 1543.* Houston: Gulf Publishing Company, 1939.

Webb, Walter Prescott. (ed.) *The Handbook of Texas.* 2 vols. Austin: Texas State Historical Association, 1952.

Weems, John Edward. *A Weekend in September.* College Station, Texas: Texas A & M University Press, 1957.

Manuscript Collections

Archives Collection, University of Texas Library

Anson Jones Papers

Thomas Jefferson Rusk Papers

Ashbel Smith Papers

Newspapers

Houston *Chronicle*

Houston *Morning Star*

Houston *Post*

Houston *Telegraph and Texas Register*

Unpublished Papers

Berryman, Marsha G. "Houston and the Early Depression, 1929-1932." M.A. Thesis, University of Houston, 1965.

Carleton, Donald. "A Crisis of Rapid Change: The Red Scare in Houston, 1945-1955." Ph.D. dissertation, University of Houston, 1978.

Davidson, Chandler. "Negro Politics and the Rise of the Civil Rights Movement in Houston, Texas." Ph.D. dissertation, Princeton University, 1968.

Dishron, Joseph A. "A Population Study of Houston and the Houston Area." M.A. thesis, University of Houston, 1949.

Garcia, John Armando. "Mexican-American Political Leadership in Houston, Texas." M.A. thesis, University of Houston, 1968.

Greer, William Lee. "The Texas Gulf Coast Oil Strike of 1917." M.A. thesis, University of Houston, 1974.

Jager, Ronald B. "Houston, Texas, During the Civil War." M.A. thesis, University of Houston, 1974.

Lindsey, Walter. "Black Houstonians Challenge the White Democratic Primary." M.A. thesis, University of

Houston, 1975.

Maroney, James C. "Organized Labor in Texas, 1900-1929." M.A. thesis, University of Houston, 1975.

Meltzer, Mildred H. "Chapters in the Struggle for Negro Rights in Houston, 1944-1962." M.A. thesis, University of Houston, 1963.

Merseburger, Marion. "A Political History of Houston, Texas, During the Reconstruction Period as Recorded by the Press, 1868-1873." M.A. thesis, Rice Institute, 1950.

Sapper, Neil Gary. "A Survey of the History of the Black People of Texas, 1930-1954." Ph.D. dissertation, Texas Technological University, 1972.

Schmidt, Ward Gary. "A History of the Desegregation of the Houston Independent School District, 1954-1971." M.A. thesis, University of Houston, 1972.

Timme, Kathryn. "A Medical History of Houston-Harris County, 1836-1918." M.A. thesis, University of Houston, 1965.

Young, William Alexander. "History of the Houston Public Schools, 1836-1965." EED. dissertation, University of Houston, 1967.

ACKNOWLEDGMENTS

I wish to express my gratitude to the Harris County Historical Society for recommending me as the author of this book. As a longtime member of the society myself, I know of no group more dedicated to the writing and preservation of local history. Teaching courses in Texas history at the University of Houston and doing research in the field served only to quicken my interest in the history of my adopted city. Therefore, I was particularly pleased and grateful when, through the agency of the society and Windsor Publications, I was presented with the opportunity to do this project.

I also want to thank Pat Butler of the Harris County Heritage Society for the excellent choice of photographs depicting the history of Houston and Harris County. A conscious effort was made to blend the text and photographic reproduction, so that each would complement the other. In this effort, I believe we have succeeded. Also, I am indebted to Lissa Sanders and Annette Igra of the staff of Windsor Publications, who provided insightful criticism resulting in a much more polished literary effort. In fact, from the very beginning of this project to its conclusion, the entire editorial staff of Windsor Publications has been helpful in many ways. My colleagues in the History Department at the University of Houston, Professor Robert I. Giesberg and John O. King, gave me the benefit of their counsel, and the staffs of the Anderson Library at the University of Houston and the Downtown Public Library have been unfailingly helpful and gracious in rendering assistance to me.

Finally, upon the completion of any work, the historian is made very much aware of those who have trod the same research path before him. In this regard, anyone writing about the city of Houston soon realized his obligation to the late Andrew Forest Muir. Professor Muir's articles on Houston and Harris County are literally gems of historical writing. The WPA writers' project book on Houston remains to this day an excellent compendium, perhaps still the best source for "what happened." On the other hand, Professor David McComb's Houston: The Bayou City emphasizes interpretation and qualified as a seminal, one-volume overview. If this book should in any way continue the tradition that the above-mentioned writers and others have commenced, the author will consider himself very happy indeed.

Stanley E. Siegel

INDEX